The Baby Thief

The Baby Thief

The Untold Story of Georgia Tann,
the Baby Seller Who Corrupted Adoption

Barbara Bisantz Raymond

CARROLL & GRAF PUBLISHERS
NEW YORK

THE BABY THIEF
The Untold Story of Georgia Tann, the Baby Seller Who Corrupted Adoption

Carroll & Graf Publishers
An Imprint of Avalon Publishing Group, Inc.
245 West 17th Street, 11th Floor
New York, NY 10011

AVALON
publishing group incorporated

Copyright © 2007 by Barbara Bisantz Raymond

First Carroll & Graf edition 2007

ISBN-13: 978-0-78671-944-0
ISBN-10: 0-7867-1944-3

9 8 7 6 5 4 3 2 1

Interior design by Sue Canavan
Printed in the United States of America
Distributed by Publishers Group West

Contents

It's hard to understand, without being immersed
in the poisonous air of then.

—Doris Lessing, *Under My Skin*, Vol. 1

Prologue

I learned of Georgia Tann in 1990 from Alma Sipple, who'd met her decades earlier. I was interviewing Alma for a magazine piece. She said she could still see Georgia: a stern-looking woman with close-cropped gray hair, round, wireless glasses, and an air of utter authority.

She gained entry to Alma's apartment in Memphis, Tennessee, by identifying herself as a social worker and orphanage director concerned about Alma's ten-month-old daughter, who had a cold. After examining Irma, Georgia pronounced her seriously ill.

When Alma said she had no money for a doctor, Georgia offered to obtain free treatment by passing Irma off as her ward. She warned Alma not to accompany her daughter to the hospital: "If the nurses know you're her mother they'll charge you," she said. Two days later she told Alma that her baby had died.

Alma didn't believe her. But neither frantic visits to Georgia's orphanage, from which she was ejected, nor desperate trips to the police station, where she was ignored, nor haunting of hospitals and graveyards revealed the truth: that Georgia had flown Irma to an adoptive home in Ohio.

When I interviewed Alma forty-five years later she had finally found her daughter, but while the reunion had been happy their relationship was fragile. Irma was uncomfortable with the television coverage of the reunion that Alma had sought, and educated enough to intimidate a mother who'd only finished sixth grade. "What can I get her for Christmas?" Alma asked me. "I'm afraid to insult her with my taste."

A year later Alma had a heart attack and called me from the hospital. She and her daughter were not in touch. "Only someone who's lost a child this way can know how horrible it is," Alma said, crying. "There's a hole in me that will never be filled."

I couldn't forget the woman who had ruined Alma's life and so many others. Georgia had arranged over five thousand adoptions between 1924 and 1950, many involving children she had kidnapped. She had molested some of the little girls in her care and placed some children with pedophiles.

Georgia had also caused so many child deaths that by the 1930s the official infant mortality rate in Memphis was the highest in the country. And the actual number of Memphis children who died was even larger than the official count, because Georgia failed to report many deaths. She also neglected to bury all of her dead children in the cemetery used by her adoption agency. "They simply disappeared," a former Memphian told me.

Still, most of Georgia's children survived, and grew up all across the country, many in her favorite markets, Los Angeles and New York. Those adopted by Joan Crawford, June Allyson and Dick Powell, and other celebrities were featured in magazines, and some have had distinguished careers. But most are seemingly ordinary people coping with the extraordinary fact of having been placed with adoptive parents unscreened for anything but wealth.

Some of these adoptive parents loved their new children and treated them well. But other children were made to serve as domestics and farmhands. Some were starved, beaten with hoes and razor strops, hung from hooks, and raped.

There seemed no bottom to the pain Georgia had caused, and I flew to Memphis, consumed by questions. And besides the questions about her and the consequences of her actions there was another one: why hadn't anyone stopped her? She had been expelled from Mississippi before moving to Tennessee. What had made Memphis ripe for her? And what aspects of her era had facilitated her crimes?

Only after situating Georgia within her context would I discover her other dimension—the one that allowed her to hurt millions more people than those she directly touched. While building her black market business, she had invented modern American adoption.

It's hard to overestimate her influence. When she began her work in Tennessee in the 1920s, adoption as we know it did not exist. Eugenicists had made Americans afraid to adopt, and agencies like the Boston Children's Aid Society were arranging a scant five adoptions a year. In 1928, however, only four years after Georgia's arrival in Memphis, she arranged 206.

She did much more than popularize adoption. She commercialized it, charging adoptive parents large fees and marketing children in nationally syndicated newspaper ads.

Worse, she stole adoptees' identities. To cover her kidnapping crimes, and to appease clients threatened by the possibility of their new children someday reuniting with their birth parents, she falsified adoptees' birth certificates, sealing their true documents and issuing them false certificates portraying their adoptive parents as their birth parents.

The practice was approved by legislators who believed it would spare adoptees the onus of illegitimacy. All fifty states ultimately falsified adoptees' birth certificates.

Georgia's legacy has endured into the twenty-first century, and the vast majority of America's 6 million adoptees are still legally denied knowledge of their roots, even after they become adults. Many can't find their birth parents or learn potentially life-saving information about their family health histories.

But finally, fifty-seven years after Georgia's death in 1950, adoptees are escaping her influence. In a dramatic legislative and court victory in 1999, people who had been adopted in Tennessee won access to their original birth certificates and adoption records. Since the passage of the Tennessee open adoption records law, adoptees have won similar legal battles in twelve other states. They won't stop until Georgia's legacy is eradicated throughout the nation.

Georgia accomplished all that her victims are fighting to undo through boldness, cunning, and the exploitation of her time and place. I began my research by studying the environment in which she had operated, paying a visit to the site of her orphanage on Poplar Avenue.

Part One

Georgia's World

1.

Georgia's Home

The Memphis I visited was very different from Georgia's. Her orphanage or Home, the local branch of the Tennessee Children's Home Society, was long gone, replaced by a rectangular structure housing the offices of the Baptist Brotherhood. Surrounding it were similarly modern and graceless buildings: a Taco Bell, Radio Shack and Payless Shoe Store, Mega-Mart and King's Den Hair Salon. There was little evidence of the beautiful shade trees that gave Poplar Avenue its name. But nearby side streets contained lovely old homes with deep lots and gardens so lush they hushed the buzz of traffic. Ivy scaled trees whose trunks were taller than the homes: pin oaks, pecans, sweet gums, snow flowers, yellow pines, dogwoods, sycamores and, arching over all, elms that had escaped the disease that killed most others in the world. The air smelled of honeysuckle and pine.

This was the world in which Georgia lived. Her brick and stucco residence was on Stonewall Court, two blocks from the Home. It still stands, and when I visited was owned by an attorney and his wife who had been kind to adoptees who'd visited, seeking some link to their past.

Georgia's orphanage at 1556 Poplar Avenue had been more imposing: three stories high, with a tile roof, columns, and spacious grounds sloping upward from the street.

Inside, polished wood floors led to a filing room, a personnel office, a private conference room for adoptive applicants, and Georgia's office. The floor also shone in the formal reception room, which had two fire-places and drapes of pale rose and blue. A small table bore a lamp with glass beads whose facets sparkled in the sun slanting through a window flanking a fireplace. Dahlias grew in urns on the wide front porch.

The rooms upstairs were more plainly appointed, but they were clean and orderly, sterile in appearance if not in fact. Georgia considered appearances important. So her three nurseries were painted pink and equipped with white metal cribs decorated with pictures of teddy bears and sleeping babies. Her aides wore starched white uniforms and crisp nurse's caps. But, as one of her former employees told me, the women weren't nurses; the head caretaker tended infants while drunk. And the outfits worn by babies when viewed by prospective adoptive parents were strategically selected. Georgia reserved the most beautiful clothing for "the bad apples," the plainest children, who were hardest to sell.

In the backyard of the Home were swings, a sandbox, and a tall, white picket fence. Two of Georgia's workers lived in an apartment over the garage; a cook and a gardener lived in the basement of the main building. All employees except the gardener and a chauffeur were female; a former resident described the Home as "a kingdom run by women." Neighbors, whose sleep was disturbed by the cries of babies being smug-gled into waiting limousines, called the orphanage a house of mystery.

Mysterious as the Home seemed to some, however, Memphis insiders had easy access. During Georgia's Christmas parties, matrons led their children upstairs. "I picked you out in this very room," they told them. While some of Georgia's clients abused their adopted children, many loved them, and gratefully donated their own services, polishing silver and hand-stitching tiny nightshirts. When she was angered by proposed adoption reform legislation, they flooded Nashville with polite, stern telegrams.

It is difficult to admit involvement with a criminal, and few adoptive parents admitted to knowledge of the source of many of Georgia's children. Many professed unawareness of the desperate, futile habeas corpus suits that were reported in the local press, and of her Home's expulsion from the Child Welfare League of America.

But when the Tennessee governor finally acknowledged Georgia's crimes in 1950, prompting mail from birth parents that was sometimes literally tear-stained, adoptive parents must have searched their souls. They could not, however, bring themselves to investigate whether their children had been stolen, and return them if they had been. Neither could Tennessee politicians. They left her stolen children exactly where they were.

2.

Georgia's Disappearance

One reason that Georgia's children remained separated from their birth parents was that returning them would have been an admission of crimes committed not only by her, but by countless prominent Tennesseans. In a successful scheme to ensure her invulnerability she had transformed potential adversaries into accomplices. These included politicians, legislators, judges, attorneys, doctors, nurses, and social workers who scouted child victims, wrongfully terminated birth parents' rights, and falsely informed mothers that their babies had been stillborn. Deputy sheriffs tore screaming toddlers from their mothers' arms.

This collaboration allowed her to operate with impunity for twenty-six years. It wasn't until she was three days from death from cancer that a Tennessee official alluded to her crimes. And this reference was prompted largely by knowledge of the imminent publication of an article written by the first reporter brave enough to call her a baby seller in print.

At a press conference held before dawn on September 12, 1950,

5

Governor Gordon Browning sidestepped every important issue, speaking not of grieving parents or dead babies, but money. Georgia had, he said, illegally made $1 million while employed by the Tennessee Children's Home Society, which received funding from the state. She had not shared her profit with the agency. "I have asked the welfare department to proceed with whatever course it can take to recover this money for the Tennessee Children's Home Society," Browning said.

Browning had actually planned to shut down Georgia's business—but apparently only after death had rendered her unable to name her politically important colleagues. One week earlier he had appointed a young attorney named Robert Taylor as investigator. But it was a token position; Browning refused to allow the idealistic Taylor to question Georgia or her helpers. Taylor was also prevented from viewing the court records of a judge who had procured children for Georgia.

Even worse, Georgia's business and private papers, which Taylor had also been prohibited from viewing, were stolen by her attorney. Taylor protested the theft, but officials allowed the lawyer to keep them for two months, and, of course, to destroy whatever he wished.

In 1951 the frustrated Taylor proposed a bill that would have given him control over the investigation. Georgia's helpers caused it to die in committee. A proposed federal investigation of the Home was quashed.

The sole result of the state's only lawsuit against Georgia's Home was the "recovery" of money she should never have made.

Georgia Tann had won. And Tennesseans had helped her. The facts are depressing, and shortly after beginning my research I became depressed too. It was a hot day, one I'd spent reviewing records regarding the state's case against Georgia's estate, reading nothing of importance. Then, from a faded sheet retrieved from a courthouse basement, I gleaned the names of eighteen of Georgia's last twenty-two wards, and their ages at her death.

Fourteen were babies, from four days to six months of age. There was also an eight-year-old boy named Jimmy Nickens, as well as the three Irwin sisters: nine-year-old Patricia, eleven-year-old Wanda, and thirteen-year-old Geneva.

These children must have been strong, for Georgia had been neglectful and abusive, keeping the babies lying almost unattended in the Home's suffocating heat, and drugging them with alcohol and sedatives to keep them quiet. One tiny, premature infant had gone untreated for a heart defect.

Her older children, who lived in boarding homes, had fared no better. Georgia had refused to allow the three Irwin sisters, whose mother had died of tuberculosis, to be tested for the disease. They and Georgia's other school-age wards were virtual prisoners, kept indoors, denied schooling, and, in many cases, hidden from their frantic parents.

The closing of Georgia's Home on December 15, 1950, gave these and other parents their first hope of a hearing, and they demanded their children's return. They received nothing, not even confirmation that their children remained alive. Only two of Georgia's last wards, who had been rejected by their adoptive families, were returned to their birth parents.

And few but the parents themselves protested this treatment. Local news articles focused upon the logistics of Georgia's amassing of $1 million. The national press scarcely covered the story. And I found no article, published anywhere, that suggested that Georgia's stolen children should be returned. The general consensus seems to have been that they were lucky to have been delivered into wealth, and that they were emotionally attached to their new parents. But at the time of Georgia's unmasking, some children had been in their adoptive homes for less than a week. And her last wards hadn't even been adopted.

With no help from the local or greater environment, parents wishing to recover their children needed considerable cunning, or luck. Twenty-three-year-old Josie Stateler distracted an aide at the Home on Poplar Avenue, stole back her fourteen-month-old daughter, and moved to Massachusetts. And the father of eight-year-old Jimmy Nickens, who was languishing in a Memphis boarding home after having been rejected by his California adoptive parents, sent several desperate letters to Robert Taylor. Taylor helped ensure Jimmy's return to his family. But other parents, even those who went to court to recover their children, never got them back.

Custody of Georgia's last wards was consigned to the Tennessee Department of Public Welfare, which evinced little enthusiasm for the assignment. "The children will be studied, and those found acceptable will be placed for adoption," said Vallie Miller, supervisor of adoptions. "We will not accept responsibility for the others."

But state workers disposed of every child. They hospitalized the infant with the defective heart, and placed several other children they deemed similarly unadoptable in state or private institutions. An "imbecilic" adolescent girl was sent to a state asylum. A one-year-old with cerebral palsy who had been rejected by her adoptive parents was also slated for institutionalization. Vallie Miller placed her instead in foster care. But a report written by Miller also indicated the difficulty faced by children who were both homeless and considered imperfect, providing a glimpse of the atmosphere Georgia had exploited to such vicious effect.

Miller referred to two other infants who if not "over-placed" might be adoptable, "although earlier one child appeared to be subnormal, and the other has required special observation because of a history of epilepsy in his maternal background. . . ."

Several other babies, "normal in every way," were placed for adoption.

So were the three Irwin sisters, whose automatic responses to social workers' questions—"Yes ma'am, we want homes of our own, even if we have to be separated"—bespoke an absolute lack of hope. Georgia had placed their three younger sisters, but Patricia, Wanda, and Geneva had been considered too old for adoption, and had been destined for a reformatory. They had endured troubles before entering Georgia's network, such as their father's desertion of the family and their mother's slow, painful death. They owned one item apiece, a rough cotton dress, and the oldest sister, Geneva, was wracked by guilt over not having kept the band of six young girls together. Vallie Miller was able, however, to place the three oldest in an adoptive home.

But that was all the state did. No one investigated the welfare of the rest of Georgia's five thousand adoptees, who were left stranded across the country. This was despite the fact that not a single child had been legally adopted.

Georgia had violated the laws of Tennessee and other states, and federal laws against kidnapping. But several politicians and legislators had adopted through her, and, anxious both to keep their children and to appease worried constituents, they quickly passed a law retroactively legalizing all of her illegal placements.

The legislation violated logic, and people with influence ignored it when they wished. Neither adoptees nor birth parents had influence. But several adoptive fathers who had divorced refused to support their children, because, they argued, their adoptions had been illegal. Some adoptive couples who were dissatisfied with their children sought to have the adoptions annulled.

In contrast, adoptees seeking their birth names were denied them because such information was forbidden to adoptees, and, Tennessee lawmakers insisted, their adoptions had been legal. Yet one of these same adoptees was later denied a substantial inheritance because she was an adoptee, not a "blood heir."

The law that legalized illegal adoptions might have been struck down, if it had been challenged in an unbiased court. But birth parents lacked the financial resources with which to fight it.

And Georgia, forgotten by all but her victims, sanitized by the legalization of her crimes, disappeared from history. I didn't originally appreciate how her escape had affected the institution of adoption and children born as late as 2007. But I understood how it had hurt some of her direct victims, such as the five siblings who'd been seized on their way home from school and sold to five families. Only the oldest, an adolescent who'd been sent to a reformatory because he wasn't intelligent enough to satisfy his adoptive parents, ever returned home.

I also learned of a nine-year-old girl named Peggy who protested vigorously after being taken from her mother. "I became a stutterer, a bed wetter, a perpetual screamer," she told a Memphis reporter in 1987. "I made life miserable for everyone."

She was sent back to Georgia, who shuttled her among eight different foster homes. Deemed incorrigible, she was returned to her mother, but continued to grieve for her four brothers and sisters, who remained in California and New York.

Many of the hundreds of adoptees I would eventually speak with were, like Peggy, driven almost to breakdown. When Georgia Tann died, Elizabeth Huber was thirteen, and experiencing an identity crisis more severe than the average adolescent's. She had arrived in California eight years earlier, ill with pneumonia and traumatized by the death of her mother. Georgia hadn't told Elizabeth of her impending adoption, but had simply flown her to Los Angeles, where she was picked up by her new parents in the lobby of the Biltmore Hotel.

Georgia represented her children as blank slates, and Elizabeth's adoptive mother was persuaded. She greeted her by telling her she was a new person named "Carol," and giving her a doll.

Surprised and confused, the child named the doll Elizabeth. It was the nicest toy she'd ever owned, but she hated it. Her anger was compounded by her adoptive mother's dismissal of her grief over separation from her younger brother. When she talked of things they'd done together, her adoptive mother said, "Those things never happened. You're 'Carol.'"

"I knew Elizabeth would never be accepted there," she said over lunch one day in 1992 near her home in the Pacific Northwest. Articulate and intelligent, she was a former model. But her poise and mental equilibrium hadn't come easily. She'd only survived, she said, by refusing to be ruled by the past.

"When I was first adopted, I was terrified," she said. She didn't know who "Carol" was or how she should act. Almost overnight she'd gone from a shack in the hills, where she was the second youngest of fourteen children, sleeping on the floor and eating orange peels for breakfast, "to this affluent home. I began talking to myself in the mirror—no one else would listen to me." She also consciously assumed moods. "When I'd go to a birthday party I'd wear a birthday party mood. But on other days I didn't know who to be."

Her confusion deepened, and as a young adult she consulted a therapist, who, suspecting a link between adoption and her difficulties regarding identity, suggested she take back her old name.

Fearful of offending her adoptive parents, she resisted his advice for twenty years. But when she reclaimed her name in 1982 she finally found some peace. Two years later she realized a long-held dream—reunion with her beloved younger brother and other relatives. "I got off the plane in Nashville and my relatives were there—all the women had orchids," she said. For the first time in forty years, she felt like she belonged.

Soon after meeting Elizabeth, I spoke with another adoptee Georgia had wronged. At age six Barbara Davidson was adopted by a man who sexually abused her. Her adoptive mother seemed oblivious, and Barbara didn't tell her. "I knew what he was doing was wrong," she said. "But I thought it was all my fault." She was also accustomed to molestation, having earlier been abused by a man in a boarding home in which Georgia had placed her, and also by Georgia herself.

When she spoke to me Barbara was deeply depressed. Without benefit of therapy, which she was afraid to seek because she feared that psychiatrists would doubt her stories, she struggled to believe she hadn't deserved her past. "I was only a baby," she told me, crying.

Elizabeth lived in Oregon, Barbara lived in Texas, and, speaking shortly afterward with adoptees in almost every other state, I realized how pervasive Georgia's reach had been. The epicenter, of course, was Memphis, where, visiting the courthouse archives, I'd see people with worn, worried faces, studying old docket books for mention of relatives stolen by Georgia. The genealogy department of the Memphis Main Library bustled with searchers. Some spoke of quests of forty years.

"Help me," some asked upon learning I was a reporter. Aware of my inability to help them search, I recalled the words of an elderly Memphis attorney I had interviewed, with some difficulty: "I understand your sense of outrage, but what is the point of writing this book? The world is full of wrongs for which there are no remedies."

It's true, of course, that nothing can compensate a mother and child who will never know each other's touch or hear each other's voice, or erase Barbara Davidson's memories of sexual abuse. But I also recalled

Barbara's words, the first time we spoke. It was an emotional, disturbing conversation, for Barbara told me things she had never even told her husband, and as she did, her voice regressed to that of the terrified six-year-old she'd been. She was furious with Georgia, but Georgia was dead. When she learned that Georgia's sole surviving long-time employee still asserted Georgia's innocence, she exclaimed, "May God have mercy on that worker's soul. She has no right to take the truth to her grave. If she would say, 'Yes, Georgia did sell and hurt children,' that would help so many people. If she would just admit Georgia was wrong, in God's name she was wrong . . .

"I wake at night," she told me, "and I still feel the ropes around my wrists."

Having conducted largely fruitless interviews with that employee, a woman in her eighties named May Hindman, I knew she would never oblige Barbara. But I believed that Barbara and other adoptees could achieve some satisfaction by forcing Tennessee officials to admit they'd been wronged. More helpful than an apology would be access to the adoption records they had long been fighting for. My article about Georgia Tann, published in *Good Housekeeping* in March 1991, had aided their efforts.

But the article that had helped some adoptees was greatly troubling others. One of the most troubled was Billy Hale.

3.

Billy

I met Billy Hale through a classified newspaper ad I placed shortly after my first Memphis visit, which, because of old-time residents' defensiveness, had yielded little information about Georgia Tann. The ad read, "If you have knowledge of Georgia Tann or the Memphis branch of the Tennessee Children's Home Society please contact . . ."

I received little response from ads I ran in major newspapers on the East and West Coasts. Few of the thousands of adoptees Georgia placed in New York and Los Angeles sought information about her in those publications. But they and other Georgia Tann adoptees who sought reunion with their families considered the classified sections of the Tennessee, Arkansas, and Mississippi newspapers—where I also ran ads—to be lifelines. I was contacted by more than 900 people, including a man who had recently discovered papers related to Georgia's business that had long been believed destroyed.

Other responses were emotional in nature. Elderly women wondered if I was the daughter Georgia had stolen. I referred them to a Memphis search expert, a woman named Denny Glad, but felt terrible for raising hopes that might never be met. Most calls, thankfully, were from adoptees, birth parents, adoptive parents, social workers, nurses, doctors, and others who simply wished to discuss their experiences with Georgia. They sent me correspondence from her, birth certificates and hospital records, and described heartbreaking letters in which birth parents pleaded for their children's return.

Almost everyone I spoke with referred me to others, and so I learned of Billy. Over the next few years he would undergo several changes, but when I met him he was fifty-three and living in Portland, Oregon; his hair was short and his voice was sad. He told me he had always been sad, though not so sad as now, and believed the reason stemmed from his early childhood. But his adoptive parents had told him his memories were wrong: his mother had relinquished him at birth, representatives of Georgia's agency had said.

Bruce and Gertrude Hale loved Billy, and raised him first on a farm near Nashville in a stone house surrounded by mountains, and then in a century-old mansion in Murfreesboro that had briefly served as the capitol of the Confederacy. Painted white with green trim, the house had six bedrooms, seven fireplaces, and three porches. On summer nights Billy would sleep on one of the porches, surrounded by stars, the sounds of frogs, katydids, and crickets, and scent from the giant magnolia out front, said to be the second largest of its variety in the South.

It was the perfect home for a child, flanked on three sides by water and bordered by tall trees from which he swung and plunged into Stone River. He and his adoptive father built a boat they sailed on a nearby lake; Billy navigated coves and hollows and beneath apple trees that stood in the water, catching blue gill and crappie and catfish and bass.

But despite his loving adoptive parents and comfortable surround-ings, Billy was always troubled. On his first day of school he grew hys-terical, crying, clutching at Gertrude's legs. She couldn't leave the classroom that day; it took two weeks before she could return home during school hours. Billy was terrified of using public restrooms and undressing in front of others; Gertrude obtained permission for him to shower privately.

Billy's memories of his earliest childhood days included having been driven, crying, in a limousine with two black-garbed women and a tear-stained little girl. He also recalled having been told he was part Cherokee, but, as the Hales patiently explained, neither that nor the car ride had occurred.

Billy felt guilty, though his parents assured him he had done nothing wrong. He empathized with anything small and weak. When he turned thirteen his father took him hunting. Billy knew he had to shoot a squirrel, but afterward felt so terrible he tried to bring it back to life. At twenty-four he married a shy, slender young woman who seldom smiled, out of embarrassment over a crooked front tooth, which he quickly helped her to have fixed. He soon had two beautiful children and steady employment as a telephone repairman.

But he suffered, as he had since childhood, from seemingly motive-less rages. When his daughter sassed him he punched a hole in the living room wall; he later broke down a door. He recognized the incongruity of both dreading and ensuring the breakup of his family, but he was unable to change its course.

When his wife divorced him, Billy broke down, and after spending three months in a psychiatric hospital begged for another chance. But his rages continued, and six years after their remarriage they divorced again.

So scrupulous by nature that he separated the nails in his small workshop by both size and color, Billy became obsessive, inventorying each square of sandpaper, bolt, and screw. With his wife gone, and his adoptive parents now dead, he felt rootless. Desperate to fix himself in time and space, he wrote his autobiography, intermixing accounts of his grammar school grades and detailed, hand-drawn maps of his childhood homes with such pleas as, "Reader, learn from my mistakes. I love you, and look forward to meeting you in the next life."

In the 1980s he met an attractive, red-haired woman named Della and, charged with the possibility of again having a family, entered into a third marriage. Then in 1992 he watched a television program that would change his life.

Ten months after publication of my *Good Housekeeping* article about Georgia Tann, CBS's *60 Minutes* had produced a segment about her. Billy had missed the original airing. But as he pulled out of his driveway on a Sunday evening six months later, on July 23, 1992, he was hailed by a neighbor, who told him that CBS was rebroadcasting the piece.

Returning his car to the garage, Billy climbed the stairs to his second-floor family room and inserted a blank tape in the VCR. The segment began with the bare facts, reported by Mike Wallace: Georgia had stolen children from the poor and sold them to the rich, and the state had done nothing to help her victims. "They simply closed the book [containing the adoption records] and hid it away. From shame? From cover-up?" Wallace asked search expert Denny Glad.

"As much as anything, to keep from having to admit that it ever happened," she said.

Billy continued watching the program, relatively relaxed. Having read my article, he was familiar with Georgia's story, which he had believed didn't directly concern him. Born five hundred miles from Memphis, he had, he assumed, spent his time as ward of the Tennessee

Children's Home Society in its orphanage in Nashville, site of the agency's headquarters. He didn't realize that Georgia, who wielded more power than anyone else in the statewide organization, regularly scouted children at the Nashville orphanage.

But when he saw a picture of the exterior of Georgia's Home, Billy was transfixed. "Della, I know that house. I know what's in that house," he said.

All night he remained on the green couch in the family room, replaying the video, suffering the flashbacks that had been triggered by the picture of the Home. He flashed on Georgia Tann, enraged; on a craggy-faced man in overalls who had huge hands; on a slim, beautiful woman with long black hair.

He went to work the next day, but was too nervous to function. Returning home, he watched the video again and again. This was the beginning of Billy's obsession with Georgia. For the next five years he would think of little else. He would leave his job. His marriage would end. All this was in the future when I met Billy two weeks after he'd watched the *60 Minutes* episode, but I didn't have to be clairvoyant to see it.

Della, exhausted, went to bed early the first night of my visit. I sat in the kitchen with Billy, contemplating what my article and the *60 Minutes* piece that followed it had wrought: a middle-aged man led to recall things he might be better off forgetting, now driven to remembering more, his mind spiraling back and back and back.

"Don't get lost in there," I begged him; Della had said the same thing. But he felt he couldn't go forward with his life until he dealt with his past. With the help of Denny Glad and support of a therapist he had begun a search for his mother, the results of which he offered to share with me.

I had little to give in return. And when, thinking of the slim, dark-haired woman of his memory, Billy asked, "Where were the courts, the police? Didn't anyone care?" I was mute. But I eventually discovered the chain of events that had encouraged Memphians to allow Georgia to hurt, ultimately, millions of people. The chain began with a natural disaster that occurred thirteen years before her birth.

4.

The Plague

The disaster that would aid Georgia was a plague that struck in 1878, devastating a city that had previously seemed blessed. Established in 1819, Memphis was strategically located on the Mississippi River, the great inland sea of nineteenth-century commerce. Covered by forests of tall trees, luxuriant vines, and brilliantly hued flowers, Memphis resembled the fantastic landscapes of Henri Rousseau, and was blessed with the fertile soil for which the Mississippi Delta was famous.

To Memphis came independent-minded planters, entrepreneurs, river pilots, and merchants. Members of aristocratic families provided the leadership of this providential mix. Memphis became a major hub of transportation and was on its way to becoming the largest inland cotton market in the world.

The city emerged from the Civil War relatively unscathed, having fallen, gently and with little bloodshed, after an hour-long battle fought on water. Trading in wartime contraband added to the wealth of the citizenry. Their town attracted thousands of immigrants from countries like Germany and Ireland, and became the fastest growing city in the land.

But while Memphis was progressive in many ways, its sanitary system was medieval. Six thousand privies drained into the Bayou Gayoso, a meandering stream in the city's business section composed of foul-smelling pools separated by dams of human excrement. The streets were unpaved, sloughs of manure and mud roamed by hogs and goats. An unappreciated danger was the superfluity of water—in wells, bayous, and rain-filled holes in the rotting wooden sidewalks. Standing water is an ideal breeding ground for the *Aedes aegypti* mosquito, which, scientists discovered in 1900, is the carrier of yellow fever.

Yellow fever, which appeared in the United States before the Revolution, was imported from the rain forests of West Africa through the West Indies and the busy port of New Orleans. Infected mosquitoes carried in the bilge water of ships bit seamen, who when they reached port infected any resident mosquitoes that bit the sailors. The newly infected resident mosquitoes then infected human Memphis residents, setting in motion a vicious cycle that stopped only when frost killed the insects. Memphis had suffered five serious outbreaks of yellow fever between 1850 and 1870, but dry summers or unusually early frosts kept the annual death toll under a thousand. During the torrid summer of 1873, however, eight thousand Memphians contracted yellow fever, and twenty-five hundred died.

The city recovered from this catastrophe, largely because its most prominent residents, having left Memphis for the duration of the epidemic, remained healthy. For the next several years the city was spared the disease, and on July 4, 1878, grateful city fathers set off a brilliant display of fireworks.

But by the time they celebrated, the *aedes aegypti* mosquito, its ranks swelled by unusually heavy rains in West Africa, had traveled by ship across the Atlantic. On July 15 the New Orleans mayor sent a terse cable, "Yellow Fever here—virulent—36 cases." Memphis officials established quarantines and cleansed streets and basements with lime and carbolic acid. Barrels of supposedly purifying burning tar were set on street corners; cannons were fired regularly to clear the air. Desperate citizens invoked ancient talismans, sprinkling chopped garlic and mustard powder in their shoes, breathing through rags soaked in turpentine. They strung bags of the evil-smelling plant, asafetida, around their necks, and waited.

On July 29 occurred the death from yellow fever of a woman in nearby Grenada, Mississippi, who four days earlier had received a package from New Orleans containing a new dress and, apparently, an infected mosquito. Memphians fumigated all mail and strengthened their blockades. But they couldn't prevent fleeing New Orleans residents from entering Memphis on skiffs or through the woods.

In late July a refugee from the South who was too weak to stand docked at Memphis and crawled into a shed, where he was discovered the next day, wracked by yellow fever.

On August 13 a local woman succumbed to the disease. She was thirty-four-year-old Kate Bionda, mother of two; her death throes, suffered in her stiflingly hot room above a snack house by the river, were excruciating.

Her first symptom, suffered six days earlier, had been a mild headache. But it soon became agonizing, and was accompanied by joint pain so severe she cried out. Her temperature soared to 106 degrees, and she grew delirious. From her body emanated a peculiar, terrifying smell, as of old rats' nests, or rotting flesh.

On the third day her temperature broke; she sat up and asked for tea, and her loved ones rejoiced. They didn't understand the insidiousness of her disease.

The symptoms of yellow fever often briefly receded, only to return with a vengeance. The whites of Kate's eyes were soon speckled with red spots. The virus was dissolving her blood vessels: fluids, leaking out, coagulated and congealed. Purple welts appeared on her skin, which was the yellow of jaundice. Her tongue and lips grew cracked, and blood oozed from her nose.

By the fifth day, blood seeped from all of her orifices, even her tear ducts; she felt blinded. She was wracked by vomiting both forceful and terrifying; what issued forth was copious, black, the consistency of coffee grounds, a mix of stomach acids and hemorrhaged blood.

From the inside out Kate capitulated. Her liver liquefied; her heart softened to mush. The rate of decomposition increased after death, reducing her to little but bones in a bloody pool.

Not even the most eminent contemporary physicians understood how she had contracted the illness. Some thought it was caused by a "miasma" emanating from the garbage-strewn Bayou Gayoso. Others believed the disease was carried by particles of dust or an airborne toxin.

Today doctors vaccinate people traveling to countries like Africa against yellow fever, and provide intravenous fluids to patients to prevent dehydration. Physicians of Kate's time prescribed peppermint, camphor, and calomel, and applied leeches to patients' stomachs. A doctor from New York who volunteered his services called these "cures that killed."

Memphians understood that the Fever would disappear with the first frost but no one knew why, or how it was spread. They assumed incorrectly that it was contracted through contact with patients, their vomit or bedding.

Each day the radius of the city affected by the Fever increased by several blocks: the flight range of the *Aedes aegypti* mosquito. A local reporter wrote of the "many bloodthirsty mosquitoes, a million or more to every man, woman and child here." But no one made the necessary connection, and the mosquitoes remained unchecked; insect repellants were unknown. Few homes had screens.

Escape seemed the only prevention. Within two days of Kate Bionda's death twenty-five thousand of the city's forty thousand residents fled to places as distant as New York City. Businesses were abandoned; dinners were left uneaten as families escaped in wagons, carriages, goat carts, on mules or horses and on foot. Men shoved aside women and children to board crowded trains. "The ordinary courtesies of life were ignored," wrote Colonel Keating, editor of the *Memphis Appeal*. "There was one emotion: an inexpressible terror."

Terror was also felt by people at stops along the railroad line, who feared infection. Armed men prevented Memphians from disembarking and local citizens from even offering them supplies. This resulted in sounds and sights that must have been hard to observe: the moans of passengers begging for water, their blackened tongues protruding from cracked lips.

And yet the illness spread. Yellow fever plagued two hundred cities and towns across the South that year, and killed more than twenty thousand people. But Memphis, with a daily toll often higher than that of all other towns combined, was the worst afflicted, and soon garnered charitable contributions from all over the country.

But as Sister Ruth, a twenty-six-year-old Episcopal nun who had traveled from New York City to nurse the ill, wrote, "Money is quite useless. There is plenty of money here, but it buys no head to plan, no hands to wash. . . ." All but two hundred of the six thousand white citizens who remained in the city fell ill; 75 percent of them died. Black residents had previously been immune to the Fever, but they too contracted it in 1878, and suffered a 7 percent mortality rate. Between deaths and desertions of political leaders, city government collapsed. Illness cut the police force from forty-one to seven; the staff of the *Memphis Appeal* was reduced to one printer and Colonel Keating, who published one-page daily newspapers consisting of roll calls of the dead.

The sounds of the city were hellish. For a while funeral bells were rung at burials, but the constant tolling became too frightening. When the bells stopped, Memphis keened with a silence broken by the footsteps of residents looking for doctors, the rumble of death wagons, and the call of the drivers: *"Bring out your dead."* The screams of patients also rent the air. Head pain accompanying the disease was so severe sufferers drew blood with their fingernails, trying to ease it. Others remained composed until overtaken by delirium, then wandered the city naked, seeking lost loved ones.

The city seemed a harbinger of hell. The inevitable sweltering summer heat was intensified by the fires, which, considered sanitizing, burned in every fireplace. Smoke from the outdoor fever pyres, smoldering tar, and booming cannons coalesced into a dispiriting yet merciful haze.

But not even the sound of cannons obscured the ever-present lamentations. These and sounds even more terrible—as those of stomach muscles ripping as a patient, bracing himself at a window, shot forth his black vomit—pierced the hearts of even the most formerly callous observers.

Of course some citizens looted the homes of the sick. But many more residents, pulled out of themselves by horrors they could never have imagined, united to help. Protestant and Catholic nuns tended the babies found coated in black vomit, futilely nursing at the breasts of their dead mothers. A madam named Annie Cook converted her bordello into a clinic and cared for the dying. Relief efforts were coordinated by a young businessman named Charles Fisher, who tirelessly treated the ill, a lit cigar clenched between his teeth, to camouflage the stench. On September 20, he sent a telegram to be read in New York City's Booth Theater, which hosted a benefit for Fever victims.

"Deaths to date—2,250. . . . Our city is a hospital. . . . We are praying for frost; it is our only hope."

Frost was expected by October 11. But that morning's temperature was a balmy 67 degrees. By then almost all of the local Catholic priests were dead, as was Sister Ruth, whose nickname among the poor had been "Sunbeam." Annie Cook had also succumbed. Charles Fisher died six days after his message was read in New York. Colonel Keating, who survived, wrote, "There were hours . . . as if the Day of Judgment was about to dawn."

Finally on October 18 came a black frost, and by October 29 new cases had fallen to almost zero. According to the Board of Health, the epidemic was over, but in the strictest sense it would never end.

Memphis had lost over five thousand of its citizens to death. Most of the thousands who had fled to cities such as St. Louis never returned. Among these were many of the city's professionals, and businessmen whose concerns, flourishing in their new locations, were constant reminders that Memphians had lost more than the loved ones in their graves. They had lost the Memphis that would have been.

Among those who had abandoned the city were the Germans who had brought to Memphis music, theater, and industry. Almost all of the Irish had died of the plague. The proportion of foreign-born citizens, which had been 30 percent in 1860, dropped to 5 percent by 1900.

Instead of reaching the expected count of eighty thousand by 1880, the population dropped from forty thousand to thirty-three thousand, plunging the city from thirty-second to fifty-fifth in national rank.

The population began to rebuild, but its composition was different from before, for the replacements for the lost Memphians were poor, often illiterate newcomers from the most rural areas of Arkansas, Mississippi, and Tennessee. They couldn't afford to pay taxes, and civic leaders were forced to declare the city bankrupt.

Added to this humiliation was the stigma of disease. Across the country health experts urged that Memphis be burned to the ground. Desperate to improve their city's image, Memphians began replacing the wood block sidewalks with pavement, and wells and cisterns with a modern waterworks. But yellow fever returned in 1879. Half of the population fled. Five hundred eighty-three people died, as did any remaining faith in Memphis.

Formerly a town inhabited by concerned citizens, Memphis became a city of transients who seldom indulged in civic-minded or even legal pursuits. So although Memphis regained its city charter in 1893, the chance of it becoming a modern metropolis, once deemed inevitable, seemed hopelessly remote. Then yellow fever struck again, in 1897.

The few remaining citizens of means withdrew to newer, safer areas. The gap between them and the newcomers living in the tenements bordering the business district widened. Criminals and gangsters flourished in the void, and the city's homicide rate soared to the highest in the country. Memphis was ripe for exploitation.

Georgia Tann would become the most enduringly harmful of the city's manipulators, and the plague eased her way. Children were less likely than adults to die of yellow fever, and hundreds of Memphis children were orphaned by the plague of 1878. Gratitude toward the sisters who cared for them inspired Memphians with an unquestioning respect for women who worked in adoption. This admiration persisted into the 1920s, when Georgia would take full advantage of citizens' gullibility. Georgia would also exploit the nuns themselves in the most terrible way, by trying to seize and sell the children the sisters frantically hid from her in attics.

The altered demographics caused by the plague also helped Georgia. Descendants of the sixty thousand rural émigrés who filled the vacuum left by the dead and departed provided her with women she considered "breeders"—single mothers whose babies she would steal.

But the epidemic helped Georgia most by breaking citizens' spirit. Formerly, Memphians had been self-assured and scornful of fools. Now they were desperate, vulnerable to the charlatan who would protect her.

He was Edward Hull Crump, and he was born in 1874, seventeen years before Georgia, into a respected Mississippi family. When he was four years old the plague spread from Memphis, killing his father and plunging Crump into poverty so extreme he was reduced to exploding inflated pigs' bladders instead of the customary firecrackers at Christmas. A natural leader, Crump developed a bullying confidence and craving for power. At eighteen he moved to Memphis.

He was drawn there for the same reason as were the other rural emigrants who surged in after the plague: impoverished as it was, Memphis offered excitement. Accustomed to a state listless with eroded red hills and swamps, Crump savored the briskness: the pungent odor of fried catfish, Mississippi mud, and raw whiskey; the incongruity of sweetly scented lilacs sold by beggars and exotic spices stored in troughs. He noted the opium dens, bagnio girls, giant wharf rats. He noted the city's aimlessness, and what it portended. Memphis needed a manager, and he loved to boss.

Crump had only a grammar school education, but he possessed an egotism and aggression that post-plague Memphians admired. Shortly after his arrival he assaulted several men, including his employer, whose business he acquired and built into a highly profitable insurance company. His fortune assured, he tackled his real goal: ruling Memphis.

His political tactics were as crude as those he had applied to business. Elected to the city commission in 1907, he monopolized municipal meetings by standing on tables and shouting, shaking his fist. By 1910 Crump was mayor, and was readying Memphis for the woman who would corrupt adoption.

5.

Mollie

While Crump began ruling Memphis, many of Georgia Tann's direct victims were born. These weren't her child victims, but their parents. While I initially knew few of these parents I spoke frequently with their children, most often with Billy Hale. Through him I learned of Mollie.

Billy's voice was flat. "I feel like I've been hit by a sledgehammer," he said. Since watching the *60 Minutes* episode he had been deluged by wonderful memories of walking down a country road hand-in-hand with his mother, intermixed with flashes of being kidnapped from her and subjected to brutal sexual abuse. He was desperate to find her.

A colleague of Denny Glad had advised Billy to run ads in Tennessee newspapers. Billy had published notices in the 1970s reading "Seeking mother who gave up a baby boy born February 10, 1939. . . ." They had drawn no response.

But during the intervening years he had learned his mother's name. His new notice, which read, "Anyone with knowledge of Mollie Mae Moore, born around 1920, call . . . ," was seen by Mollie's brother Harrison, who lived in Pattonsville, Virginia, near Tennessee's eastern border. He called Billy and asked, "Are you Mollie's baby?"

"Yes," Billy answered tremulously.

Harrison drew a deep breath. "She looked for you all her life, Bill."

Mollie was dead. Billy had found her and lost her in the same minute. His sorrow was compounded by what he learned of her life after his abduction: of the several days she'd spent in jail for protesting his kidnapping, and of how, when she married a man who treated her as badly as she believed she deserved—for she never forgave herself for losing Billy—she was afraid to risk bearing another child.

"She kept a scrapbook for me," Billy said, "and a birthday card she never got a chance to send. My picture was on her bedstead and in her wallet, and anyone who spoke to her for five minutes heard about me. She believed I'd come back. She called out for me when she was dying."

She died of cancer in Kingsport, Tennessee, on October 1, 1984, eight years before Billy spoke with Harrison. Billy had been on a business trip near Kingsport the week of her death. "If only I'd known," he told me hoarsely.

Billy had recently spent nine days with his Uncle Harrison and five cousins in Virginia and Kingsport, where he had been born. He memorized every sight: the farmhouse where he and Mollie had lived when he was a toddler, the pond on which they'd skipped stones, the face of the now-middle-aged neighbor with whom he'd played.

He also visited Mollie's grave, and sent me a photograph of the simple tombstone and family pictures of her at different stages of her life. There was a snapshot of her kneeling in the grass, holding Billy, on a sunny day. Billy is ten months old, plump, and looks impossibly happy; her face holds so much hope.

Billy was haunted by her face, and guilt for not trying harder to find her. He couldn't eat or sleep or concentrate; he was in trouble at work. "I've got to get my life together, get it together," he told me. And in tones offering no foreshadowing of the price he would pay, he said he would no longer bury his memories. He would, in fact, write the story of Mollie's life.

Over the next months Billy wrote hundreds of pages of information gleaned from his memory and that of his mother's surviving siblings. He called his book *Lost Love*. Like most authors he had difficulty finding a publisher, and eventually he gave up. But, hopeful of memorializing Mollie, he sent me his manuscript and the scrapbook she'd kept throughout the years of their separation.

Mollie was born in 1919 with black hair and brown eyes that mirrored those of her mother, Stella, who in turn resembled her father, whose father had been a Cherokee chief. Escaping the Trail of Tears in 1838, Mollie's great-grandfather settled near Tennessee's Great Smoky Mountains. But once that area became a federal reservation hemmed in by guards and barbed wire, there was little to do but dream of the past and drink. The children of the Cherokee drifted away and intermarried.

Growing up decades later in Jacksonville, Florida, Mollie seldom thought of her heritage, but she had beautiful high cheekbones and a reverence for nature. She was the seventh of fourteen children, born after Sadie, Ovedia, twins Robert and Mary, Virginia, and Frances, and before the seven youngest boys: twins Harrison and Henry and Frederick and Sederick, Julian, Gaylord, and Frank.

Her paternal grandfather had sharecropped in Wisconsin, and her father, Frank, had mined coal in eastern Tennessee as a young man. By the time of Mollie's birth, weakened by black lung disease, Frank worked as a house painter. Seeking employment, he moved his family from Florida to Ohio and then back south, where they lived in a two-room log cabin located on a hillside that afforded a panoramic view of wooded, southwestern Virginia. Stella was too overworked to note the region's loveliness, but Mollie was entranced. She practically lived outdoors, gathering flowers and playing hide-and-seek, kick-the-can, and baseball, with a ball made of shredded rubber from inner tubes, covered by an old sock. When she grew too old to play with her corncob doll, she sat under a tree, sewing tiny doll-sized dresses.

The children seldom attended school; Mollie had three years of education. They carried water from the spring, picked blackberries and sold them from a roadside stand, and grew corn in their small plot. They fed the chickens and gathered their eggs; Mollie and the younger boys milked the cow. But the primary reason the Moores denied their children schooling was a sense of futility.

Mollie was practical too. She didn't ask for store-bought clothes. She didn't panic when a big black snake slithered through the only door of the playhouse she and Frances had made of fallen branches. She swiftly fashioned a back door. She remained calm the night four men came, reeling and swearing, to their rented house in Kentucky. It was 1932, and she was twelve. Her father was away, and her brother Robert aimed a shotgun out of the kitchen window and ordered them to leave. They refused, and Robert was forced to shoot at one man, grazing him. Meanwhile Mollie kept the younger children from hysteria. But even she grew nervous when the men returned three days later. She screamed with the others as they hid under beds while the men shot up the house. Miraculously they missed every single occupant. Still, Mollie began dreaming she was cursed.

It was a frightening thought, and she blotted it out with her farm work and music. She had taught herself to play the guitar, and had what everyone agreed was a voice as lovely as Jeannette McDonald's. She sat outside in the evenings, strumming her guitar and singing.

She had always been pretty; by thirteen she was beautiful, tall and slim with glossy waist-length hair worn in a braid down her back. Several boys from the area wanted to come calling, but she didn't want any local boys. She hoped to find the kind of man she'd never met: handsome, romantic, kind—a man who didn't hit. She modeled herself after her brother Robert's wife, who was pretty and patient.

Mollie visited her sister-in-law every day, rocking her baby and singing him to sleep. When she was older she planned to have her own baby, named William Leroy, after her nephew. She wouldn't presume he would share her interests. But if he did, she'd explain the difference between marsh and wire blue grass, and the lavenders of thyme and mountain spurge. She'd sit with him beneath persimmons and magnolias listening for the mockingbird; she'd show him tracks of the great black bear. She would never let him be lonely.

6.

Georgia's Youth

Georgia Tann was obsessed with women of Mollie's social class. She was most interested in the frequency of their pregnancies, about which she had contradictory feelings. She was contemptuous of their fertility and privately referred to them as "cows." Yet she envied them for their ability to give birth.

And while Georgia felt superior to these young women she also identified with them. This connection touched the most painful part of her self. Early in my research I ascertained that Georgia had been hurt during her early years. Anxious to understand her, I drove from Memphis to her hometown of Hickory, Mississippi.

My timing lacked felicity, for when I began the three-hundred-mile ride the temperature was close to 100 and pain from an ear infection was a constant, throbbing presence. I was scarcely outside Memphis when I crossed the state line into Mississippi, traveling south on Highway 55. It was as generic an interstate as any, so signs I was venturing into the Deep South were subtle: an intensification of heat and atmospheric closeness, roadside mud changing from Memphis's drab brown to Mississippi's fiery red. The vegetation became vaguely tropical: Virginia creeper, cane, buck vine, cypress, and gum. The few animals I saw were roadkill.

Reaching the outskirts of the state capitol, I turned onto Route 20, traveling east past occasional roadside stands to Hickory, which had a population of 470—a town so tiny it didn't appear on my road map, but lay between Jackson and Meridian. All I knew of these larger cities was that they had been near the sites in the 1960s of the murders of three Civil Rights workers and Medgar Evers of the NAACP. Much has changed since then, and I was neither on Civil Rights business nor black. But awareness that I'd be considered more an outsider here than in Memphis accompanied me, as I honed in on my tiny target, as inexorably as the pain in my ear.

Earlier attempts to speak with Hickory natives by phone had met with mixed results. Some residents couldn't understand my Northern speech. One man, to whom I'd repeatedly tried to explain myself, handed the phone to his wife with an exasperated, "Mabel! There's some damn foreigner on the line!"

And while many of the twenty-five Hickory residents with whom I spoke patiently recounted decades-old events, several male citizens refused to talk to me. Two who'd worked as handymen in Georgia's Memphis orphanage adamantly swore they hadn't.

Not everyone had been straight with me in Memphis, of course. Once, as I bent to record what one of several public officials had said, I sensed him, winking at the others. As I left his office, he phoned the next person on my list.

I never learned how he ascertained the order of my visits. I had learned that the more graciously some Memphis public figures spoke to me, the less I could rely on the truthfulness of what they said. I'd thought I hated this artificial politeness, but, dealing with Mississippians, I mourned its absence. It was as if their coarser, hotter clime had stripped them of a veneer Memphians consider essential. In Mississippi tempers were short, and feelings raw.

"We're a clannish group till we get to know you," a Hickory woman had earlier told me over the phone—the time between "now" and "till" being measured in generations, not years. Being in a comparative hurry, I was delighted to discover that eighty-five-year-old Maisie thawed more quickly than did some other locals. By the end of our first conversation she had not only offered her interpretation of the moral of Georgia's tale—which, referring to the reduced circumstances in which her heirs had been left, she expressed as, "Sin will find you out"—but offered to do some "sleuthing" for me.

Throughout the next several weeks Maisie had called me frequently with tidbits gleaned from a local courthouse and Georgia's former neighbors. She also sent me an article about Georgia recently written for *The Meridian Star* by a local reporter, who, in a phone conversation, explained why so few in Hickory would speak with me. "They resent how Mississippians have been portrayed in the national media as barefoot, watermelon seed-spitting rednecks," she said. She said that Hickory residents felt their town was known for only one thing, spawning Georgia Tann, and that they were embarrassed.

The reporter's status as a local, she emphasized, had been crucial to her inducing residents to talk to her for her piece. But she hadn't approached the cabin of Jack Kendricks, who had served as Georgia's mother's chauffeur. When I asked her why—for I too wanted to speak with him in person, earlier attempts at phone conversation having been thwarted by his deafness—she said matter-of-factly, "Some folks around here shoot first, ask questions later."

Shoot even an insider like her? It was a sobering thought.

Both she and Maisie stressed the importance of my having a local liaison when I visited Hickory. The reporter and I set a lunch date, after which she'd introduce me to several residents. Maisie, who eagerly awaited my trip, would be my main guide. "I have a '72 Cadillac; we'll meet and go rambling," she said.

I was looking forward to having someone to ramble with that scorching July morning as I approached Hickory, following several solitary days in Memphis. Hickory had no hotel so, as Maisie had suggested, I checked into a motel in nearby Newton, a town set upon subtle elevations, less hills than swells, and soil faded from northern Mississippi's red to the yellow of mid-state. My attempts to call Maisie and the reporter were stymied by the fact that I couldn't make long-distance calls from my motel and that Hickory, ten miles away, was considered long-distance. Driving into Hickory, where my call to Maisie resulted in a busy signal, I decided to look around on my own.

It seemed foolish to have arranged escorts. Hickory didn't look sinister, but simply tired. An old lumber camp and former sawmill town, it was founded in 1815, when its forests of ash, hickory, poplar, and magnolia were virgin. The mill provided employment for most of the town's residents, and folks considered themselves, compared to other Mississippians, fairly prosperous.

Today, however, the mill is gone. The town's gas station has closed, and citizens look to nearby Meridian for their needs. Hickory's one-block center resembled a ghost town, and I was so impressed by its quiet, and so diverted by my ear pain, that I had overlooked one of its odder characteristics: there were no street signs.

This would make finding interviewees difficult. I looked for something that resembled a city hall. A man in a rocker directed me to a temporary-appearing structure, an unpainted partition joined to a building. Entering, I found myself in a narrow passageway; on my left was a square cut in the wood—a crude window—through which I looked into a sparsely furnished office. A ceiling fan rotated desultorily; flies buzzed overhead.

The three adults inside looked up. I asked for a street map. A heavyset man in a T-shirt asked, "What you need that for?"

"I have to find particular houses," I answered. He looked blank. "There are no street signs . . ." I said.

"Oh yeah," he said, and laughed. "The high school kids took 'em down last year, and we haven't gotten around to putting them back."

"Well, may I have a map," I asked again. I must have been the first person to make this request, for not one of the three seemed to know if a map of Hickory existed. After ten minutes the heavyset man produced what looked like the original plans for the town, but they were useless, showing few streets, and those few lacked names.

Luckily, however, the three city hall employees knew everyone in town. I copied down such directions as, "Go three streets south, turn right at the huckleberry bush," and, after a brief stop at what seemed a convenience store, where I bought aspirin and fruitlessly asked for over-the-counter ear drops, I set off to my first appointment.

It was with a gracious older woman who lived within sight of the old Tann homestead where Georgia had been raised, and which Georgia had visited frequently throughout her life to see her widowed mother, Beulah. "I hear you tried to buy ear drops at the five and dime," she said as she poured me iced tea.

The store didn't resemble a five-and-ten-cent store—it smelled of old meat—but the woman was kind, and I nodded. Less defensive than some other residents with whom I'd spoken by phone, who insisted, implausibly, that Georgia had been "pretty," "real friendly," and "the sweetest thing," that they had "thought the world of her" and wished they'd "knowed her better," my hostess made no judgments about her, but simply told me the birth and death dates of Georgia's Hickory relatives and of how Georgia had tried unsuccessfully to persuade a local woman to send her young daughter, who had Down Syndrome, to Memphis, where Georgia said she would teach her to talk. My hostess had no idea why Georgia had wanted to teach the girl to speak, or considered herself qualified to do it.

She was on firmer ground discussing Georgia's Hickory homestead, which in its prime during the 1930s had been the largest and most beautiful in town, with servants' quarters and a brick courtyard, a large wraparound porch, fountains, imported palm trees, and a room-sized, walk-in cooler that provided the only refrigeration in town.

The palm trees and much else had been paid for by Georgia. "Folks here did wonder," she admitted, "how she afforded it."

We were briefly interrupted by a man my hostess had arranged to meet me, since he had, as a teen, done errands for Georgia. "She was a boss-man, she ordered me around," he said, but he knew little else about her.

"Heard you tried to buy ear drops at the five and dime," he said as he left, and my hostess and I began the short trek to Georgia's homestead. En route we passed parched shrubbery that I viewed through a sort of haze. My companion, clad like me in lightweight cotton, looked crisp. But between the oppressive heat and my fever, which was spiking, I was slick with sweat. The sidewalk undulated upward; the ringing in my ear rose to a roar. Passing several small houses I wondered how many locals knew of my store visit, and whether, behind faded curtains, eyes watched me now as I made my dazed way.

Georgia's homestead was less imposing than I had imagined it, mostly because, although it was occupied, by the owner of the five and dime, it had been allowed to deteriorate: its white shingles needed paint, and its grounds were overgrown by poison ivy. I stepped gingerly, trying to imagine the courtyard with flowers and hedges blooming, the fountain spouting water, the brilliantly colored parrot Maisie had described squawking at my approach . . .

It took more imagination than I could summon at that moment, and soon afterward I bade my hostess good-bye and drove back to the phone booth to call Maisie. She answered on the first ring.

"Maisie, it's Barbara, let's ramble," I said.

"I'm sick," she answered flatly.

"What?"

"I'm sick, I can't see you," she said. She wouldn't say what she was sick with.

"Maisie, I'm right here, I'll bring you lemonade," I told her.

"I can't do it." She sounded scared and, suddenly, too old to press. I wished her well, said good-bye, and dialed the reporter's work and home numbers. I couldn't reach her. Feeling a queasiness that had nothing to do with my ear pain, I proceeded to my next appointment.

I held great hope for this interview, which was to be with a ninety-nine-year-old woman whose mind, I'd been told, was as clear as glass, and who had vivid memories of Georgia, who'd been her contemporary and neighbor. I knocked on her door, which was opened by one of her sons, a large man in his sixties wearing bib overalls. He led me into the tiny, stiflingly hot living room, where a sweet-faced woman sat in a wheelchair. Crossing his arms over his chest, he stood facing me, on her right. A slightly shorter but otherwise identical-appearing brother stationed himself on her left.

Introducing myself, I asked her a question. Her sons cut her off.

"Georgia's mother was the most respected woman in Hickory," said the taller one.

"Her daddy was a federal court judge," said the other.

Their comments were apropos of nothing; I hadn't asked about Georgia's parents.

"The Tann home was the second one built in town—"

"There were no streets then, only paths through the woods—"

The room spun as I tried to extricate the sweet-appearing old lady from her boys. But they stood firm and clamored on with such inconsequentialities as Georgia's brother Rob liking to hunt possums.

"Thank you," I told the elderly lady as I rose to leave. The taller man came over and, putting his hands on my shoulders, pressed me back into my chair. "Now, Missy," he said. "Not so fast."

I'm not large but I am strong and could have immediately escaped, but I sat there feeling boneless as he raved about outsiders butting in, snooping around. His brother yelled about the Civil War. "You Yankees brought the niggers down here, through underground tunnels. We used 'em, and we took the rap!"

I looked for help to the old lady, who seemed to have lost her sweetness. Wrenching away from her son, I left, and once again called the reporter at *The Meridian Star*. "She's not available," someone told me.

I told myself not to become paranoid. My left hand pressed to my ear to counter the pressure inside it, I drove to my next interview.

This source lived twenty miles from Hickory, in a remote area that I realized could prove menacing. But she'd sounded friendly when she'd phoned me and, driving down twisting dirt roads in shade provided by redwoods and pines, surrounded by wood scent so sweet it almost distracted me from my ear, I felt myself relax.

Her home was a run-down cottage that appeared to have been built at two different times, of two kinds and colors of shingles. I knocked on the screen door, and a man of about seventy appeared. He wore shorts and a stained undershirt. He carried something long.

I'm delirious, I thought.

"I'm here to see—" I said.

"She doesn't want to talk," he answered. He raised his shotgun level with my face.

For a moment I stopped breathing. Then I ran to my car, in which I peeled back down the dirt roads, through Hickory to Newton and then west on Route 20, on the way to the Memphis airport and freedom, away from the shotgun and poison ivy and, most draining of all, the eyes. They seemed to have stolen my self, my confidence, caused me to forget who I was.

Even if I'd been born there, I thought confusedly, I would never have been accepted. I wouldn't have quilted or canned well enough. I would have read too much.

A siren shrilled behind me. I pulled over to the shoulder, where I was ticketed for driving eighty-seven miles an hour. I drove more slowly afterward, of course, but it wasn't until I landed in Cleveland, Ohio, where I then lived, that I felt competent, in control. The person, I thought, I had long ago made myself. Someone who would ask whatever questions she wanted, and, if she chose, never again enter a five and dime.

Recovery of my sense of control had been contingent upon leaving Hickory. Over the next months I realized that Georgia had, to an infinitely greater extent than I, been robbed of choice in her hometown. It was her desire for autonomy that drove her to sell children.

* * *

Few watching Georgia grow up, however, would have ascertained her frustration. She seemed charmed. Her mother, Beulah Yates Tann, was from a prominent Philadelphia, Mississippi, family whose roots stretched back to frontier times. Georgia's father, George C. Tann, had an even more distinguished lineage: his grandfather had served under William Henry Harrison at the Battle of Tippecanoe, and his father was a Confederate war hero. George himself was the most educated man in the county, an aficionado of classical literature and judge of the Mississippi Second Chancery District Court.

But while George was respected he wasn't well liked, for he was arrogant, argumentative, and domineering. He was also, recalled a former neighbor, "a womanizer. Oh, me! He'd go out of town to see women, or have them come right to his office in broad daylight. I don't know how Beulah stood it."

Setting a pattern Georgia would follow, he was an emotionally cold person who evinced little affection for children but became known for finding homes for orphans. Social work would not be Georgia's first choice of career; her father's child-placing work was even less intentional. The poor, rural Mississippi of the nineteenth century lacked a centralized agency responsible for homeless children, and chancery court judges like George were charged with their care. The scarcity of orphanages often forced magistrates to send children to workhouses or state asylums, and as insensitive as George was, he was apparently frustrated by his lack of options.

"I wish I had a judge, a schoolteacher and a good, far-seeing minister to sit as a committee and help me decide what should be done with these children," he frequently told his young daughter. Her earliest memory was of him "always bringing children home with him" for temporary care.

Georgia's second cousin told me that Judge Tann kept and adopted one of these children, who grew up as Rob Roy Tann. Rob was born three years before Georgia, in 1888. Other relatives claimed that Rob was not adopted, but born to George and Beulah. Since Mississippi doesn't keep birth records from before 1912, and the state's adoption records are sealed, I couldn't verify Rob's origins.

But Georgia was named after both of her parents—her given name was Beulah George. The fact that Rob wasn't given his father's name suggests that Rob joined the family after his younger sister's birth. Another possibility is that Rob was adopted before Georgia was born, but that George didn't want to give his name to an adopted child.

Whatever Rob's origins, he was different from George, Beulah, and Georgia. He was thin; they were heavyset. "And Rob was a gentleman," an elderly Hickory man who'd operated the town's service station told me. "I thought a lot more of him than the others."

Rob was also physically weaker than his sister, prone to ear infections and mysterious fevers. While serving in World War I, he suffered what was then called shell shock and for the rest of his life suffered from tremors. He died of tuberculosis at age forty-six. A former neighbor recalled him lying on his mother's porch during his last summer. "Every time she wiped his brow, he thanked her," she said.

Rob may have been his mother's favorite. Georgia was her daddy's child. With her wide brow and unusually low-set ears, she resembled him. She was even more like him inside: imperious, brilliant, a natural leader.

Perhaps it was inevitable that two such similar people would clash. One reason for their conflict may have been George's discomfort over Georgia's sexual orientation. It's impossible to discern how much either understood about it during her childhood. Homosexuality was seldom spoken of then in the South, and the word "lesbian" was virtually unknown. But both sexes had clearly demarcated roles, and Georgia never conformed to the image of Southern womanhood. Big-boned and broad-shouldered, with a blunt, masculine manner, she occasionally appeared in public in flannel shirts and trousers, unacceptable clothing for women. She wore her hair severely pulled back, and as an adult sometimes had it cut as short as a man's. She evinced no interest in marriage.

And unlike most other girls of her time Georgia wanted to pursue a career, the masculine-seeming profession of law. George wanted her to become a concert pianist. Conflicts between parents and children are sometimes of little consequence. That the disagreement within the Tann household led to so much can be partly attributed to the tenacity of the characters involved. George was known for his iron will, while Georgia possessed an extraordinarily strong personality and drive. Under any circumstance, she would have made a mark, and, had her early life been easier, she might have accomplished much good. But she became so preoccupied with self-protection as to become selfish, narcissistic. Georgia lacked empathy. This made her dangerous.

Georgia was little more than a baby when she began suffering the insults that would shape her future and those of millions of others. She was an active child who loved to run and play. George, however, forced her to spend long hours in the parlor, practicing the piano. "I was glued on a piano stool at five, and I didn't entirely get away from a piano until I was grown," she told a friend, Memphis reporter Ada Gilkey, in 1935. But although Georgia despised playing the piano, she played it, hopeful that compliance would earn her something she desperately wanted. "All the time," she said, "I wanted to be a lawyer. . . ."

The main route to becoming a lawyer in the South during the early 1900s was to "read law" with an established attorney. "[A]nd I read law with my father and passed the state bar examination in Mississippi, but he wouldn't let me practice because it 'wasn't the usual thing' [for a woman] and I was the only girl in the family."

Her father's refusal to let her practice the law he'd taught her may have been the ultimate frustration, but Georgia had probably long resented submitting to George. It was not her nature to be compliant. Arrogant, condescending, so confident that if she hadn't actually become famous she would have been grandiose, Georgia would control everyone in her life but George. And while she was unable to defy him by practicing law, she searched hard for an alternate profession.

Had Georgia been born much before 1891, she would have had almost no choice of profession at all. Women were considered intellectually inferior, fit only for marriage and bearing children. Even women who wished to remain single often married, since they had no way of supporting themselves. Some married, homosexual women found solace in "romantic friendships," passionate, loving and often sexual relationships with other women. It wasn't widely recognized until the twentieth century that women could be homosexual, and romantic friendships were sentimentalized and considered ennobling. Both heterosexual and homosexual women were often forced to channel their intellectual drives into activities like gardening or needlepoint.

Georgia and other independent-minded young women would expand their options through education in women's colleges. The first such school was Mt. Holyoke College, established in Massachusetts in 1837. Martha Washington College in Abingdon, Virginia, from which Georgia would graduate, opened in 1860. By 1880 forty thousand women, representing one-third of the university student population of the United States, were enrolled in 153 colleges and universities.

A large number would remain single. A study cited by Lillian

Faderman in *Odd Girls and Twilight Lovers: A History of Lesbian Life in Twentieth Century America*, found that 50 percent of female college graduates between 1880 and 1900 were unmarried, compared to 10 percent of American women in general. It's unclear how many college graduates remained single out of choice, and how many were simply considered too educated to be suitable wives. But women's colleges provided welcome refuge for young women like Georgia, who desired autonomy. For the first time in history, large numbers of women lived and learned together, heady with the excitement of pioneering and anxious to work at a profession.

Georgia's experiences in college must also have assured her that she could have a personal life that didn't involve marriage. Many female professors lived in "Boston Marriages," domestic and often love partnerships with other women. They wore rings and called each other "Sister." Georgia would follow both of these practices with her partner, Ann Atwood Hollinsworth.

As a college student, Georgia would probably also have been aware of loving relationships between female students. What were considered "crushes" between girls at women's colleges were ubiquitous, and had many names: rave; spoon; pash (for "passion"); smash; gonazo ("gone on"); flame. Crushes between young women were so accepted that all-female dances were held at Smith and Vassar during the early twentieth century. Students attended in pairs, with one partner dressed in a feminine manner, the other in male attire.

I don't know if Georgia had a love relationship during college, but she graduated with no apparent inclination toward marriage. To support herself she needed a job in one of the two acceptable careers for women: teaching and social work.

Georgia majored in music, and after graduating in 1913 taught school briefly in Columbus, Mississippi. But she lacked the requisite patience for teaching, and may well have considered it an old-fashioned profession.

Social work, however, was in its infancy. Georgia was also familiar with social work, having long practiced a form of it herself. Charity work was a refuge during her adolescence, perhaps providing an excuse for her absence from local parties and dances. While other girls primped for them, she donned starched, long-sleeved blouses and skirts that swept the floor, and visited the local poor.

Georgia may have been motivated in part by altruism. But at an early age she began depersonalizing the adults and children she helped. This depersonalization was encouraged both by the Southern culture, which deprecated poor whites, and Georgia's increasing self-absorption. But even empathetic people sometimes become callous to protect themselves from pain. And although Georgia may never have been particularly empathetic, she was affected by her encounter with a drugged baby.

The child's mother was addicted to morphine, a major ingredient of cough medicine sold over the counter. During the early twentieth century, authorities often sent drug abusers to insane asylums as punishment, and when Georgia was very young, a Mississippi sheriff institutionalized this mother, along with several of her children.

"Hours later," Georgia told Memphis reporter Ada Gilkey, "the mother cried out something about her baby as the effects of the dope began to wear off. Officials at the institution called my father about it. The whole family had retired, but we got up and drove into the country. And there, under a pile of filthy rags in a corner of a shack, we found a pitiful baby which had evidently been given a little of the dope."

The Tanns brought the baby home. Georgia nursed the baby and, quite possibly, grew attached to it. But eventually it and the other children were sent to an orphanage.

This incident, Georgia said in 1935, first informed her of the plight of young, neglected children. The experience may also have encouraged her to avoid further emotional involvement with a child. For a woman who would work for decades in adoption, and who took great pride in her placements, Georgia seemed curiously immune to children's charms. "She had no favorites among the babies" in the Home, her former employee, May Hindman, told me. "She was businesslike and treated them all the same." Georgia's two grandchildren, who live in California and Texas, said that she had been emotionally cold even to their mother, June, the daughter Georgia adopted in the 1920s.

"My mother promised to raise us very differently from how Georgia had raised her," Georgia's granddaughter Vicci told me ten years after June's death. "She said Georgia was a cold fish—she gave her material things, and nothing else." When June began to menstruate, she ran to Georgia in the middle of the night, terrified that she was dying. "Georgia turned her over to the maid and went back to sleep. The maids raised her," said Vicci. "I don't know why Georgia bothered to adopt her."

The reason would become clear in time. It would involve her father, the most influential person in her life. Georgia's feelings toward him were a mix of love and hate, of wanting to prove herself to him and to defy him. The incident involving the drugged baby was a prototype of her relationship with George, evoking admiration for his stature in the community, and, quite possibly, rage at him for ultimately institutionalizing the baby.

Georgia's experience with the drugged infant also affected something of greater significance than her relationship with her father: her treatment of poor, white, often single mothers. Some of the disdain Georgia felt toward them was probably related to class differences. But the incompetence of the drugged baby's mother may have made Georgia feel justified in her contempt.

Utterly unappreciative of ambiguity, she considered the world to be inhabited by two, widely divergent types. Poor people, including the single mothers she called "cows," were bad; wealthy people, whom she described as "of the higher type," were good. Some of this obtuseness may have been simulated, meant to excuse her crimes. But Georgia would argue, and would seem to believe, that poor people were incapable of proper parenting. Their children needed rescue. Georgia would save them, by seizing them and placing them for adoption.

An incident that occurred when, according to Memphis reporter Ada Gilkey, Georgia was a mere "slip" of a girl may have further inclined her toward social work—and also taught her how to wreak mild revenge on her father. A policeman who knew of her work with the poor asked for her help. An infant had been left in a basket on a doorstep, and the policeman didn't know how to care for it.

Georgia traveled with the baby and the policeman in the patrol car to the Meridian courthouse, where the child would be declared legally abandoned. As she emerged from the Black Maria, or paddy wagon, with the infant in her arms she met her father and several attorneys from New York. Embarrassed, George gulped, "Gentlemen, this is my daughter."

"Laughing introductions were made, and in the years that followed Judge Tann was to 'get used to' most anything where his daughter was concerned," Ada Gilkey reported in 1935. Georgia, she wrote, would never forget the expression on George's face, or how he'd fought to maintain his composure.

Around 1906, when Georgia would have been fifteen, she arranged her first adoption, of two children she found huddled in a corner of her father's courtroom. He had placed them "in the protection of" the

Mississippi Children's Home Society, which, like other orphanages of the time, would have been more likely to warehouse them or place them in foster care than to arrange their adoption. Within three weeks, however, Georgia persuaded a respected Mississippi couple to adopt the five-year-old boy and his three-year-old sister.

Georgia discussed this placement with Ada Gilkey in 1935. The article that ran in the Memphis *Press-Scimitar* didn't reveal how the children had become separated from their birth parents. But Georgia's description of the family is telling, indicative of the attitudes that would inform her business, and that she would incorporate into the institution of adoption. "The father was a man of intelligence but of a mean disposition that was always getting him into trouble," Georgia said. "The mother was from an 'ordinary,' poor family. The children were sweet, attractive in appearance. The girl now has a degree in music. The boy has finished his law degree and begun his practice. Each was given an opportunity—and made the most of it."

Referring to this incident in 1946, a Memphis reporter wrote, "Miss Tann had found her life's work."

Georgia certainly did find her vocation early, although it's impossible to know whether her realization of it was triggered by these first adoptions, rather than by the rescue of the drugged baby, the ride in the Black Maria with the abandoned infant, or an incident lost to history. Her father's work and her environment would have constantly reminded her of the needs of homeless children.

"When I was growing up, there were orphanages all over the South," attorney and former investigator Robert Taylor told me. The attorney who after Georgia's death vainly tried to conduct a thorough investigation into her black market dealings, Taylor was born in Tennessee in 1915, almost the same year Georgia began her earliest professional social work.

Finding adoptive homes for institutionalized orphans could have kept Georgia busy for decades. Unfortunately, she wouldn't be satisfied with merely finding homes for homeless children—she'd become obsessed with finding adoptive homes for children who already had homes. She would acquire these children through kidnapping or deceit, and if she saved them from anything it was poverty.

Georgia considered poverty the worst possible condition. "It was her upbringing; she was from a very snobbish family that looked down on people in those shanty houses who got their hands dirty for a living," Andre Bond of Biloxi, Mississippi, told me.

Georgia felt she was taking children from "trashy people and elevating the children," Christine Nilan of Nashville said. Christine had been adopted through Georgia by a cultured, educated family whom Georgia frequently visited. "It was as if she thought, 'There's something that doesn't belong over here; I'll put it over there,'" Christine told me.

Georgia often boasted about having placed children with "high type" adoptive parents, and she expected grieving birth parents to be comforted by this fact. When a young mother begged for the return of the three children Georgia had stolen in 1939, Georgia told her that her appropriation of them was for their welfare, that they'd receive "good homes [and] splendid educations." Georgia's attorney, Abe Waldauer, a cultured, educated adoptive parent himself, also equated affluence with happiness. In a May 1935 letter to a Mississippi lawyer representing a father who was protesting Georgia's placement of his child for adoption, Waldauer wrote, "The child is fortunately placed in a home capable of lavishing every affection and advantage which wealth can give."

The woman who believed the end justified any means may have considered the means warranted even when they killed a child. She seemed undisturbed by the deaths of scores of children in her care. A child who died as a result of her social engineering would, at least, not have to grow up poor. And there were always more children to rescue.

Of course, Georgia's career provided her with benefits other than the satisfaction of making poor children middle class. She became wealthy, and influential, because of her own accomplishments and reflected glory. "She liked being on a first-name basis with the prominent people who adopted her children—movie stars, directors, politicians," former investigator Robert Taylor told me. She wasn't above exaggerating her connections to prominent people, Taylor added. Near the end of her life she hung autographed photographs of clients Joan Crawford and June Allyson in her hospital room. The autographs were forged—signed, at Georgia's direction, by her employees. She also instructed her workers to send her get-well cards, and to sign the actresses' and President Truman's names to the cards.

And around 1906, fifteen-year-old Georgia Tann may have had an intimation of the rewards she'd reap from her future profession when she accomplished what her father had considered impossible: the adoptive placement of the young brother and sister she'd found in his courtroom. Eight years later, having graduated from college, rejected teaching, and having been forbidden to practice law, Georgia chose social work as her profession.

It was a profession that offered opportunity. The photographs of New York City street children taken by Jacob Riis had led to an out-pouring of private, volunteer activities, which resulted in the establishment of Humane Societies, Juvenile Courts, and institutions for orphans. Over 460 orphanages were established in the United States between 1890 and 1910. When Georgia graduated from college in 1913, Mississippi had three professional, religiously affiliated orphanages. An orphanage operated by the Fraternal Order of Masons was located in Meridian; Georgia had volunteered her services there during summer vacations. In 1912 the first state orphanage, the Mississippi Children's Home-Finding Society, was also established in Meridian. Georgia obtained employment with this organization, and after its headquarters was relocated to Jackson in 1916 took a position there as field agent.

One of her duties was the placement of orphans in foster homes. Adoption was so uncommon then that even the most altruistic social workers believed the only way to spare homeless children incarceration in spartan institutions was to place them in "work" homes in which they earned their keep by performing menial chores.

Georgia would prove far more resourceful than other social workers in arranging adoptions. She also reaped very different benefits from social work.

Ethical workers found satisfaction in helping others. Georgia considered social work a vehicle through which to achieve power, adulation, wealth, and prestige—goals that would seem unattainable to even the most ambitious social workers today, who would be constrained by agency policy. But the field's lack of regulation in the early twentieth century left children vulnerable, particularly in Mississippi.

Children adopted elsewhere were generally their adoptive parents' heirs. Mississippi residents, however, were allowed to adopt with the condition that the children wouldn't inherit from them, a condition deplored by the state's ethical social workers, who realized these children would be treated as servants. Georgia's supervisors at the Mississippi Children's Home-Finding Society had begun providing financial aid to the relatives of orphans, so that children could remain with their families of birth.

Georgia, who lacked her colleagues' scruples, considered adoptive placement a business. In another departure from previous adoption practices, she considered her clients to be the prospective adoptive parents who would make her wealthy, rather than the babies she placed. She was equally unconcerned with the rights of birth parents. In 1992 I spoke with a woman whose grandmother, Rose Harvey, may have been one of the first mothers Georgia harmed.

Rose encountered Georgia in 1922—approximately sixteen years after Georgia's first adoptive placement. By then she had apparently stepped over the line; she wasn't simply finding adoptive homes for orphans, but for children she'd kidnapped. One spring morning she drove her Model T to a cabin in Jasper County, near her Hickory hometown. Asleep inside was Rose Harvey, who was young, poor, widowed, and pregnant, and suffering from diabetes. Her two-year-old son Onyx played on the back porch. Georgia lured the sturdy black-haired, brown-eyed boy into her car.

Georgia's father, George C. Tann, signed papers declaring Rose Harvey an unfit mother and young Onyx an abandoned child. Onyx was placed with an adoptive family headed by a man named Rufus Rasberry. Shortly afterward Onyx's three-year-old brother was also taken from his mother and placed with Rufus's brother, Clyde.

Heart-stricken and incensed, Rose sued to regain her children, unsuccessfully; George may have intervened. But Georgia's child-placing practices may have angered some local residents. She was run out of town shortly after placing Rose's little boys for adoption—I have been unable to learn if this case or some other, unknown one was the cause. Her father had friends in Memphis. After working briefly for a Texas orphanage, she got a job with the Memphis branch of the Tennessee Children's Home Society, and moved there in July of 1924.

7.

Georgia's Memphis

The city to which Georgia moved perfectly matched her needs. She wasn't subtle. Blunt, assured of her right to do anything she wished, she made little effort to hide her crimes. Citizens of the Memphis that existed before the yellow fever plague of 1878 would have run her out of town. But by 1924 Edward Hull Crump had rendered Memphians spineless, afraid to criticize him and his friends.

Crump began this change shortly after his successful mayoral campaign in 1909, during which he promised to purge Memphis of prostitutes and gangsters. He didn't rid the city of them, however; he managed them, charging them $50 weekly fines and allowing them to stay in business. Crump knew that attaining his goal of ruling Memphis would require citizen support. He courted everyone, providing black residents with parks and athletic fields, poor white citizens with free milk, and young professionals with political positions.

But he did more than appeal to every person; he indulged every part of every person, who had impulses both noble and base. The base, he believed, were stronger, although few citizens would admit it. He didn't pierce their denial. By fining the owners of gambling parlors and bordellos he feigned giving conservative Memphians what they claimed they wanted—control over crime—while allowing them to indulge in whatever vice they wished.

Memphians understood that they were no longer supposed to perceive their entire city, the good and the bad, but only what Crump wanted them to see. The broken campaign promise they first ignored must have seemed unimportant. The fact that Crump was making money from crime was harder to rationalize.

Not—and Memphians I spoke with insisted that this made it bearable—that he took the money home. His cut of vice profits—money extorted from Dutch Mary, the madam; Joe Bernadino of the Bernadino Syndicate; and Jim Mulcahy, owner of the Memphis Cotton Club, money collected into little black bags on Wednesday afternoons by city workers whose efforts were coordinated by Crump lieutenant Frank "Roxie" Rice, whose tobacco juice perpetually ran down his shirt—provided a governmental slush fund. The fund, which financed elections and city improvements, was augmented by contributions from city workers.

Workers had to contribute, or lose their jobs. And beating Crump at the polls would have been difficult. He banned voting machines, requiring that Memphians hand their ballots to people loyal to him. Within hours he knew how every citizen had voted. And any city worker who had voted wrong was soon unemployed.

Memphians told themselves not to mind. Memphis was improved. Crump paved the city's streets, and reduced taxes to the lowest rate in history.

And while previous mayors had ignored details of city government, Crump toured Memphis by day and even by night, noting every broken lamppost and quickly having it repaired. He made Memphis pretty, organizing society women into highly competitive beautification committees.

For the first time since the plague, citizens traveling outside the city could identify themselves as Memphians without embarrassment.

And those who cooperated with Crump found their lives so easy. When a young attorney named Gerald Stratton asked for his support in the 1930s, Crump smiled and said, "I'll catapult you into public office." Instantly Stratton became a state legislator. Two years later he was state senator, and two years after that he was elected to the lucrative post of county court clerk.

Then Gerald asserted himself in 1942. After increasingly frustrating years of obeisance, he criticized Crump's support of the poll tax. Stunned and furious, Crump demanded he resign from office. Gerald refused, and was harassed by threatening phone calls and police surveillance. Most upsetting to him and his wife, Roswell, however, was the shunning.

No one spoke to Gerald at work or on the street. Roswell was blackballed from the Junior League; the local chapter of the Red Cross wouldn't let her donate blood. They were treated like lepers. Then one Sunday morning a man in a black sedan tried, or pretended to try—in Memphis it was hard to know the difference—to run them over. At forty-two years of age, Gerald suffered a heart attack.

He and Roswell left Memphis, spending the next twenty-six years in Boston, Massachusetts. Then they moved back to Tennessee, settling in Nashville, where I visited Roz in 1992. She told me she was proud of her late husband for speaking his conscience. She said he was one of very few Memphians to do it. "Of course we did end up poor—Gerald left behind his law practice. But he took courses at Harvard and practiced law in Massachusetts; I got a job in a hotel. We opened up and got in touch with the whole bigger world."

The Crump Machine that hurt the Strattons would greatly aid Georgia Tann. The Machine's base was the city's municipal workers, who during political campaigns were required to march in parades, attend nightly rallies, and canvass neighborhoods. To them were added young attorneys who rode crowded streetcars, making impassioned speeches for Crump.

Above the base was the Machine's middle tier, made up of henchmen like bagman Frank "Roxie" Rice. For thirty years, he served as campaign manager, slush fund coordinator, and director of the Memphis bloc of state delegates, who served at Crump's whim and voted however he wished.

Victims spoken of in whispers, like the union organizer whose body was said to have been found facedown in the Mississippi, and the criminals who were escorted to the state line for beatings and never seen again in Tennessee or any other state, were believed to have been dealt with by the brawny Roxie. His office in a remote courthouse corridor was inaccessible to anyone outside Crump's inner circle. He was said to live on cigarettes, whiskey, and Coke.

When Georgia met Crump in 1924, he was fifty and seemed the most assured man on the planet. He had easily survived the only threat to his leadership: legislation passed by conservative citizens in 1916 that ousted him from the office of mayor. He resigned instead, named his successor, and had himself elected county trustee, a lucrative post. Then he tightened his grip on the city. From his post as trustee, and later his private business office, Crump pulled the strings that animated the politicians who pretended to govern. No one was nominated for any office without his approval. No one with his approval lost a city election or, eventually, a statewide contest: by 1940 he would mastermind 102 political contests without defeat.

In 1922 he tested his power, not declaring for a mayoral candidate until the night before the election. Then he whispered five words: "Rowlett Paine is our man." Phones jangled; Crump's Boys told the bootleggers, the bootleggers told the waitresses, the waitresses told the customers, and when the votes were counted Crump's power was confirmed.

With elections this farcical his Boys scarcely needed to campaign. But Crump's hold over Memphis was more psychological than physical, and he understood the importance of letting citizens pretend they had a choice. So even during the many years when his candidates ran unopposed Crump acted as if they might lose, raising money, printing posters, burning bonfires at midnight rallies.

Crump also capitalized on Tennessee's poll tax—a tax on voting which was intended to disenfranchise the state's many black citizens. He paid their poll taxes and bussed them to the polls, where they voted for his candidates. White Memphians pretended not to notice. Obliviousness seemed particularly essential after the gubernatorial election of 1928.

Crump longed to determine the outcome. In an unsuccessful effort—his last such until 1948, when his statewide hold was broken—he voted more black citizens than ever before. Local reporters attempting to photograph this were beaten by the police, then jailed for "threatened breach of the peace"—an offense (or the potential of one) for which they could not post bail.

Memphians allowed themselves to notice enough of this to note that they should never notice anything again. Decades before *1984* was a flicker in Orwell's brain, Memphians learned to see without seeing, to act as if they were asleep even when they were awake. Scarred by their beatings and time in jail, some reporters left the city—Turner Catledge went to Manhattan, where he became managing editor of the *New York Times*. Of those who remained in Memphis, however, many slept, too.

So did the judicial system. Members of the Memphis Bar Association had averted their eyes since 1915, after observing Crump fire a sheriff who refused to tamper with a jury. Rather than risk political suicide, they backed any candidate he picked. Everyone knew whom to support, a Memphis judge recalled decades later. "It always was a Crump man." Except when it was a woman.

8.

The Little Wanderers

*B*oss Crump was so helpful to Georgia that I initially considered her manipulation of him to have been her greatest coup. Instead I discovered her primary achievement to have been something I hadn't considered necessary: the creation of an adoptive market. When Georgia began her child-placing career, almost no one adopted children.

I was more surprised by this fact than I should have been: I'd written several articles about adoption. My pieces, however, had concerned the institution as it existed in the 1990s, when the demand for healthy white American infants exceeded the supply. I had assumed that the number of adoptions in the first third of the twentieth century had been proportionately consistent with the number arranged during the final third, when the U.S. population included 6 million adoptees.

I had been naive or, if I'd had an intimation of the truth, afraid to face it. My analysis of Georgia's physical setting had been performed at little emotional cost. Placing her within the context of the history of the care of homeless children would, I feared, be more difficult. It would in fact bring me uncomfortably close to Georgia, and cause me to question how heinous she was. Sitting in the Cleveland Public Library one dark February day, I read facts so appalling they made her crimes seem almost benign.

It was an unwelcome thought, not only because I was more comfortable considering the outcome of her actions to have been absolutely pernicious, but because of what it implied about the suffering endured through the years by the most vulnerable among us. Over the next week I realized that more than defensiveness had impelled an elderly Hickory woman to say, "We thought Georgia was doing a wonderful thing" for the children. I recalled a Memphian's boast that she hadn't given her children to garbage men. Poised at a road I didn't want to travel, I nervously considered to whom she had, directly or indirectly, provided babies.

The lives of unwanted children, always bleak, were revealed to have evolved from an even more lamentable state as I researched further back in history, to a point when babies were routinely murdered at birth by their parents. Infanticide was practiced and condoned in ancient Greece, endorsed by Aristotle and Plato.

Some sickly, disabled, or female infants were suffocated, drowned, or dashed against rocks. More often unwanted children were "exposed," abandoned in marketplaces or on hillsides. Most died of starvation; others were forced into slavery or maimed for exhibition.

Infanticide gradually became less acceptable: by the Middle Ages Europeans who killed their children were subject to death by decapitation, impalement, or torture with glowing tongs. Some infanticidal women were burned as witches; others were enclosed in sacks full of vipers and drowned in "sacking ponds," like the Säcklache in Zittau, Germany.

But poverty was so pervasive and contraceptive methods so ineffective that the killing of children continued. According to Rachel Zinober Forman, author of *Let Us Now Praise Obscure Women*, a study of single mothers in the United States and Britain, infanticide was the most common crime in Western Europe between the Middle Ages and the eighteenth century.

Along with this practice, however, evolved more compassionate means of treating orphaned or unwanted children. An orphan asylum was built in what is now Trier, Germany, in the sixth century. The first orphanage in our country was established by Ursuline nuns in 1727.

But such institutions were rare. People were reluctant to support homeless children financially, and in Europe and the United States even young single parents were legally obligated to raise their babies. Bastardy Acts, including legislation passed in 1741 in North Carolina, which included what became the state of Tennessee, authorized imprisonment for any parent failing to support a child born outside marriage. Several states passed laws forbidding separation of infants younger than six months from their mothers. Matrons of maternity homes forced residents to breastfeed their babies, so the mothers would bond with them and keep them.

Orphans and foundlings were forced to earn their keep by working as servants or slaves. With trepidation I read of the auction of seventeen homeless children in Newton, Massachusetts, in 1793, having five minutes earlier learned of the murder of an orphaned twelve-year-old Boston servant in 1655. Bruises covered the boy's body; his back had been ripped open by lashes. His master was found guilty of manslaughter, but sentenced only to being burned on the hand.

There was no mention in any of my books of what became of the seventeen auctioned Newton, Massachusetts, children.

Infanticide, institutionalization, auctioning: these and other methods of caring for unwanted children overlapped in time and coexist today in some countries. But there has also been some progress, with relatively fewer child deaths and more humane care of orphans.

Another means of caring for children was indenture, which originated in England. Indentured children worked for host families in exchange for lodging and food. While the hosts weren't expected to treat the children as family, they were required to educate them and provide them with several acres of land at the end of their servitude at twenty-one. But provision of the benefits was not enforced: few children received an education or any land, and many were abused.

Indentured children were considered nuisances, and the British deported many of them to their colonies. Four indentured youngsters traveled on the *Mayflower* in 1620. Life in the New World, arduous at best, was particularly difficult for unprotected, overworked, indentured children—only one of the *Mayflower* orphans survived his first Plymouth winter. Concern regarding the high mortality rate suffered by these children was outweighed by desire to keep them off the public dole: indenturing was popular, and, with the limited use of institutionalization, contained the problem of homeless children for a time.

But the Industrial Revolution in the 1880s and the influx of 35 million European immigrants to the United States swelled the ranks of the poor, some of whom were unable to care for their children. Many desperate mothers gave their babies to workers at foundling asylums. Lacking sufficient employees, however, workers at many orphanages boarded the babies with uneducated women who killed them with neglect.

Abandoned children found by the police were usually dead. Those discovered alive in New York City were taken to Bellevue Hospital, where they were randomly assigned religions and names. An infant found in an alley would be named Charlie Alley; a girl found under a cherry tree near a hill would become Cherry Hill. Infants whose discovery coincided with a sensational murder trial were named after the victims, witnesses, or perpetrators. The abandoned children were cared for by prisoners and, if they survived until age four, sent to poorhouses.

Filthy institutions in which children mixed with criminally insane adults, poorhouses were condemned by reformers as "living tombs." The subsequent building of more orphanages must have seemed like progress.

But though some children's asylums were undoubtedly good, those I read about seemed little better than poorhouses, with infant mortality rates 50 percent on average, and, in places such as New York City's Randalls Island, as high as 100 percent. During the particularly terrible year of 1895, 129 foundlings were admitted. One was adopted; four were reclaimed by their parents: every one of the remaining 124 babies died.

The odds of child deaths couldn't have been higher than in this orphanage. But in terms of sheer cruelty, nothing equaled what occurred on baby farms.

Baby farms were homes or apartments where, for a small fee, uneducated women housed babies whose parents were unable to raise them. Some baby farmers received periodic payments; others were paid in a lump sum. Those receiving a one-time fee had no financial incentive to keep the children alive, and some farmers starved, suffocated, or drowned them.

Death rates on baby farms whose owners had insured the lives of their charges were particularly high, a fact that inspired an 1895 *New York Times* editorial urging that life insurance for children be declared invalid, as it was a "temptation to inhuman crimes." Nevertheless the killing of children for insurance benefits continued, and sentences for farmers found guilty of exposing babies to the sun for so long their skin blackened and they died of dehydration, fatally poisoning children with whiskey or cracking their skulls against walls, were abysmally low. One baby farmer who killed "at least" fifty-three children received a three- to seven-year sentence.

Residents of poorhouses and baby farms who survived to adolescence often fled. It's difficult to know how many children, orphaned, abandoned, or having run away, were on their own by 1872: the number of street urchins was estimated to be thirty thousand in New York City and six thousand in Boston. These and other cities teemed with the young homeless, who begged, stole, sold newspapers, and sometimes prostituted themselves for food. They were the "apple boys" and "flower girls" who peddled their goods on street corners; the "singing girls" who boarded docked ships at night to entertain the men with music and were sometimes raped; and the true-life counterparts of Hans Christian Andersen's "The Little Match Girl," which I had never been able to read as a child without crying.

Reading now of where these children slept—on steps, in filthy cellars, the iron tubes of bridges in Harlem and burned-out safes on Wall Street, of how ten would pile together for warmth in winter or jostle for spots near grates through which hot air blew, generated by underground presses—I felt like crying again, and not simply for these now long-dead waifs. What I had been avoiding was gaining on me. I kept putting a particular face to the singing girl, and a name.

I drove home from the library that evening through streets full of salt-encrusted vehicles and gray with slush. Viewed after reading of baby farms and rat-infested tenements, my home seemed more luxurious than I usually found it. It was located in the comfortable kind of suburb I had once vowed I would never live in and that I appreciated, then, for its safety and good public school.

Even families so sheltered, of course, have problems, and mine had its share, but not that night, when all was perfect, with a fire in the fireplace, my husband, having arrived home unexpectedly early from a business trip, warming sauce and cooking pasta, the children working on, and occasionally helping each other with, algebra and geometry problems.

I tried not to think about my luck; I feared I'd jinx it. And I didn't tell my family what threatened me and how it might affect us. I did explain that homeless children had been so poorly valued in the past that the name of a Nashville orphanage—the Home for Friendless Children— had elicited no protest, and that even social reformers of the nineteenth century had called the children "ragamuffins," "little wanderers," "street Arabs," and "guttersnipes."

These terms hardly inspired people to want to raise these children. In the library the next afternoon I was reminded that the institution of adoption—which throughout its history in the United States has been regulated on a state-by-state basis, and which has existed legally since Massachusetts passed the country's first adoption law in 1851—was not immediately popular. At the beginning of the twentieth century adoption was still rare, and adoptable children were beginning to seem not more but less desirable because of belief in an ideology that, imported from England, insisted they were genetically flawed.

Developed by Charles Darwin's second cousin, Francis Galton, the eugenics movement promoted the maintenance of a genetically healthy population by means that included sterilization of people deemed unfit to procreate, and was meant to counter the fact that poor, uneducated Americans were bearing more children than were cultured ones. Some particularly prolific breeders were among those considered most "abnormal"—single mothers.

The books and articles I read never explained why these mothers were considered abnormal: I gathered that the magnitude of their sin was considered sufficient proof. Their abnormality was supposedly manifested in their "feeble-minded" intellect, "depraved" morals, or physical abnormalities. The author of a 1918 study titled "The Unmarried Mother: A Study of 500 Cases," described single mothers as "repulsive" and "misshapen." A physician writing in the journal *Mental Hygiene* claimed that some mothers were "excessively equipped sexually."

Researchers found what they expected to see: the 1918 study of five hundred unmarried mothers pronounced one-third retarded and most of the rest "moral monstrosities," "melancholic," "demented," psychotic, or epileptic. Young women for whom no shred of evidence of illness could be found were labeled "probable epileptics" or "pre-insane." Their babies, according to eugenicists, would inherit their worst traits.

Not even idealists such as the Reverend Charles Loring Brace believed the children could escape their inherited taint. "It is well known to those familiar with the criminal classes," he wrote in his influential book, *The Dangerous Classes of New York*, published in 1872, "that certain appetites or habits, if indulged abnormally and excessively through two or more generations, come to have an almost irresistible force, and, no doubt, modify the brain so as to constitute almost an insane condition." Referring to a nine- or ten-year-old girl, "given up, apparently beyond control, to licentious habits and desires," he warned, "the 'gemmules,' or latent tendencies, or forces, or cells of her immediate ancestors were in her system, and working in her blood, producing irresistible effects. . . ."

These effects, he believed, would soon be felt by everyone. The title of Brace's book referred to the children of the poor, who he believed formed a dangerous underclass that, if unreclaimed, would poison all of society.

These children were generally considered unworthy of adoption. But Brace and others felt they could be prevented from destroying the nation by serving time in "God's own country"—on farms in the Midwest. Brace, a Yale graduate from a prominent New England family, founded the New York Children's Aid Society in 1853. His organization and the New York Foundling Hospital, which was run by the Sisters of Charity, were responsible for the most massive resettlement of the Eastern poor in American history, the Orphan Train Project. Brace and his workers swept through New York City streets, gathering up orphans and children of the poor and shipping them out west. Between 1853 and the early 1930s, approximately 250,000 children were "resettled."

The Orphan Train resettlement differed from indenture in that custody of the children remained with Brace's organization, not with the farmer who would expose them to the fresh air and farm work that would effect their redemption. But, like indenture, it depended for its success upon the kindness of strangers. The scope of Brace's vision, combined with a lack of resources, precluded investigation of those who took in children, and seldom allowed for supervisory visits. His methods were bare-boned, involving the deployment of scouts who traveled out west, searching for areas in obvious need of free labor. Notices were posted, such as, "Wanted—Homes for Children—A Company of Homeless Children from the East Will Arrive at Troy, Missouri, on Friday, February 25, 1910."

What happened next was seen differently by the different parties. Brace, who believed so strongly that children were benefited by resettlement that he couldn't understand why some poor parents refused to allow theirs to ride the Train, described the process like this:

"On a given day in New York the ragged and dirty little ones are gathered to a central office from the streets and lanes . . . are cleaned and dressed, and sent away, under the charge of an experienced agent. . . . When they arrive in the village a great public meeting is held. . . . Farmers come in from twenty to twenty-five miles looking for the 'model boy' who shall do the light work at the farm . . . ; housekeepers look for girls to train up; mechanics seek boys for their trades. . . . Thus, in a few hours, the little colony is placed in comfortable homes. . . ."

Orphan Train riders found the journey much more complicated and frightening. Most were headed for states and towns they'd never heard of. Since the Train made several stops, at each of which a portion of the children was "resettled," many were separated from siblings and friends. At the stops, the children were taken to a courthouse, church, or opera house and placed on an elevated platform. Signs identifying them by number were sometimes hung around their necks. Farmers examined the children's teeth and checked their muscles, then marked down the numbers of their first, second, and third choices. Some children were made to tell jokes, or do acrobatic stunts.

The children must have felt like slaves at auction, and, receiving in this strange new environment no indication of their worth other than audience reaction, experienced extreme humiliation if they weren't selected quickly. Robert Petersen, an Omaha attorney who rode the Train to Blair, Nebraska, at age six in 1923, later recalled the terrible Saturday night when no one wanted him, and the happiness he experienced two days later when he was selected. He was doubly fortunate in that the farming couple treated him not as a farm hand, but as a quasi-legal son.

Few Train riders were treated as sons and daughters. Interviewed in the 1980s by authors of *We Are a Part Of History: The Story of the Orphan Train*, ninety-three-year-old Mary Goth of Clinton, Missouri, recalled, "My experience was that of a servant. My foster mother was cruel—oh, she was a cracker jack." As Mary matured and planned to leave to get a paying job, her foster parents schemed to have one of their sons impregnate her, so she would remain their maid.

The worst hardship suffered by Orphan Train children was the separation from their parents. One little girl who'd been placed in a comfortable home wrote to an Orphan Train worker, "I would give a hundred worlds like this, if I could see my mother."

Despite the pain of these children, Brace's experiment was considered a success, and there was little criticism of the fact that resettled Train riders worked long hours in their country homes. Most poor children, even those who lived with their parents, labored at home or in the fields and, after the Industrial Revolution, in factories.

Employers bragged about the intricate piecework produced by children's nimble fingers. Some Americans were shocked, however, to learn that these children were as young as four. Reformers took note and by 1900, twenty-eight states passed legislation protecting child workers. The laws were vague and difficult to enforce, but, combined with the passage of compulsory education legislation and steadily rising income levels, they obviated much of the need for children to supplement their parents' income. Child labor began to seem wrong, even for orphans.

With less emphasis placed on their earning potential, children began to be valued as children. They also seemed to be growing scarce. Between 1850 and 1915, the annual birth rate for native white Americans dropped nearly 40 percent, from 42.8 to 26.2 per thousand, with the average married couple producing three children, not the eight they would have a century before. Some contemporary accounts attributed the decrease in fertility to tight corseting. The apparent shortage of children made each one seem more precious.

The stigma regarding adoption persisted, however, fed not only by tales of bad "gemmules" but by the skepticism of social workers who insisted that orphans be studied for a year before adoption, to ensure their fitness for placement.

Many adults strongly desired to parent, however, and there had always been some willing to raise children born to others. While some procured children through orphanages, others obtained babies through secretive means. The earliest such instance of which I read involved a childless, elderly knight named Thomas of Saleby and his elderly wife, who lived in Lincolnshire, England, in the seventeenth century. Anxious to have an heir, and aware of the impossibility of adopting in England, which because of a belief in the importance of maintaining bloodlines didn't have adoption legislation until 1926, they obtained a baby girl from a village woman and Thomas's wife pretended to have borne her. The couple stood fast, keeping the baby even after their bishop threatened to excommunicate them for fraud. (Thomas, who realized how much his wife loved the child, is said to have told the Bishop, "I fear the wrath of my wife more than I fear the wrath of God.")

The subject of a February 1921 *New York Times* article went further than Thomas's wife. Over the previous thirteen years, fifty-one-year-old Mrs. F. E. A. South of Atlanta, Georgia, had not only secretly obtained eleven children, but fooled even her husband into thinking she'd borne them. "They range in age from two months to thirteen years," the reporter wrote, "and live in complete ignorance of their true origin," although obviously not for much longer. Mrs. South had procured them secretly, continued the reporter, because of her "great desire for babies," which explained why she had acquired them but not why she'd lied about it. His readers wouldn't have needed that explained. In 1921 adoptable children were still considered tainted, not simply by the public in general but in many cases by the husbands of would-be adoptive mothers. There is no mention in the *Times* piece of whether Mr. South would have welcomed these eleven children into his home if he had known they weren't biologically his: when interviewed he was apparently still in shock, insisting that his wife's confession was "an infernal lie."

While similarly skirting the issue of American males' aversion to adoption, an article published in 1921 in *Sunset, The Pacific Monthly*, noted the increasing frequency of women deceiving their mates. "It is not uncommon for a woman to call upon a [maternity home] worker, announce that she has informed her husband of the stork's impending visit, explain that the husband is . . . on a business trip [and] present a rush order for a child."

Surprisingly often, the husbands were duped. But in 1926 Mrs. Nat Bass of Brooklyn, New York, felt compelled to confess her deception to her husband, and the district attorney, when the baby farmer from whom she had purchased an infant was investigated for fatally starving and beating twenty-two children. Fearful the farmer would reveal her name, Mrs. Bass admitted to faking both a pregnancy and a minor traffic accident, which, she had claimed, necessitated she be treated at the baby farmer's "clinic." When her husband arrived, she lay in bed with a newborn baby boy.

Mrs. Bass's belief that her husband would accept only a birth child, not an adopted baby, seems to have been accurate, for although authorities were willing to allow her to keep eight-month-old Nat Jr., her husband rejected him. "I don't want the child," he said. "I won't keep it in my home. I did love it, because I believed it to be my own son. . . . You'll have to take the child away."

The baby became a public charge, which meant he could be sent to Randalls Island. "The poor little thing," understated the prosecutor, "got a very bad break in life."

Reading this, I could almost literally see the split, see the thousands of children languishing in orphanages and on baby farms; the thousands of infertile adults who desperately wanted a child, but, because of a belief in eugenics, were afraid to adopt one. Between them was the void I had sensed when reading the books on adoptive history, which noted that the number of adoptions had increased threefold between 1934 and 1944, but never mentioned why this had happened or that, in one Southern city, the number of adoptive placements had spiked decades before that. As I researched the history of the care of homeless children, the void had grown progressively less empty. In it, summoned as if by some perverse part of my subconscious, was the woman forced to seek the prestige, money, and power she would never achieve in law in the unlikely venue of social work, led by a sense of opportunism and specific psychological urges to the subcategory of adoption.

She developed both her business and the institution of adoption by doing something unprecedented: making homeless children acceptable, even irresistible, to childless couples. She accomplished this by insisting, when most child placement workers apologized for the unworthiness of adoptable babies, that they were neither children of sin nor genetically flawed. They are, she said repeatedly, blank slates. They are born untainted, and if you adopt them at an early age and surround them with beauty and culture, they will become anything you wish them to be.

Georgia didn't actually believe the children were blank slates, but she made her sales pitch with conviction, evincing the bravado that would later allow her to decry black market adoptions while arranging them herself.

But she didn't rely on her ability to persuade. Even as she proclaimed, "Rearing and environment mean much more than inheritance," she falsified children's records, transforming them from the offspring of parents she considered poor white trash to the children of debutantes and medical students. She portrayed her children as more genetically perfect beings than most adoptive parents could have borne themselves.

And Georgia virtually guaranteed the success of her placements. "One hundred of our children turn out, on average, much better than 100 children [raised in their families of birth]," she said. "The reason is that ours is a selective process. We select the child, and we select the home."

People other than Georgia learned how to exploit the previously underground market for adoptable children, and baby farmers began selling children for as much as $100.

Nationally, adoption remained rare in the 1920s. The Orphan Trains traveled west until the early 1930s. But by 1935 Georgia had waiting lists with the names of couples from across the United States, Canada, and South America.

I sat hunched in the library reading room recoiling from my discovery that Georgia Tann had invented modern American adoption. I was almost afraid to learn what her proximity to the institution said about it, or her.

Adoption, a respected institution that has brought millions of people joy, reflected more flatteringly than I wanted it to on Georgia, softening her edges, making haze of her essence. I was accustomed to thinking of her solely as having hurt children, demeaned them, sold, even killed them. I was accustomed to focusing on those she stole, who lost parents, siblings, histories; whose mothers lost not only babies but their babies' babies—grandchildren—and on and on: unimaginable, immeasurable, unquantifiable griefs. But an unknowable percentage of the more than five thousand children Georgia sold had in fact lost their parents to death, relinquishment, or abandonment, and, without her intervention, might well have died on baby farms.

This, for so many Memphians and, that February day, even for me, was the sticking point: she did help some children. She helped them, admittedly, for ignoble motives. And even when she helped them she did it accidentally, since by requiring only that adoptive parents pay her fee and failing to investigate their characters, she never knew whether she was putting babies into cold or abusive situations.

Some of her children, however, ended up with wonderful adoptive parents. Did the fact that she occasionally, uncaringly, inadvertently, helped children exonerate her, even in part? I knew it didn't, but that day I felt it did. I felt a chink in my defenses through which Georgia could wound me.

I was vulnerable, too, on the other side of the Georgia Tann:adoption equation. This side, I sensed, was even more tainted by proximity to her than she was shown to advantage by it. The reason was more than intellectual aversion to seeing a respected institution sullied. I am a person who often feels guilty for things not remotely my fault. Conversely, I sometimes feel more than accountably grateful to people like Thomas Edison for inventing the lightbulb. I am a person who would feel that adoptive parents are indebted to the person who popularized the institution from which they have profited. And I didn't want to owe Georgia Tann anything—least of all, my adopted child.

I have two children: Beth, who when I sat in the Cleveland library that day was sixteen, and Tim, who was fifteen. They are wonderful, loving children, the kind of people who, if I met them as strangers, I would want as friends.

When they were very young, I had tried to forget which was the adopted one. I did this not for a noble motive, but out of cowardice. Being a mother is hard, I knew from having watched my own, and being a child more difficult than many adults like to recall. And I sensed that the fact of adoption might make parenting more complicated, and growing up more difficult for the adopted child.

I didn't want to worry about this so I shoved it under, nervously, and between the nervousness and the burying I hurt Beth.

How easily, I see in retrospect, I justified ignoring her adoptive status. "I don't want to raise an 'adopted child,' just a child," I thought blithely when she was an infant.

Pretending that the fact of her adoption had no effect on Beth or me predisposed me to believe it had no relevance to my work, even as I wrote the *Good Housekeeping* article and began researching my book. My interest in the subject of Georgia Tann was professional only, I had assured myself, even as part of me realized that my reaction to her was informed by my status as an adoptive parent.

Regarding my research, I had attempted an impossible balance, getting close enough to relate the story with some empathy while staying far enough away to avoid intersection with it, and especially its protagonist— a futile gesture, as she could have told me.

Now my personal life and research had collided, forcing me to accept who I was. Throughout my research, I had identified with Georgia's victimized birth parents rather than with her wealthy clients. But I too was an adoptive parent, profiting from the institution she popularized, profiting from another woman's misery—the loss of her child.

It was frightening to be so unmasked. And I had more than my own feelings to worry about. Having acknowledged Georgia's connection to my family, I understood I would have to mention it in my book. How would that affect Beth? I pictured her: smart, strong, popular, but with the vulnerability that even the most self-confident adoptees possess. Beth considered adoption a private matter, too private, I'd always felt, though I realized that believing she might become more comfortable with her adoptive status by talking about it for my book might be the ultimate justification.

I didn't know how to broach the possibility with her.

Feeling trapped inside my head, I shifted my gaze from the knothole on the table before me to the tables beyond mine, and further to the decorative scrollwork and chandeliers I loved. I took ten minutes to get a drink of water, relishing every second spent, every step taken down curving stone stairways hollowed by other people's footsteps. Sitting back down, I retreated gratefully into research, deciding to begin exploring Georgia's effect on adoption by considering the validity of her sales pitch: adoptable children are blank slates.

Several adoptees had told me how this statement had hurt them. It wasn't simply that they, like all children, entered the world with genes preordaining them to certain intelligences, personalities, appearances, and talents, but that many, adopted past infancy and occasionally at ages as advanced as sixteen, arrived in their new homes after having been immersed in a specific culture and, more significantly, traumatized by separation from their birth families.

Not even the youngest of them was "blank." Georgia, however, sent six- and seven-year-olds with no musical ability to couples who, because of her falsification of their records, expected them to become concert pianists. She sent children of limited intelligence to college professors intent upon sending them to Yale.

"Can you imagine those children trying to adjust to homes like that?" Denny Glad had asked me. "Can you imagine the frustration of those adoptive parents?"

Of course I couldn't, any more than I could ever know exactly how many children had been rejected and returned to Georgia, or had been placed in detention homes, or had run away.

I had talked to adoptees dealt these fates. And I'd read an article in the February 1933 issue of *American Mercury* magazine in which one wrote eloquently of her frustration. "The danger that threatens an adopted child is not his uncertain heredity, his obscure background, or doubtful legitimacy, but the fact that his adoptive parents take him ready-made and then expect him to grow and evolve according to specifications which they set down as definitely as they select his sex or the color of his hair. When in any way he disappoints them, the trouble begins."

I wondered if Georgia's blank slate assertion still hurt adopted children. While it seemed unlikely that contemporary adoptive parents would believe her claim, most people hope their children will share their interests. It's unfair to expect this of either adopted or biologically related children. But those raised by parents whose genes they share are more likely to resemble them in interests and talents. Adopted children have, of course, no genetic coding from their adoptive parents. I recall the surprise with which I watched Beth develop, and am grateful she was so determined to do it her own way. But if she'd been less assertive, would I have tried harder to mold her?

"When I adopted my own two children, the agency worker told me my nurturing would affect them nine times more than their heredity," a child psychiatrist I spoke with for this project told me. Knowledgeable as she was herself, she tried to believe the worker, until her children taught her the truth.

It was her clients that Georgia sought to serve; it is (and this is a half-step forward) the needs of children and adoptive parents that adoption workers consider today. Birth parents remain the most neglected members of the adoption triad; perhaps I shouldn't be surprised that it took me until the following day, Friday, of that February week to begin realizing how much Georgia had hurt them.

Their babies were, she said, born innocent—blank slates. By virtue of either their single or poor status, their parents, however, were tainted. According to Georgia and the theories of reformers, children raised by these tainted parents would quickly be tainted too. Single mothers, who before their children became marketable would have been forced to raise them, were suddenly considered incompetent to keep them. This message was clearly conveyed by Georgia and her lawyer, Abe Waldauer. Writing to Georgia in 1937 about a mother who had sued to regain the baby Georgia had stolen, he boasted that his cross-examination had reduced the young woman to mincemeat. Her "own counsel has indicated," he wrote, "that I have convinced her of her own unworthiness."

The predictable corollary to this was that white, wealthy, infertile, married couples felt entitled to the children others bore out of wedlock. It was as if single mothers bore children solely to fill childless couples' needs.

Illegitimacy, which had formerly been considered a nuisance, began to seem a societal blessing—when the children so born were white. Not until decades after Georgia's death would large numbers of white couples seek to adopt children of other races. But, aided by promotional techniques, the most effective of which exploited the children's appearance, Georgia's version of adoption—the placement of white children with white parents—grew popular.

Throughout the 1930s and '40s, as Georgia's influence extended outside Tennessee, the separation of babies from white, single mothers quickly became institutionalized. There were seventeen hundred separations of babies from young single women in Minnesota in 1949; in 1925, when these babies had widely been seen as undesirable, there had been only two hundred. And while the later partings were, outside Memphis, usually accomplished by methods less coercive than stealing, single mothers faced extreme pressure. One, whose social worker refused her any choice, communicated her frustrations in a letter to President Truman in August of 1950.

"With tears in my eyes and sorrow in my heart I am trying to defend the rights and privileges which every citizen in the United States is supposed to enjoy under our Constitution. . . . [J]ust because I had a baby under such circumstances, the welfare agency has no right to condemn me and demand my child be placed."

Exactly ten years and three months earlier, a young single mother had poured out her own anguish regarding the seizure of her child by Georgia Tann. A letter written by Mary Owens to a social worker she futilely hoped would help her recover her child reads, "Please help me to git my baby back. I am so heart broken about the way it has bin taken frome me until I am about to have a nervous break down. . . . After all it is our own darling baby and I would gladly lay down my life just to see her one time. . . . Miss Tann said she would all ways let me hear about her but it is just like asking about the dead. . . . Please help us as it is even hard to try to live. . . ."

Her babies died like flies.

—Investigator Robert Taylor

Part Two

Georgia's Crimes

9.

Georgia's Methods

Once I acknowledged my family's connection to Georgia and adoption, I found Mary Owens's letter almost too painful and personally resonant to read. Beth's birth mother had certainly felt sadness like Mary's. Mary's daughter must have cried, as Beth did, for the mother she had lost.

My husband Bob and I had seen Beth's mother in her hospital room two days after she had given birth. It was an unusual meeting for the time, required by the judge who was to give Beth's adoption legal standing.

I would later be grateful for the meeting, but I approached it with fear. My lawyer had called it "the confrontation," and if Beth hadn't been in the intensive care nursery it would have involved her, Bob, me, Beth's mother, and Beth's grandmother, who would have transferred Beth from her mother's arms to mine.

But the meeting was less emotional than I had anticipated, for only the adults were present. And though, as our attorneys had cautioned, no names were exchanged and scarcely a word was spoken, I was later able to open the door a little, to say, "Your mother wore jeans and a white shirt. She was pretty; she seemed nice." I was so nervous I blanked out her face, but her hair was brown and her eyes were blue-green.

Beth's eyes are the same striking color. She was a lovely baby. Georgia would have quickly sold her.

The energy that enabled Georgia to sell babies with alacrity when others couldn't give them away impressed Memphians from the first day of her arrival. Besides working long hours in her cramped downtown office in the Goodwyn Institute, site of the local branch of the Tennessee Children's Home Society, she visited merchants door-to-door, soliciting donations and espousing the benefits of adoption. It benefited not only children, she emphasized, but taxpayers, who would be spared the cost of maintaining orphanages. She mentioned the tax aspect often, and in the 1930s claimed to have saved Memphians $218,000 by arranging two thousand adoptions.

I don't know when Georgia revealed her ultimate goal, which had nothing to do with tax money: heading a national child-placing monopoly with branches in every state. But in a speech made in 1949 in her branch office in Los Angeles she said, "I want to hear from every family in the United States which would like to adopt a child, and from everyone who knows of a child who should be made available for adoption."

Not even she could achieve such control. By 1949 she was, despite her denial of it, close to death: the Los Angeles branch would be her only satellite location. But she had realized her childhood desire for money and fame, having become the most prolific and best-known adoption arranger in the country. She was also the country's most respected arranger, due to her ability to deceive people who didn't know her well. Georgia delivered speeches in Washington, New York, and other major cities, and was lauded by a national magazine as "the foremost leading light in adoption laws." Eleanor Roosevelt sought her counsel regarding child welfare; President Truman invited her to his inauguration; Pearl Buck asked her to collaborate on a book about adoption.

Georgia garnered national notice early; on September 19, 1929, five years after her arrival in Memphis, she was mentioned in a *New York Times* article regarding the director of an orphanage for black children.

Headlined "Welfare Worker Lays Alleged Forms of Punishment in Memphis Home to Woman Head," the article read, "Miss Georgia Tann, executive secretary of the Tennessee Children's Home Society, charged today that negro inmates of the Settlement Industrial Home were punished by being placed on hot stoves and made to stand on hot coals and in hot ashes. . . .

"The social worker's report . . . alleged that Bessie Simon, superintendent of the institution, was responsible for the alleged tortures and that one little negro's face was seared with a red hot poker for punishment. She said Bessie Simon was collecting money for orphans and running a boarding school at the same time. . . ."

It was an instance of the pot tarnishing the kettle: Georgia, too, abused children and received boarding money from temporarily incapacitated parents. She was also doing something even Bessie hadn't done: collecting boarding money from unsuspecting parents whose children she had already sold.

Georgia never publicly acknowledged the contradiction between her words and her behavior; she may not have admitted it to herself. Introspection would have robbed her of the aplomb that served her so well. Shortly after her death a reporter for the *Nashville Tennessean* described a speech Georgia delivered in 1944 to Memphians critical of her adoption practices.

"Her narrowed eyes gleaming with what appeared to be genuine anger, she brushed fingers through her silvery, short-cropped hair in a characteristic gesture," and acted as incensed as her audience by "'the thriving black market in babies. . . .'" But she admitted no part in baby selling, blaming instead "'Doctors, lawyers and private individuals [who] are arranging adoptions without a license to do so. . . .'"

According to reporter Nellie Kenyon, "Those who heard Miss Tann's stirring talk applauded her. They left the meeting with her words of warning ringing in their ears."

Georgia's propensity for deflection helped her greatly. So did her political clout. She had won Crump's support quickly upon arriving in Memphis, and constantly reminded citizens she had it, and that she would report the least resistance to her wishes to him. This bought her all the protection she needed. Police officers ignored parents whose children she had stolen; judges ruled against the parents in habeas corpus suits.

Judges also approved her illegal adoptions: one judge approved fourteen in a single day. But the judge most useful to Georgia was Juvenile Court Judge Camille Kelley. While pretending to advise parents struggling with illness, unemployment, or divorce, Judge Kelley secretly severed their parental rights and transferred custody of their children to Georgia. Kelley provided Georgia with a large number of children—20 percent of the more than five thousand children Georgia placed for adoption. A former court worker recalled Georgia perching "like a solitary vulture" in Kelley's courtroom.

Marie Long witnessed the collusion between Georgia and Camille Kelley in 1935. Fifteen-year-old Marie was living on a farm with three sisters and a brother when their mother, near death from cancer, asked the welfare department to board them until relatives could care for them. A worker drove them to Juvenile Court, where they met Georgia: "She had a tight-lipped, hatchet face," Marie told me. "She was hateful-looking, mean." They also met Judge Camille Kelley, who seemed the drab-appearing Georgia's opposite: smiling, perfumed, frilly, wearing silk, pearls, furs, and orchids even in court. She told the children they would be temporarily housed at the nearby St. Peter's Orphanage.

On the way five-year-old Christine, the youngest, sat on the lap of twelve-year-old Bessie, her second mother. Marie promised the others she would keep them together, no matter what. But when they arrived at the orphanage the court worker accompanying them grabbed Christine and dragged her into a waiting car. "Bessie!" she cried. "Bessie! Bessie! Bessie!"

"I can still hear her screams," Marie told me. "I begged the nuns at St. Peter's to tell me what had happened. Finally one said Georgia Tann had flown Christine out of state, to be adopted."

The help Camille Kelley gave Georgia was extensive enough, and required enough deadening of conscience, to suggest motivation beyond deference to someone protected by Crump. Former investigator Robert Taylor told me that Georgia bribed Judge Kelley and others, including the nurses who falsely told mothers their babies had died.

And many Memphians told me that Georgia had paid off Crump. "Her business contributed to his campaign coffers," said an elderly pediatrician. "She paid off the city to lay off her," another long-time Memphis resident said. And it's true that Crump extorted kickbacks even from churches, and made civil servants give him 15 percent of their pay.

But whether or not a financial arrangement existed between Georgia and Crump, he received more than money from her. She reflected well on Memphis during the years outsiders believed her to be "the foremost leading light" in American adoption. And she was even more solicitous of Crump's friends than she was of her ordinary clients. His cousin adopted through her, as did U.S. congressman and Memphis mayor Walter Chandler, judges, state representatives, and state senators. An elderly social worker described the speed with which Georgia met the needs of the head of the Memphis delegation to the state legislature, who had been awaiting the birth of a grandchild. When his daughter delivered a stillborn baby he called Georgia, who quickly brought a new-born to the delivery room. The legislator's daughter, who had been anesthetized for the delivery, never learned of the substitution.

"Miss Tann did for me what God himself couldn't do," said one of her board members, who had adopted through her. Grateful clients were particularly inclined to support her. But Georgia received help from people other than Crump and adoptive parents. The aid of Ann Atwood Hollinsworth, her lifelong partner, was crucial.

Eight years younger than Georgia, Ann was twenty-five when they moved to Memphis. She was never officially employed by Georgia, and worked as secretary for the Boy Scouts of America. But she spent her free time typing Georgia's business correspondence and ferrying adoptive babies across the country. She helped raise Georgia's adopted daughter, June, and gave Georgia a domestic life. Ann's "love for Miss Tann seemed sincere," wrote reporter Nellie Kenyon of the *Nashville Tennessean* shortly after Georgia's death. "She registered grief and pain at the death of the woman" she called "Sister." Ann lived for forty-five years afterward, dying in 1995 at age ninety-six. She seldom talked publicly about Georgia, but in the 1980s told a Memphis reporter that she had been "the most generous woman who ever lived."

Georgia provided financially for Ann, and may well have loved her: when the two fought and Ann checked into a hotel, Georgia sent her candy and flowers. But theirs was not a relationship of equals; Georgia dominated Ann as she did everyone else.

Georgia was a formidable woman. People saw her as larger than life. "She was a relentless, cold-blooded demon, a female smiling Buddha, a very wicked woman," I was told by a Memphis pediatrician who'd tried vainly to curb her in the 1940s. "She got bigger and bigger the more power she had. She was pompous, self-important—she was like Hitler, riding around in a big Cadillac driven by a uniformed chauffeur. She terrorized everyone."

Another of her contemporaries described her as "enormous" and "massive."

But although Georgia was big-boned and heavyset, she wasn't gigantic: she was about five feet, five inches tall and weighed about 155 pounds. She looks surprisingly ordinary in photographs: a plain and almost pleasant-seeming woman. She achieved this mundane appearance, an elderly Memphis attorney told me, "only because of her skill in projecting a positive image."

It was her combative nature, rather than her physical appearance, that intimidated others. She argued frequently about personal and professional issues, and never backed down. In articles written after her death, Tennessee reporters described her as fiery-tempered, pugnacious, "domineering, tyrannical. . . . Her ability to make those to whom she talked see her point was commanding. . . . Her word was law. . . ."

Her manner inspired instant obedience, particularly in children. "Oh, we were scared to death of Georgia," said a Hickory resident who as a child observed the adult Georgia visiting her mother, Beulah. "When she spoke, we minded. She was just that way."

She haunted Billy Hale in his dreams. When I spoke to him shortly after he'd viewed the *60 Minutes* episode on Georgia Tann, he described how she'd struck him for touching the glass beads of a lamp in the Home.

Georgia must have seemed only marginally less frightening to adults than to children; almost no one criticized her publicly until she was safely dead. Even then, such criticisms were few, and often juxtaposed with laudatory comments. A Memphis pediatrician described the surreal experience of reading the front page of a Memphis newspaper on September 15, 1950, the day of her death. It was three days after the press conference at which the governor had revealed that she wasn't the "angel of adoption" she'd pretended to be. "It was the strangest front page I've ever seen," the doctor told me. On the left side was an article describing her crimes. "On the right there was a eulogy with tremendous use of Roget's Thesaurus, praiseworthy words, saying what a wonderful woman she was."

Her obituaries were fawning, considering the circumstances, but accurate in many respects. "Miss Tann put her heart and soul into her work," wrote a reporter for the *Commercial Appeal*. "It was both her business and her hobby. It was not only her public life—it was her private life as well."

And Georgia was intelligent, directed, focused. Her devotion to work, which would have been noteworthy in anyone, seems particularly remarkable when her physical problems are taken into account. Injuries resulting from a car accident that occurred before she moved to Memphis had caused one of her legs to be shorter than the other, and despite the aid of an orthopedic shoe she walked with a limp. She suffered from arthritis and often used a cane. For the last five years of her life she suffered from cancer, for which she refused surgery, and treated with what Judge Camille Kelley called the "dope"—probably morphine—that enabled her to work.

Georgia seems to have lived in her head, solely by her wits and will, and to have ignored her body. It was a means to accomplishing her mission, and she meant it to project confidence, authority, success, and professionalism. She wore tailored suits or black skirts and print blouses, and black shoes with low Cuban heels. Her nails were manicured, but she used no other cosmetics. She wore one piece of jewelry, a two-carat diamond ring, on the fourth finger of her right hand. Her hair was fine, cropped, parted severely and worn off her face. Her eyes were blue, and projected willpower and resolve.

"Even her friends called her fearless," wrote reporter Nellie Kenyon shortly after Georgia's death. "Her determination to rule was as strong as the iron burglar-proof bars on the windows of her home. . . ."

Her fearlessness was best illustrated by the way she coped with three threats on her life, including one from a man who snuck into her bedroom at night. Georgia awoke and scared him away. These incidents "grew out of baby adoption cases," Nellie Kenyon wrote. "Concerning the last threat she calmly told reporters: 'I wasn't afraid.'"

And at least twice, Georgia was hit by parents whose children she'd stolen. She was unperturbed. Such boldness was less often associated with women than men, and Memphians repeatedly described her to me as mannish.

Georgia's partner, Ann Atwood Hollinsworth, complemented her in looks and temperament. Ann was short, thin, and nondescript in appearance: "I never could recall what she looked like," said an adoptive mother who saw Ann frequently.

May Hindman, who performed adoption-related work for Georgia for fourteen years, recalled Ann as a snobbish and artistic woman who painted landscapes. Ann had grown up in Meridian, Mississippi, near Georgia's hometown. Her parents and Georgia's were good friends.

It's unclear how well Georgia and Ann knew each other when the much-younger Ann was a child. But by 1920 they were co-workers in

Jackson, Mississippi, employed by the Kate McWillie Powers Receiving Home for Children, which was affiliated with the Mississippi Children's Home Society. Twenty-one-year-old Ann worked as housemother. Georgia, then twenty-nine, was supervisor of the Receiving Home.

Letterhead for the Mississippi, Children's Home Society lists Georgia as "Miss George Tann." U.S. Census records placing Georgia at the Powers Home in 1920 list her simply as "George Tann."

Georgia had previously gone by the female version of the latter part of her given name—Beulah George. Why she chose to be known as "George" while working in Jackson, Mississippi, is unclear. The use of "George" may have been an expression of her sexual orientation. But it seems more likely that she used the name "George Tann" to imitate, or almost to become, the other George Tann, her father.

I don't know whether Ann called Georgia "George" in Jackson, or whether Ann moved with her to Texas after Georgia was run out of Mississippi for her child-placing methods. But Ann accompanied Georgia when she moved to Memphis in 1924. By then Georgia had a young daughter, June, whom she'd adopted as an infant in 1922. Ann also had a child, a son, Jack, who was born around 1924.

In Memphis, Georgia changed her name again, back to "Georgia Tann." Ann had by then also changed her name, from "Ann Atwood" to "Ann Atwood Hollinsworth." A slightly different version of the surname—"Hollingsworth"—was common in Ann's hometown of Meridian, but I found no evidence that Ann was ever married. A Hickory resident described Ann as "one of those poor young women Georgia helped," a single mother. If this was true, Ann would have been embarrassed by it, and may have adopted her new surname to make herself appear to have been more respectably widowed or divorced.

Whatever the source of Ann's new name, and however she, Georgia, and the two children came together, they were a family, and Georgia treated Jack as a son. She provided for his and June's education at Miss Lee's Private School in Memphis. When he died in an air crash in the early 1940s, Georgia went into seclusion with Ann for several weeks.

Jack was an intelligent young man, and, had he lived, he would probably have assisted Georgia in her business, as did Ann, June, and Georgia's mother, Beulah. Beulah frequently boarded some of Georgia's wards at her home in Hickory. After June graduated from the University of Mississippi she sometimes helped Georgia by transporting children to adoptive homes.

Georgia was fortunate in having the support of Crump and her family, especially in the beginning of her career, when she faced even more challenges than the enormous one of creating a market for adopted children. One hurdle was Tennessee's adoption statute. Passed in 1852, only a year after Massachusetts enacted the first adoption law in the country, the Tennessee statute required childcare institutions to investigate prospective adoptive parents and supervise adoptees in their new homes. To facilitate supervision, adoptive parents were required to be state residents. To ensure that birth parents' surrenders of their children were voluntary, the statute required that the surrenders be confirmed by the action of a court.

Had Georgia been held to the standards of Tennessee law, she would have been compelled to operate ethically. But she perverted adoption, first by weakening Tennessee law, and then by revolutionizing adoption practices across the United States.

Unlike the authors of the 1852 Tennessee statute, Georgia had no interest in protecting the rights of adoptees or birth parents, only in pleasing her clients—adoptive parents. She didn't investigate their fitness, allowing virtually anyone who was financially comfortable to adopt a child.

For thirteen years she also, extra-legally, allowed nonresidents to adopt her children. By the 1930s ethical social workers in Tennessee were complaining about this violation of state law. Fortunately for Georgia, Boss Crump controlled the state legislature, and in 1937 a law was passed legalizing adoption by out-of-state residents. She usually ignored the aspect of the new law that required them to travel to Tennessee to finalize the adoptions.

For as long as possible, Georgia also disregarded the provision of the 1852 statute that required a judge's verification of birth parents' surrenders. Ethical social workers criticized this violation too, so in 1941 the law was changed again. The new legislation allowed surrenders to be witnessed by a notary public. Georgia and her workers were notaries, and they routinely claimed to have witnessed willing surrenders of children whose parents had never relinquished them.

Georgia further consolidated her hold over adoption in Tennessee by seizing control of the statewide organization that employed her. She did this by exploiting her relationship with Crump and weaknesses within the Tennessee Children's Home Society.

The oldest child-placing organization in the state, the Society had branches in Knoxville, Chattanooga, and Jackson, Tennessee, as well as Memphis. It was based in Nashville, in a Victorian mansion that had been converted into the best-equipped, most modern childcare institution in the South. But its officials lacked backbone. The statewide director, Fannie Elrod, allowed herself to be bullied by Georgia, and through the years ignored increasingly frequent complaints about her.

And although the organization had enjoyed a good reputation prior to Georgia's employment, it was soft at the core: like her, it was violating state law. A provision added to Tennessee's adoption statute in 1917 required child-placing agencies to be licensed by the state. For some reason, representatives of the Tennessee Children's Home Society consistently refused to apply for a license, a fact that made every adoption arranged by the organization, and every adoption arranged in Memphis by Georgia Tann, illegal.

The illicit nature of her adoptive arrangements didn't bother her. She considered herself above the law, free to make her own rules. And the agency's policy of noncooperation with the state suited her perfectly. Secrecy would be an essential hallmark of her business; she would refuse to divulge information about her adoptive placements to the Tennessee Department of Public Welfare, to Welfare Departments in states in which she placed children, and even to Fannie Elrod, her supposed boss.

But Georgia was concerned about a fact that negated her position as head of local child placement. Georgia wished to arrange adoptions, but when she arrived in Memphis the local branch of the Tennessee Children's Home Society only handled foster care. Another Memphis agency, the Children's Bureau, handled the few adoptions that occurred. Georgia was determined to reverse this situation.

A social worker employed by the Children's Bureau during the 1920s described the speed of Georgia's attack. "She wielded a whip," the worker told me.

She added that she and her supervisor, the well-regarded French social worker Elise de la Fontaine, had immediately disliked Georgia. "To people not involved in social work, she probably initially seemed fine," she said. "But if you stood in her way you saw her real side. She was ruthless." Cold, haughty, boastful of her political clout, Georgia simply appropriated wards of the Children's Bureau and arranged for their adoption.

This worker had been furious at Georgia's lack of scruples. "She placed with no regard to whether children would be happy in their adoptive homes; it was hit and miss," she said. Georgia's only concern was the number of placements. "She was trying to place every child in Memphis. She wanted to get her hands on every child she could."

Within a year of her arrival in Memphis in 1924, Georgia had control of virtually every local child available for adoption. The Children's Bureau was reduced to providing only foster care. Georgia was unstoppable, the former Children's Bureau worker told me. Georgia's hold over Tennessee adoptions became so absolute that when this worker and her husband, a prominent Memphis physician, sought to adopt a child in 1940, they had no choice but to adopt one through Georgia Tann.

Georgia's dominating personality and political contacts served her well, allowing her to surmount professional obstacles while also confronting personal problems. One difficulty was the condescension with which she was viewed by the wealthy Memphians she cultivated as clients.

"She was no one you would have wanted to know socially," an elderly Memphis matron told me.

"She didn't even perm her hair," said another.

"She was," said a third, "not attractive in any way."

It may be difficult imagining a woman as tough as Georgia being hurt by these opinions, but she probably was. While she'd been an outsider in Hickory because of her career aspirations, she had been admired for her social position. But Memphians disparaged her as "country." She didn't dress fashionably, or know how to dress her daughter June, whose expensive outfits were so ill chosen that Memphis matrons pitied the child. "June was frumpy and quite uninteresting, not an interesting child at all," an elderly Memphis woman told me. Georgia enrolled June in

Miss Lee's Private School and sent her to Ole Miss, where she joined a sorority, but she, too, remained an outsider. "She moved on the fringes of the Southern debutante circle," Attorney Lewis Donelson told me. "Like her mother, she was always trying to be accepted."

Georgia was also distinguished by the unconventional nature of her domestic unit. It's difficult to discern whether she was considered an outsider because of her sexual orientation, largely because most of her contemporaries referred to her homosexuality only indirectly. "I never knew how to take her; she wore mannish clothing," or variations of it, they'd say. Then, segueing to talk of her political connections, they'd give the impression of having prudently ignored a lifestyle they might otherwise have condemned. Georgia encouraged this seeming obliviousness by misrepresenting her relationship with Ann, and even with June. Unmarried women weren't supposed to adopt children in the 1920s, and in some states were legally prohibited from adopting. So Georgia portrayed June as her adoptive sister, who had been adopted by her own parents, George and Beulah. She forced June to address her as "Sissy."

June, who understood that Georgia was her adoptive mother, must have been confused by the charade. Almost all adoptees have difficulties regarding identity, and most desire knowledge of their roots. But June's genetic heritage would remain a mystery. She learned nothing about her parents, who Georgia claimed had died of the flu, or about the circumstances of her adoption, which she assumed had been arranged through the Texas home-finding society for which Georgia had briefly worked. Georgia was vague even about June's date of birth. She generally claimed that June had been born on June 7, 1921, and June believed that to be her birth date. But in correspondence with her attorney in 1934, Georgia wrote, ". . . I took a baby [June], personally, for adoption" in February of 1921.

It's unclear why Georgia at least once misrepresented June's date of birth, and which date was correct. But it's patently true that Georgia frequently falsified the birth dates of many children she placed for adoption. In every case of which I learned, she reduced the children's age. She did this to satisfy clients' wishes for the youngest possible babies, and to make the children appear bright, even precocious. While Georgia reduced the ages of babies only by weeks or months, she frequently subtracted years from the ages of older children. Many adoptees were shocked, upon reuniting with their birth parents, to discover their true ages.

As Georgia increasingly augmented her supply of orphans with kidnapped children, she falsified their ages to prevent their birth parents from finding them.

Georgia also lied about her relationship with Ann Atwood Hollinsworth, portraying her too as an adoptive sister who had been raised by Georgia's own parents, George and Beulah. That Georgia and Ann were related by adoption was actually one of the few things Georgia said that contained some truth. But Ann hadn't been adopted by Georgia or anyone else before she moved to Memphis in 1924, and she never became Georgia's adopted sister. In 1943, however, Georgia adopted Ann as a daughter. Georgia was fifty-two, and Ann was forty-four years old.

The adoption took place on August 2 in Dyer County, a rural area that was the site of many of Georgia's illegal adoptions involving children. The legal record states that the "petitioner, Georgia Tann, desires to adopt Ann Atwood Hollinsworth. The said Ann Atwood Hollinsworth is a full orphan of the state of Tennessee.

"Petitioner further states that she has reared and educated the said Ann Atwood Hollinsworth, and desires to make her her legal heir by said adoption. . . . Petitioner prays that the court decree that Ann Atwood Hollinsworth be adopted by her, with the right to inherit and succeed her estates, both real and personal, as if born to her."

Even when considered within the context of Georgia's unorthodox and duplicitous adoption transactions, her adoption of Ann seems strange. Her contention that she had "reared and educated" Ann was of course false. Georgia's reason for the proceeding was probably exactly what it appeared to be: to ensure Ann's right of inheritance. It was not uncommon then for women to adopt female companions for this reason. Georgia may also have wished to codify or celebrate her union—in the only way possible—with the woman she loved.

Georgia's lies regarding her personal relationships, which prefigured the dishonesty and secrecy with which she would taint the institution of adoption, may have seemed somewhat necessary regarding her relationship with June. Prevarication concerning her involvement with Ann must have seemed even more crucial. And it was more critical during the period after World War I than it would have been before.

People such as Richard Freiherr von Krafft-Ebing—an Austro-German psychiatrist and author of an influential study of what he termed sexual aberrance—began declaring that partners in Boston marriages were not, as had been previously believed, asexual, but homosexual. This idea quickly became part of popular culture. "Intimacy between two girls was watched with keen, distrustful eyes," wrote Wanda Fraiken Neff in her 1928 novel, We Sing Diana. "Among one's classmates one looked for the bisexual type, the masculine girl searching for her feminine counterpart." Romantic friendships and Boston Marriages were now deemed lesbian partnerships, and the women themselves "inverts," of the "intermediate," or "third" sex. Lesbians were said to be hermaphrodites, sexual deviates, genetic anomalies possessing male souls trapped in women's bodies.

Earlier in the twentieth century, Georgia could have settled into a domestic relationship with Ann in virtually any city in the country without fear of censure. Arriving in Memphis in 1924, however, she had cause for concern. She was such an example of what sexologists called "the mannish lesbian" that she could have been wearing a label. Krafft-Ebing described a supposedly typical case:

"Even in her earliest childhood she enjoyed playing at soldiers and other boys' games; she was bold and tom-boyish and tried even to excel her little companions of the other sex. . . . [After puberty] her dreams were of a lascivious nature, only about females, with herself in the role of the man. . . .

"She was quite conscious of her pathological condition. [She had] masculine features, a deep voice, manly gait, . . . small breasts; she cropped her hair short and made the impression of a man in a woman's body."

According to Krafft-Ebing and other sexologists, "inverts" such as Georgia were not only biologically tainted, but had been corrupted by their experiences in women's colleges and settlement houses. Georgia had been reticent about her private life before 1918. During her years in Memphis she became even more secretive.

While Georgia kept secret her private and much of her professional life, she blatantly promoted her business. Faced with the challenge of inspiring wealthy, infertile couples to adopt children previously deemed unworthy, she procured the most beautiful babies she could find and dressed them in elaborate layettes of organdy and lace. Then she placed one infant, or two, in a simulation of twins, in a ribbon-bedecked wicker basket, and visited her targets.

Most of her earliest clients are dead; I don't know under what pretense Georgia displayed children to them. It's likely that her approach to these couples was subtler than it was to political targets like Mildred Stoves.

Age ninety-one when I spoke with her, Mildred described working in the 1930s for the Memphis Department of Public Welfare. "And one day Miss Tann just stopped in my office with this beautifully-dressed, beautiful baby and said, 'Miss Stoves, I have a child for you.'"

What did she do?

"Well I refused it," she answered. "Miss Tann did seem surprised. But I was young; I wasn't married: what did I want with a baby?"

She admitted that many other social workers, all like her employed by agencies Georgia considered rivals and in most cases also unmarried, had been unable to resist the gift of a rosy, sweetly-powdered babe. Mildred Stoves was perhaps less impulsive than they. She may also have been more prescient. For although these workers doubtlessly received lifetimes of pleasure from their adopted children, they also experienced terror when Georgia blackmailed them. Employed by such organizations as the Department of Public Welfare, the Children's Bureau, and the Traveler's Aid Society, these adoptive parents soon realized that Georgia was a criminal. But criticizing her was almost impossible when, as she threatened, it would result in her reclaiming their adopted child. Or in letting "his mother know where he is"—since any adoptive parents who read newspaper accounts of local habeas corpus suits had to have been aware that the children they'd adopted through Georgia might have been stolen.

Georgia lured people into impossible situations, victimizing, occasionally, even those who profited from her. Among this otherwise-privileged group were physicians, attorneys, judges, and university professors. Such early, strategic placements provided her with names for what Candy Debs, who'd been adopted by a California legislator, described to me as "a hit list, a sales tool." The list would eventually include Joan Crawford, June Allyson and Dick Powell, Pearl Buck, Lana Turner, and New York governor Herbert Lehman. These prominent adoptive parents made adoption seem fashionable.

Georgia was not only the first American to make adoption popular, but also the first to attract clients she described as "high type" or "of the better sort." Unlike the rural couples who had put indentured servants and Orphan Train children to work, her adoptive parents, she boasted, would send their children to college. And most of her clients did provide their adopted children with an education. In placing children with adoptive parents generally willing to treat them as children, not hired help, Georgia was a pioneer. Today's adoptive parents continue to treat adopted children as part of their families. It is one of Georgia's few positive legacies.

An unknowable number of the children Georgia placed in new families had been kidnapped from their old ones—either directly, often literally from their mothers' arms, or indirectly, by means of illegal court orders. She employed the direct method more often in the 1940s than she had in the 1920s. She had fewer customers in the early years, and a large supply of more easily obtainable product.

There were more than twenty-eight institutions caring for dependent children in Tennessee in 1929. None of these belonged to Georgia, who wouldn't have one until Memphian Fred Smith, the founder of the Dixie Greyhound Bus Line, donated the mansion on Poplar Avenue that became her Home in 1943. But from the beginning she treated every orphanage and maternity home in the state as her private preserve. Adoptee Christine Nilan recalled Georgia's frequent scouting at the Tennessee Children's Home Society Orphanage in Nashville. "I can still hear her steps down the hallway and see her funny hats. She had big feet and wore black lace-up shoes. She always went upstairs to see the babies. There would be masses of them one day; they'd be gone the next."

During her visits, Georgia photographed the babies she was interested in, and then showed their pictures to prospective clients. After the children were placed, Georgia displayed the photographs on the walls of her office.

A disproportionate number of the children in these pictures were blond and blue-eyed. While Georgia presumably preferred such children because she thought her clients would, she favored that coloring herself. Her own adopted daughter, June, was born with blond hair and blue eyes. And in the 1940s Georgia surprised June, who by then had had two miscarriages, with an adoptive daughter—a blond, blue-eyed baby, too.

The former Children's Bureau social worker who had been appalled by Georgia's adoption methods in the 1920s attributed her success in locating such a specific type of child to her use of spotters. Prominent among them was the superintendent of a Memphis orphanage that housed over one hundred children. She informed Georgia of the arrival of particularly attractive children with an alacrity that convinced the Children's Bureau social worker I spoke with that the superintendent was being bribed by Georgia. Another social worker told me that the superintendent was dismissed from her job in 1950 because of her relationship with Georgia.

Juvenile Court Judge Camille Kelley wasted no time in transferring custody of the scouted children to Georgia Tann.

Judge Camille Kelley also frequently visited a local Catholic orphanage run by the Sisters of the Good Shepherd, noting the names of marketable children with an eye toward seizing them by court order and transferring their custody to Georgia. A former orphanage worker told me, "One of the nuns [who worked at the orphanage during the 1940s] said, 'We knew something was rotten.' This nun's superior would tell her, 'Judge Kelley is coming,' and she and the other sisters would scramble around, trying to hide the prettiest children from her."

This probably hindered Georgia little, if at all. An effective if terrible marketing technique ensured steady increases in her number of placements.

One of the adoptees I spoke with was Jim Lambert, who'd been physically and emotionally abused after being adopted through Georgia in the 1930s. In our first phone conversation, he told me that his adoptive parents had chosen him after seeing him advertised in a Memphis newspaper.

After we hung up, I pulled out a folder I'd labeled "Georgia's Christmas Baby Ads," which contained some of the approximately 400 child advertisements she'd run between 1929 and the early 1940s. All were repugnant, and several seemed prurient. One, which ran on the front page of the Memphis *Press-Scimitar* in November of 1930 under the caption "Wants Home," was accompanied by a photograph of a small girl standing with her hand on her hip, wearing a short dress and disconcertingly mature facial expression. A caption described her as "a solemn little trick . . . with big brown eyes. Madge is five years old and 'awful lonesome.'"

Another ad, published on December 7, 1935, and headed "Yours for the Asking!" included a close-up of a five-year-old boy holding a large ball.

"How would YOU like to have this handsome boy play 'catch' with you?" the caption read.

"How would you like his chubby arms to slip around your neck and give you a bearlike hug? His name is George, and he may be yours for the asking."

I'd read these ads before speaking with many adoptees, and they'd disturbed me then. It was even more difficult to view them after speaking with people like Jim Lambert, whose advertisement had brought him so much pain.

Two-year-old Jim and his two sisters, Pat and Betty Jo, were taken from their mother by Georgia Tann in 1932. Pat was placed in foster care; Betty Jo was sent to a Texas adoptive family; and Jim was placed with a Chicago couple.

The couple soon divorced. Jim stayed with his adoptive father, who married a woman who so resented Jim's presence that she hung him by his shirt from a hook in the basement for an entire afternoon. At age nine Jim was sent to a Mississippi boarding school; a few years later he was transferred to Gailor Hall, which he described to me as "a kind of Memphis Boys Town." While there he received a letter from his adoptive father. "He didn't want me anymore," Jim said.

He spent the rest of his childhood in a dizzying number of places— the Porter Home and Leath Orphanage in Memphis; Memphis Juvenile Court, which had jail-like quarters for children; and foster homes. Georgia Tann eventually sent him to the Texas couple who had adopted his sister Betty Jo.

But the Texas couple, who Jim said had been working Betty Jo "like a slave," overworked him too. He ran away, was caught, and returned to Memphis, where he endured yet one more foster home before enlisting in the Air Force at seventeen. A strong, resilient man, he built himself a good life, and when I spoke with him in 1993 he spoke proudly of his loving, forty-one-year-long marriage, his five children, and his reunion with his sisters.

But his birth parents had died before he'd found them, and he'd never regain the childhood he'd lost. "I feel angry, frustrated, like I was cheated out of a whole lot of life," he said.

* * *

Jim and hundreds of other children had also been peddled more crassly than pet stores sell puppies. Georgia's baby-selling ads were so exploitative that when I first viewed them, I'd been surprised that responsible newspapers had published them.

Eventually I acquired both an understanding of 1920s Memphis and the place of that city within the larger context of a country quite different from ours today. I read a nationally syndicated news article published in 1929 that, like much of what had originally seemed extraneous research, was curiously related to the Georgia Tann story. The piece dealt in a matter-of-fact manner with an infant ward of a Knoxville, Tennessee, orphanage living not in that or any other children's institution but in the home economics department of the University of Tennessee, where he served as a "flesh and blood textbook" for students who had changed his name from "Richard House" to "Richard Practice-House." That this piece amused rather than offended readers helped me understand the reception Georgia's ads received when they began appearing in Memphis that same year.

According to an article published in the *Press-Scimitar* in 1937, inspiration for Georgia's twelve-year-long ad campaign was, from her standpoint and that of her partner-in-invention, the product of fortuitous coalescence. Georgia, wearing one of her customary dark suits, print blouses, and wide-brimmed hats, was sitting in her fifth-floor office on a December afternoon in 1929 speaking of a professional problem to Memphis friend and reporter, Ada Gilkey. Georgia had appropriated more children than she had been able to place for adoption and was paying to board them in institutions and private residences. Aware that her agency's state funding would soon be reduced because of budgetary cuts caused by the Depression, she worried about making ends meet.

Ada had a problem that day, too: a blank space where the idea for a series of heartwarming, Christmas-related stories should be.

The minds converged, and the idea for the annual Christmas baby giveaway was spawned.

I call the articles that resulted from this conversation "advertisements," for that is what they constituted. But the papers that ran the ads received no advertising money, and the reporter who may only have been incredibly naive garnered only bylines and, eventually, embarrassment. Georgia, however, began reaping financial dividends from the advertisements just ten minutes after the first one appeared.

"Want a real, live Christmas present?" read an article introducing the campaign, published on December 9, 1929.

"A present guaranteed to add two-fold to the joy of the holidays?

"Well, here's your chance, for 25 children, ranging in age from three months to seven years, will be presented to as many lucky families Christmas Eve. . . . *The Press-Scimitar* is making special arrangements with Miss Georgia Tann, Executive Director of the Memphis branch of the Tennessee Children's Home Society, to place these babies. . . ."

A variation of the ad appeared the next day, accompanied by photographs of two of the babies to be given away. "See if you can pick out the boy in this picture. No, you missed! It's the other one, the curly head on the right, and his playmate on the left is the girl! She is eight months and the little boy is one year old. They have golden hair, blue eyes and good dispositions.

"Applications should be sent to the *Press-Scimitar* Adoption Editor. Say whether you want a boy or girl, brunet, blond or red-head.

"Blonds, by the way, are in the majority."

Readers' reaction was enthusiastic. Within ten minutes of the ad's publication Georgia and the newspaper's Adoption Editor received dozens of calls from people requesting one or both of the children.

And that was simply for those two babies. But Georgia ran different ads, featuring different children, every day that December of 1929 and, during each subsequent year until the early 1940s, every day from the beginning of November until January 1.

They were captioned:

"Could YOU Use a Christmas Baby?"

"Which [of three infant boys] Will You Have for Christmas?"

"Living Dolls [three baby girls] for YOU."

"Are You in the Market for a 14-Month-Old Boy?"

"Put Your Orders in Early."

"Dan, Jimmy, Ray . . . Want One of Them?"

Georgia's ads included, of course, many, many other captions—more even than I am aware of, for I found reading them so depressing that I chose not to view all of the pertinent microfilms. I left the Memphis Main Library early, trusting in my ability to gauge the effects of the ads without making myself read every single one.

Those effects were both immediate and local and, ultimately, much further reaching. The longer I consider them the more blurred becomes the line between them, so skillfully, so seemingly effortlessly did Georgia expand her influence.

Her earliest ads ran in the *Press-Scimitar* only. They resulted not only in the adoptions of all twenty-five of the 1929 Christmas babies but, once she'd exhausted her current supply of children, also in compilation of a back list of prospective adoptive clients, a waiting list of sorts. The ads garnered Georgia increased donations and local celebrity. Most significantly, the Christmas baby stories, which quickly became the newspaper's most popular feature, helped Georgia remove the stigma from adoptable children by bringing them enticingly, intriguingly, adorably into readers' homes.

Even Memphians previously unpersuaded by Georgia's blank slate theory regarding adopted children looked forward to each day's

Christmas ad. Would the picture be of one baby, or several? Would the child be a newborn or a toddler or somewhere in between; would he, or she, be smiling? sleeping? bouncing in a baby swing, teething on a crib rail, cuddling a doll, a toy bear or, for reasons known only to Georgia, a porcelain figurine? Would the child be dressed in lace, or simply a diaper, or, as was Master Paul, advertised on December 14th of that first year, nothing at all? ("Our photographer caught the young gentleman a la nude, but he wasn't the least bit perturbed. . . . He is seven months old and blond. . . .") Elderly citizens saved their favorite pictures. Young matrons' bridge parties were enlivened by spirited but friendly arguments over whether Baby Bonnie was cuter than Master Paul.

Georgia's ads made adoption a household word in the region, and adoptable children, their faces illuminating the newspapers that shared table space with readers' coffee cups and jam pots, began to seem part of their family. Throughout Memphis and such nearby cities as Little Rock, Arkansas, and Jackson, Mississippi, infertile couples' last particle of resistance crumbled. Adoption applications soon filled half of Georgia's two-room office suite. By 1935, she had placed children in all forty-eight states, as well as in Mexico, Panama, Canada, and England.

She had also crafted a technique that survives to this day: the advertisement of children for the purpose of sale.

Her intention was very different from that of the editors of the *Delineator*, which from 1907 to 1911 had conducted a Child Rescue Campaign that involved publishing pictures and descriptions of adoptable children. The magazine sought to find homes for children, not to make money by selling babies. Organizations such as AdoptUSKids, a project of the U.S. Children's Bureau, which seeks adoptive parents for children in foster care, continue to use pictures and profiles of waiting children responsibly today.

AdoptUSKids's descriptions of waiting children include significant information regarding their backgrounds, such as whether they've spent time in an institution, or will need help coping with physical or psychological problems.

Georgia, on the other hand, revealed nothing about her children other than their physical appearance and age (and the age she reported was often wrong). She spent no time screening adoptive parents, and placed one infant in an out-of-state adoptive home only one day after the child was advertised.

Unfortunately there are many unscrupulous brokers around the world today who follow Georgia's lead. Their methods have changed: they are less likely to advertise in newspapers than on the Internet. But like Georgia, today's brokers often steal children from their mothers, or coerce the mothers into relinquishing them. They also copy Georgia's practice of concealing information about children's backgrounds. And like Georgia, they often become wealthy from their sales.

It took me a while, and placement of Georgia within the context of other adoption arrangers of her time, to appreciate her commercial brilliance. Not even larger, long-established agencies located in populous areas effected as many adoptions as she did. In 1928 Georgia, who as yet had neither orphanage nor staff, handled 206 adoptions. That same year New York City's Spence Alumnae Society and the Alice Chapin Nursery, which would later merge to form the Spence Chapin Agency, together arranged only eighty-three. The average annual number of adoptions arranged during the 1920s by the Boston Children's Aid Society was five.

It's difficult to determine how much of Georgia's greater productivity can be attributed to her marketing techniques, and how much to her criminality. Reputable social workers had a finite number of children to place: those orphaned or relinquished by their parents. Georgia placed for adoption any child she wished.

I soon discovered that Georgia's influence was so great that even ethical social workers would, by the 1940s, place for adoption many more children than they should have. Georgia transformed adoption in other ways as well.

Her ability to make adopted children seem appealing as children, not as potential laborers, attracted clients she called "high type"— wealthy and cultured. The children they desired differed from those sought by clients of Charles Loring Brace. Three times more Orphan Train boys than girls were chosen by Brace's farmers, who wanted sturdy field hands. The farmers preferred older children to toddlers. Brace didn't even attempt to place infants.

Georgia's clients sought babies, the younger the better. And many were eager to adopt little girls.

Georgia's influence upon the frequency of adoption was local at first. But when the Christmas baby series was syndicated in the 1930s, what I can only term the humanizing of adoptable children began to spread. While that humanizing would not be complete during the ads' run, and while some babies adopted through Georgia Tann and others would long be considered inferior to birth children, adoptable children became regarded as semiacceptable substitutes. The number of Georgia's adoptive applicants rose throughout the 1930s. This enabled her not only to place more children, but also to gain personal wealth.

She didn't openly affix price tags to children, but instead charged fees for transporting them to their new homes. Georgia directed prospective adoptive parents to make the checks out to her, not to the Tennessee Children's Home Society, and to send them to her private post office box in Memphis. The fees included travel expenses for a worker and the baby to be adopted, and were due in three installments.

When Georgia received a request for adoption, she quickly determined the prospective clients' financial status and social standing. If these met her standard, she or a worker usually made a cursory visit to the prospective parents' home. She charged California residents $168.72 for this visit, and New York City residents $228.81. Adoptive parents in other areas were charged fees somewhere between these figures.

The next installment of Georgia's fee was due upon delivery of the child. Georgia enjoyed handing babies to happy, excited couples, and she often made this trip herself. California residents were charged $360; New Yorkers paid $268.81.

The interval between this trip and the next was longer than that between the first two, which was sometimes as brief as two days. Often a year would elapse between the second and third trips—enough time to justify Georgia's claims of careful assessment of the children's adjustment before finalization of the adoption.

In reality, she made no assessment before having her workers make the final trip, bearing adoption certificates that the new parents signed in preparation for Georgia's presentation of the paperwork to a Tennessee judge. California residents were charged $202.72, which brought their total bill to $731.44. New Yorkers paid $268.81, for a total of $766.43.

This was a considerable amount in the 1930s, equivalent to $11,000 in today's money. And some couples paid Georgia as much as $10,000, equivalent to $140,000 today.

If these couples had adopted from reputable agencies, they would have paid almost nothing. Some probably didn't understand this. I don't know how many realized how Georgia achieved her profit—by charging the same transportation costs several times over. Seldom did she or her workers visit one family or ferry one baby only. Instead, Georgia or a minion would fly to Los Angeles with four infants crowded together in a handheld wicker basket and, often, with toddlers and older children in tow. With the children, she would check into a suite at the Biltmore Hotel. Soon afterward, she would bring them to the lobby and give them to their new parents.

Issues regarding guilt, not necessarily complicity but tacit, passive concurrence, interest me perhaps more than they should, given my connection to adoption. But often—especially after speaking with Memphians who insisted to me that Georgia began with good motives, and that none of her clients realized she was operating illegally—I found myself wondering whether the people picking up children in the lobby of the Biltmore Hotel did not notice each other's presence. Did they not know the cost of air tickets or hotel accommodations and realize that their check, alone, would have covered Georgia's expenses? And that if the other couples paid as much money as they, Georgia would have a considerable amount left over? (She would in fact make more money from one trip than the couples in the lobby could easily have known, for she would, the next day, make several preliminary and adoption finalization visits, collecting, at each stop, checks covering the full cost of her air and hotel fare.) In at least one case, Georgia received eleven times her actual expenses.

Some adoptive parents knew that Georgia's charges were padded, their adopted children told me. But it must have been relatively easy for prospective adoptive parents to overlook this and to justify paying suspiciously large sums of money—especially (and Georgia knew this would happen) after they had seen their baby. Most of her adoptive parents, as unscreened and often poorly prepared as they were, loved their new babies. Would any price have seemed too high?

I understand this more than I want to. My daughter's adoption was private. The cost involved was small, just over $2,000, and included several days' medical expenses for Beth and legal expenses for her mother. I would have paid more. And if I had later learned that some of that cost had gone to something other than legal and medical charges, I, who wanted a baby so badly, would not have cared.

The ground becomes stickier after this. Even adoptive parents with absolutely no inkling they were fattening Georgia's wallet must have wondered at the cautionary words that sometimes accompanied her delivery of babies. "Keep your heads down," she or her aides would tell the adoptive parents. "Lose yourselves." Georgia told some adoptive parents that the child's mother was looking for her child. Of course she also told them that she had obtained custody of the child for cause.

Georgia's clients apparently believed her, but some must have had doubts. Especially those who lived in Tennessee, where birth parents were desperately trying to persuade judges, the police—anyone—to help them find babies Georgia had stolen. Adoptive parents also must have seen newspaper accounts of habeas corpus suits filed by birth parents.

And what would I have done if I'd been a Memphian who'd adopted through Georgia? Would I have tried to learn whether my daughter had been stolen from her parents? And if she had been stolen, would I have returned her? I want to believe I would have, but could I have?

The opportunity to overcharge for travel expenses soon led Georgia to reverse her early practice of placing most of her children with Memphis couples. By the late 1940s she was sending 90 to 95 percent of them out of state. And the more locales her babies were in, the higher, through word of mouth, grew the number of people seeking to adopt through her. To satisfy the market she'd created, she stole more and more children.

Georgia's methods were blatant enough to initially make me marvel that they were tolerated, even by Memphians under Ed Crump. I may have been overestimating Memphians, or underestimating Crump, who robbed citizens who displeased him of their jobs and, often, their homes. It had not been simply Gerald Stratton, the former county court clerk who'd criticized Crump's support of the poll tax, who had been driven from the city. Pharmacist J. B. Martin, a black man who, refusing to be "voted" by Crump's Machine, supported Republican Wendell Wilkie for president in 1940, was forced to flee to Chicago. There, like most displaced Memphians I learned of, he prospered, eventually becoming part owner of the Memphis franchise in the Negro Baseball League. His accomplishments, however, like those of the other emigrants, brought him no hometown honor, and when he returned to watch his team play, Crump had him ejected from the ballpark.

Attorney Ben W. Kohn was beaten and arrested for backing a Crump opponent.

Another attorney was banished for referring to Crump by the name which, bestowed upon him by out-of-town journalists, was avoided by prudent local citizens: "Boss."

These three men left town even though they practiced professions that in most cities would have made them relatively invulnerable to political pressure. Local city workers were even more tightly bound to Crump. And the sad truth is that many of these workers—most of whom were parents themselves—were led, by fear of Crump and an understanding of his and Georgia's relationship, to help her steal the babies of their neighbors.

I find this fact more damning than the refusal of local adoptive parents to investigate whether their children had been stolen from their birth families. This is encouraged by my less-than-ideally objective viewpoint. But there has to be a difference between those who averted their eyes to keep children they loved, and those who, for political reasons, participated in Georgia's roundups.

Roundups were conducted by groups of varying sizes that included her and/or one or more of her subordinates. They were accompanied by an ever-changing assortment of Memphians—Juvenile Court employees, social workers, and deputy sheriffs. Armed with papers signed by Judge Camille Kelley, the groups descended upon the apartments, homes, farms, even houseboats of poor parents, rounding up their children, looking them over, and carrying off those Georgia deemed most marketable. (The reason most often cited in Judge Kelley's authorization was that their parents were providing a "poor home environment"; Georgia wasn't required to explain why she often seized only the youngest members of a sibling group, not all.) The children most vulnerable were newborn to age five, although Georgia sometimes took children as old as sixteen. Some of her clients preferred adolescents; among the more disturbing entries in Tennessee docket books are those indicating the adoptions by single, out-of-town men and women of sixteen-year-old boys and girls.

Georgia, search expert Denny Glad had told me, "aimed to please." So much so that she sometimes stole children to order, I learned from a 1939 habeas corpus suit. The subject of that suit, four-year-old Kirby Gribble, had been sighted by a spotter.

By 1939 Georgia's spotters included not only her staff of six women, certain nurses, physicians, attorneys, and Judge Camille Kelley, but also social workers employed by agencies other than Georgia's own. One, an employee of the Memphis Family Welfare Agency named Sarah Semmes, had long been counseling a thirty-one-year-old widow named Grace Gribble on providing for her six children, who ranged in age from three to ten.

Grace trusted Sarah Semmes, was accustomed to her visits and, when she dropped in that hot day with a middle-aged woman named Helen Rose, assumed that Helen worked for the Family Welfare Agency, too.

Grace signed the six papers that Sarah Semmes claimed would get her children free medical care under the Widow's Assistance program. But to Grace's surprise Helen Rose pocketed the papers and said matter-of-factly, "I'll take the three youngest children now."

Grace screamed as she realized Helen Rose was employed by Georgia Tann. She almost fainted when she realized she had signed relinquishments surrendering her children for adoption.

Anywhere other than in the Memphis of the time, Grace's surrenders would have been deemed null and void. But as Grace cried that day and the two women and a driver carried her three babies off to Georgia's limousine—Helen Rose carried four-year-old, red-haired, blue-eyed, weeping Kirby and said, "We have an order for a boy of this age and type"—she realized the futility of fighting. Still, she rushed to Juvenile Court and, spying Georgia Tann, grabbed her arms.

"Where are my babies?" she cried.

"They're on their way to a much better life than you could provide them," said Georgia. "You should thank me."

Crying, Grace pleaded for her children.

"Forget them," Georgia said.

It took Grace seven months to find a lawyer willing to take her case. Meanwhile her three youngest children attempted to adjust to new homes in three separate states. Doris Ann, aged six, had been placed with an Orlando, Florida, newspaper publisher and his wife who wanted a companion for their biological daughter.

Three-year-old Cricket, the luckiest of the three, was adopted by a Memphis physician and his wife, who loved him.

Hand-picked, four-year-old Kirby was rejected within a year by the Blytheville, Arkansas, couple with whom he was placed. Returned to Memphis by train with $1 in his pocket, he was transferred to Nashville, where he spent seven years in foster homes before being adopted by a heavy-drinking Saginaw, Michigan, couple.

The trial resulting from Grace Gribble's lawsuit against Georgia Tann, which took place on April 29, 1940, was an exercise in warped thinking. The issue at hand, which should have been whether the young widow had willingly surrendered her babies for adoption, was transformed into whether Grace's finances equaled those of their adoptive parents.

In vain, Grace's lawyer protested that the issue was not who could provide the children with more comfortable lives but "Who is their legal parent?" The overriding issue—"How much can Georgia get away with?"—was never publicly articulated. But it was answered in the presiding judge's order, which stipulated that Grace's children would remain with their adoptive parents. Regarding the children's grieving mother, he said, "[T]his is one of the sad tragedies of life that even a mother must endure for the best interests of her children."

Grace was a particular person, one who had previously enjoyed a meager but reasonably satisfying existence in her one-story stucco home on a neighborly street named Media, and ever afterward was so bitter and angry her friends eventually stopped visiting. Regarding her inability to get back the children Georgia had stolen, however, Grace resembled virtually every targeted parent.

I know in fact of only one parent besides Josie Statler—the young woman who shortly after Georgia's death distracted an aide at the Home on

Poplar Avenue, rescued her stolen daughter, and fled to Massachusetts—who retrieved a child Georgia had kidnapped. In a documentary produced by a Nashville television station a woman named Vickie described coming home from school in the 1930s to find her parents near collapse. Vickie had an eleven-year-old brother named Luther. "They got him," her father gasped. But somehow he learned the location of the boarding home in which Georgia was hiding Luther, and after watching the home for days spotted the owner taking her charges for a walk. Hiding in the bushes, he whistled "whippoorwill," a family signal. Luther ran to his father, who spirited him home and, that very day, moved his family to Arkansas.

I was unable to locate Vickie, and so I don't know how her father succeeded where so many other parents failed. Was he unusually loving, or resourceful? Did someone tell him where Luther was being held? His story ended happily, yet it leaves me with a lingering despondency. I imagine the tone with which Vickie's father choked out, "They got Luther." It is a tone so quintessentially, sadly, of Georgia's time in its contradictory mix of shock at the randomness of the raid and acceptance of its inevitability.

10.

Georgia's Adults

Losing children to Georgia may have been inevitable for many poor Southern parents, but it was never easy. "It was agony," said Evelyn Quillen, whose four-year-old daughter was kidnapped from a childcare center in 1948. "I prayed constantly that she was alive."

For most of us, such pain is blessedly unimaginable; Georgia herself may well have been, as one elderly Memphian described her, "as evil as she could be." In destroying families, she was also absolutely relentless, stealing babies from playgrounds and houseboats, luring children walking home from school with the promise of ice cream.

A favorite method was the one that had robbed Grace Gribble of her three babies: duping parents into signing surrenders for adoption. She must have had an easy time with Harry Waggerman. A German immigrant who knew no English, he gratefully signed papers he believed would procure temporary care for his beloved six-year-old daughter.

Georgia immediately sent Fannie to Illinois. Despite two court battles the widowed father never saw his little girl again.

Harry was tricked into signing a surrender in a courtroom, but the most common settings for this kidnapping method were hospitals. Georgia had spotters who worked in the maternity wards of local hospitals, and they alerted her when poor young women went into labor. "Georgia Tann's workers stood outside the door [of the delivery room] waiting," Dr. George Lovejoy told me in 1993. "The minute the baby was born they would take the papers in and have the mother sign them, and the baby would disappear."

Eighteen-year-old Mary Reed, who gave birth to a baby boy in 1943, was a typical victim. She was still almost unconscious from the heavy dose of anesthesia then routinely given to women during childbirth when she signed a "routine paper" presented by a woman dressed in white. The woman was one of Georgia's helpers, and Mary's newborn was soon flown to New Jersey.

Heartbroken, Mary brought a habeas corpus suit against Georgia. But her own doctor, who was also Georgia's private physician, testified that Mary had understood the nature of the relinquishment papers she signed, and she never got her baby back. In fact she never even saw him until 1992, when he was forty-eight. A pilot named Steve Popper, he found her after reading my *Good Housekeeping* article on Georgia Tann and seeking the help of Denny Glad.

"Oh, honey, I've been waiting for this day all my life, ever since you were born I've been waiting for this day," Mary said.

Few of the separations caused by Georgia have ended in such happy reunions, and she separated so many families, in so many ways. While Georgia sometimes had her own workers trick mothers into signing releases for adoption, she also often had actual nurses tell mothers their babies had been stillborn. Irene Green was one of many mothers who, as groggy from anesthesia as she was, knew this was a lie. "I heard my baby cry!" she insisted. The nurse told her she was wrong. When Mary frantically demanded to see her baby's body, the nurse told her it had been "disposed of."

Irene may have understood the hopelessness of her situation even more fully than did some other victimized mothers. Two years earlier, Georgia had stolen her three other children—Jim Lambert, who'd been adopted after having been advertised in the *Press-Scimitar*, and his sisters Pat and Betty Jo—and she'd been unable to recover them.

By the time her four children grew up, regrouped, and searched for Irene, she was dead, having left little behind but her Bible. In it she'd recorded their names and birthdates, and the inscription: "The children of a broken-hearted mother. I have no one to love me now."

Parents duped by Georgia were sometimes unconscious for reasons other than having been anesthetized. When a twenty-seven-year-old mother "surrendered" her daughter, Earlene Phillips, for adoption, she resided in the Bolivar Home for the Feeble Minded.

Earlene's mother was there only because she'd been impregnated by her older sister's husband. The husband, "a little country doctor, had my momma committed so no one would know about me," Earlene said. "Then she had a nervous breakdown."

Depression and heavy medication prevented Earlene's mother from understanding the nature of the papers Georgia's worker had her sign. But the young mother soon recovered to spend a lifetime mourning the loss of her child.

* * *

Georgia was aided in her kidnapping by more than cruelty and energy. She was a skillful liar, as exemplified by a story related shortly after her death by thirty-one-year-old Edward Russell. A divorced, unemployed veteran with custody of his three children, he traveled from Tiptonville, Tennessee, to Memphis in 1949 to ask Georgia for help. "She was very kind," he said. "She told me she thought the answer was for me to leave the children with her at the Home, go to California" to look for work "and that she would send the children out as soon as I was located. I remember her exact words: 'We will send them to you immediately after you have established yourself and can take care of them.'"

He left for Los Angeles the next day, quickly found a job, and asked Georgia when she could send his children. "She assured me they were in good health and in good hands and not to worry." Two months and countless phone calls later, he was still childless. "So I finally quit my job and came back to Memphis to get them. I went straight to the Home and asked Miss Tann for my children. And the only thing she said was that she thought it best to keep them.

"I was stunned. I couldn't believe it. I begged her to let me see them and she refused." He hired a lawyer and met with Georgia the next day in the office of her attorney, Abe Waldauer. "I pleaded to see the children. And it wasn't until then that Miss Tann told me that the babies were placed for adoption [in California] two months earlier. She said two were with one family, and the other with another family. . . ."

A year later, having remarried his wife and instituted what would be a lengthy habeas corpus suit, he was still stunned by Georgia's deceit. "I had no reason to believe she would trick me," he told a Memphis reporter. "I admired her. She seemed so interested in my case. She had a kind, soothing voice and I trusted her."

A former member of the famed 32nd Infantry Division in the South

Pacific in World War II, Edward Russell had been missing in action for eight weeks and reported dead for five. Nothing he'd suffered during the war, however, was as painful as what Georgia had done to him. "We've just got to get our children back. They're the whole world to us," he told the reporter.

But he'd lost them forever. The children remained with their adoptive parents.

In her quest to obtain marketable children Georgia was also aided by circumstance. At least one irresponsible parent simply abandoned her daughter to her. In 1991 the daughter, Barbara Davidson, described one of the worst days of her life. Her mother, who had divorced her alcoholic husband and married a man who hated children, told six-year-old Barbara to don her prettiest dress.

"I remember her taking me to this mansion," Barbara told me. "We walked up the outside steps and I tried to keep hold of her hand: I could hardly reach her fingers. She told me to play upstairs with the children; she had business to take care of, and then we would go home. But when I came out no one was there and no one was going to take me home and I began to cry. A woman in a black dress told me, 'Shut up, shut up, you are never going home. Shut up.'"

Shortly afterward, Barbara was sent to the California home in which her adoptive father would sexually abuse her.

Barbara Davidson's mother was an aberration: the only parent I learned of who simply, callously, gave her child away. The other parents who surrendered children to Georgia didn't do so willingly, but were compelled to by poverty and the betrayal of the social agencies that should have helped them. Such forced relinquishments increased during the Great Depression.

Georgia's range of interest was narrow: her babies, her clients, and her family. Her attentiveness to local politics was motivated only by self-interest; national issues concerned her not at all. So while she profited greatly from the 1929 Wall Street crash it's likely she did so instinctively—but, unfortunately, to great effect.

The city's economy depended upon cotton. The stock market failure reduced demand and caused a worldwide glut of the fiber, decreasing its value from 29 cents to 6 cents per pound. The collapse of the cotton market, which sharply reduced riverboat trade, devastated poor Memphians. The Fisher Body Company closed its local plant, throwing twelve thousand men out of work; the Ford Motor Company suspended operations. Employers cut workers' hours to 20 per week and fired six thousand Memphis women, giving their jobs to men.

The city's financial problems were exacerbated by the influx of thousands of sharecroppers and tenant farmers from Missouri, Arkansas, western Tennessee, and the Mississippi Delta. Many soon joined desperate native Memphians in application to the city's welfare organizations, often seeking help for their children.

But by 1929 these institutions were honeycombed with Georgia's spotters. Instead of providing parents with vocational advice, they urged them to surrender their children to Georgia for adoption. Some parents relinquished their babies rather than let them starve. Others agreed to board their children with her while they searched for work, only to suffer the same fate as had Edward Russell.

They were left suffering not only the loss of their children but guilt over their gullibility. "She knew how to spot the dumb ones," one robbed mother told me sadly. But these parents weren't dumb, and probably would have lost their children even if they hadn't boarded them with her.

Once Georgia knew the parents were poor, they were doomed. And almost anything gave them away, such as application for the free milk that was routinely given to the needy. Former investigator Robert Taylor told me that the man who distributed it, Aubrey Clapp, was a spotter. Clapp gave Georgia the names, ages, and addresses of any children whose parents applied for assistance.

Georgia robbed every birth parent she could, but she most often victimized single mothers. They were made vulnerable both by their single status and Georgia's identification with them.

The young women had no obvious similarity to Georgia. But both they and she were part of a socially unacceptable group, whose members were excoriated in similar terms. Unmarried mothers were "moral deviants possessed of 'excessive sexual equipment.'" Lesbians were "sexual deviants, genetic anomalies of the 'intermediate' or 'third' sex." Georgia never publicly acknowledged her homosexuality, but she must have been aware of it, and, in the repressive climate of the time, may have felt shame and anger at being gay. I believe she displaced those emotions onto single mothers and, by robbing them of the children that made them outcasts, symbolically expunged part of herself.

That Georgia's identification with single mothers also caused her to envy them is suggested by an incident related to me by Vallie Miller, the former Supervisor of Adoptions for the Tennessee Department of Public Welfare who had been brought to Memphis from Nashville after Georgia's death to help make plans for Georgia's last twenty-two wards. During that time she spoke with an adoptive father who had received his new child at Georgia's private residence on Stonewall Court.

He knocked on the door, and instead of the expected maid Georgia herself appeared. She looked unusual: instead of her habitual tailored clothing she wore something white and diaphanous; it looked like a nightgown. She led him to her bedroom. The bed coverings were also white.

Nervously he approached where she directed: toward an upper bed corner, where a tiny mound was surrounded by pillows and draped with a coverlet. She raised an end, and there was a newborn baby girl. His baby, he realized. And Georgia's? That is what he believed she was pretending . . . "This baby is perfect in every way," she said. He received her and swiftly left.

I learned about another of Georgia's stranger acts from a 1950s news article entitled, "Marriage Racket Laid to Miss Tann: Expectant Mothers Brought to Arkansas to Marry 'Unknowns.'" A court official in Marion, Arkansas, reported that Georgia had during the 1940s frequently been driven with pregnant women to the court clerk's office in Crittendon County, twelve miles from Memphis. Outside, Georgia would meet with one of an ever-changing assortment of shiftless-looking young men. She'd then usher the man and woman inside, where they would be married by a justice of the peace. Georgia would pocket the marriage certificate, send the young man on his way with a payment of $20, and return to Memphis with the pregnant young woman.

Why? Reproved by the Arkansas court official, Georgia had explained that she wanted to give a name to the unborn child. But Georgia, who routinely falsified children's histories, hardly needed to arrange bogus marriages in order to declare a child legitimate.

I believe that Georgia arranged sham weddings in order to vicariously experience what she couldn't have. Georgia wanted everything: most obviously the power that was usually accessible only to men, but that she achieved through her adoption business. Her father's thwarting of her legal ambitions was the important theme of her life. She bested him, becoming more prominent in her field than he ever was in his. She maintained control of her daughter, as he had of her. She was, a Memphian hinted to me, a womanizer, betraying Ann with another woman.

But it wasn't enough. Georgia was a woman unable to directly partake of the traditional source of female power: marriage and the bearing of children. Her adoption business helped her here too, allowing her to hover outside delivery rooms, hear a newborn's first cry, and swiftly bundle the baby away. She could say, as if she had had much to do with it, "This child is 100 percent normal and healthy."

Then this essentially cold woman could dispense with all responsibilities by giving "her" baby away. On to the next birth and adoption.

In formulating a business that served both her pathological needs and her desire for power, Georgia was nothing if not resourceful. Her selfishness, energy, and connections made it impossible for any targeted family to stay intact. But the quality that made her most dangerous was her gift for self-promotion. It enabled her to further revolutionize and corrupt adoptive practice by robbing birth parents she would never even meet.

In the centuries before Georgia began her business, single mothers of all races were both allowed and expected to raise their children. Georgia inverted this custom in Memphis almost overnight, regarding white mothers and white babies. (Neither she nor most other adoption workers of her time tried to place nonwhite children for adoption, the theory being until recently that there was no market for nonwhite children.) And she lost little time in nationally publicizing her justifications for removing white children from poor homes. Through speeches and in syndicated newspaper articles, she extolled the cultural and educational benefits enjoyed by adopted children.

Social workers more altruistic than she were soon persuaded that the "best interest" of poor, illegitimate children was adoption. These benefits came to be considered so great, and their absence so punitive, that single mothers who wanted to keep their babies were considered selfish. And while it was usually only Georgia and her later imitators who literally stole such children, social workers throughout the country began urging single women to relinquish their babies, supposedly out of love for them.

Struck down were the laws that in some states mandated that single mothers breastfeed their babies for six months. Enacted before adoption had become popular, the laws were meant to encourage the mothers to become emotionally attached to their babies and to want to raise them, rather than send them to orphanages funded by the public. Once these mothers' babies became marketable commodities, however, officials wanted to separate the two, rather than to keep them together.

By the late 1930s single mothers were not only being prevented from bonding with their babies, but often even from seeing them. Mothers were sometimes blindfolded during labor. Some social workers urged pregnant young women to sign forms allowing doctors to circumcise their child, if it turned out to be a boy, so that the workers could keep mothers uninformed even of their baby's gender.

By the time adoption became nationally popular in the mid-1940s the reversal was complete, and for the first time in history, white single mothers were expected to surrender their babies for adoption. That relinquishment was endorsed by leaders of such reputable organizations as the Child Welfare League of America, the American Public Welfare Association, The Salvation Army, Catholic Charities, and most psychiatrists and psychologists led dissenting social scientist Clark Vincent to predict a future in which the newborns of all white single mothers would be seized by the state. "Such a policy would not be enacted or labeled overtly as 'punishment.' Rather, it would be implemented under such pressures and labels as 'scientific finding,' 'the best interest of the child,' 'rehabilitation goals for the unwed mother' and the 'stability of family and society.'"

This scenario had actually been advocated five years earlier by Georgia Tann client Pearl Buck, who had asked Georgia to collaborate on a book about adoption. Georgia dictated only two chapters before dying of cancer; her exposure as baby seller apparently discouraged Buck from using them in her book. But the author continued to share Georgia's attitude toward single mothers, and in a 1955 article for *Woman's Home Companion* Buck advocated legislation forcing them to surrender their babies for adoption.

Such a law was never passed. But the social pressure on single mothers was so great that, reluctantly and with great pain, they began relinquishing their children en masse. By the 1950s, 90 percent of white maternity home residents surrendered their children for adoption.

To virtually everyone but birth parents and adoptees, adoption came to be seen as the perfect solution for infertility. The availability of contraceptives and abortion would eventually be considered threats to this solution. But in the 1940s and '50s, when, partially because of social unrest associated with World War II, more single women became pregnant annually than ever before, sources of supply for the adoptive market seemed assured—if never, according to some particularly avid proponents of adoption, sufficient. Some suggested setting up baby breeding farms. Supposedly, they were joking. But the sentiment that impelled this suggestion was prevalent enough to cause sociologist Leontine Young to decry the view of unmarried mothers as "mere breeding machines, a means to an end."

Georgia Tann's popularization of adoption did more than rob single mothers of their children; it isolated many women during their pregnancies. This was another reversal, since throughout the years when young mothers were expected to keep their babies, the new mothers' parents, who anticipated helping their daughters in their new roles, had allowed them to wait out their pregnancies at home.

But as adoption became more common, prospective grandparents who expected their daughters to relinquish their babies became reluctant to let their neighbors know that the young women were "in trouble." Increasingly they hid their daughters in homes for unwed mothers.

Maternity homes had existed since the early nineteenth century in the urban, eastern part of this country, and since the 1870s in most of the rest. Originally established by Evangelical reformers to rehabilitate prostitutes and other "fallen women," the institutions housed them and their babies for as long as two years, during which the mothers were instructed in childcare, a trade, and religion. Most facilities met their costs through charitable donations.

But after 1935 rising rates of single pregnancies resulted in the building of more maternity homes than most communities could finance, and residents were forced to pay for their confinement by cooking, laundering, and scrubbing floors, sometimes for as long as six months after giving birth.

The young women's maternity home stays were painful for reasons other than the hard work that was often required. They were allowed no contact with friends or boyfriends, and often made to use fictitious names. When they went into labor they were sometimes tied down and forbidden anesthesia.

These young women did not publicly protest, but many recorded their feelings in journals written during their pregnancies. One entry, included in *Wake Up Little Susie*, a book about single pregnancy in

America between 1945 and 1965, describes the panic of missing a period when single pregnancy was such cause for shame.

"Two weeks went by. They dragged at a snail's pace. Day was joined to day like links in a heavy chain which coiled around me and dragged wherever I walked. . . . I lifted heavy weights. I jumped from the height of the table to the floor until I didn't have the strength to climb back on the table again. At night I sat in hot mustard baths and slept with my head pounding from the effects of quinine. I drank tansy tea and swallowed capsules of turpentine until all I wanted to do was retch out my insides and die. I thought of dying. With all my heart I wanted to die. . . .

"When I didn't come around during the second month, I was desperate. My face became gaunt and haggard. My eyes sank deep into their sockets. My clothes were always damp with sweat. 'I'll kill myself,' I would murmur into the darkness at night. 'I'll take poison and kill myself.'"

Georgia probably never knew this young woman. But she exploited the despair of many like her, enticing her victims with such classified newspaper advertisements as, "Young women in trouble, call Miss Georgia Tann." She and her workers frequently visited doctors in Tennessee, Arkansas, Mississippi, Alabama, and other states, offering their pregnant, single patients free room, board, and medical care for the duration of their pregnancies.

She allowed the young women anesthesia during childbirth. She exempted them even from singing hymns—boarding them in private homes whose owners cared less about saving their souls than collecting the $40 per boarder Georgia paid them each month.

Georgia didn't spell out the terms of her bargain. She often told young women they would have a month after their deliveries during which to decide whether they would keep their babies. Some pregnant women chose names for their unborn children, only to awaken from anesthesia to learn that their babies had been stillborn, or were on their way to adoptive homes, courtesy of papers the mothers had been made to sign while drugged.

Other young women, who understood what free lodging, labor, and delivery would cost them, acquiesced out of financial desperation only. There were probably still others who, feeling trapped and unprepared to parent, initially accepted Georgia's coercion, her relieving them of the responsibility of choice. (These were the young women so many Hickory residents had insisted to me that Georgia had helped.)

There are areas grayer than any I want to visit, and one of them is here. I avoided it when I first realized Georgia's role in uniting the children who were languishing on baby farms with the infertile adults who, because of the babies' supposed genetic taint, were afraid to adopt them. Avoidance of more nuance than I could countenance had led me to ignore why these children had been languishing in institutions in the first place. The time before Georgia, when mothers had not only been allowed but legally enjoined to raise their children, had been less Utopian than I had wanted to believe. Poor, overwhelmed, pregnant with their seventh or eighth child, some had seen no recourse but to give their infants to baby farmers. They wanted, needed, a better option.

Georgia's clients were generally more humane than baby farmers. The institution she created and popularized filled a need. Her selfish motives resulted in some good.

But Georgia had no right to steal children, or to sell them, or to place for adoption children whose parents wanted to raise them. And she didn't treat the institution of adoption with the care that it deserved. How many even of the young women originally grateful for the option of relinquishing their children later regretted capitulation motivated by what they would have considered their weakness? How many of them suffered from lack of support in determining what they really wanted to do?

"Giving up my baby has been the bitter regret of my life," Ann Cardell said in 1975, when she was sixty-three. Age eighty-five and lost to Alzheimer's by the time I learned of her, she was revealed to me through the words of the child she had surrendered to Georgia for adoption. A Maryland psychiatrist named Gordon S. Livingston, he easily evoked the fragility of the moment when the two first saw each other after thirty-seven years. Ann herself appeared fragile, fine-boned, slender; her hands shook as she passed him a cup of tea. But as she spoke Gordon became most aware of her intense self-discipline, evinced by her carefully modulated voice and, even more, by the mechanism she had employed to bear his absence all those years.

She was the only child of a Vicksburg, Mississippi, farming couple who had sacrificed for her education. She had never married.

"Your father," she told Gordon, "was the only man I ever loved." She was twenty-six when she met him, and working as a teacher. "He was a wonderful dancer," she said. She didn't seem bitter that he'd abandoned her when she learned of her pregnancy.

"I went to Memphis to have you," she said. "I couldn't shame my parents." She had hoped that the woman who boarded her during her pregnancy would be able to adopt him, but Georgia sent him to a Chicago doctor and his wife.

Back home in Mississippi, Ann regretted her decision, becoming gaunt and depressed before finally discovering a way of coping with her loss. She pretended she hadn't lost Gordon. She kept him with her in her mind: watched him grow from infant to toddler to boy.

"By 1944 you were six and starting first grade, the very grade I was teaching," she told Gordon, he wrote in an article for *Reader's Digest*. "I couldn't wait for school to start. I saw you in every child's face. When I administered IQ tests I hoped the boy with the highest score was you. When I comforted a crying, defeated child, I feared he might be you.

"You grew so quickly that year," she said. "You were aggressive and vulnerable, cocky and easily wounded. I learned you needed an atmosphere of tolerance and love. I tried to give it to you by giving it to all those children.

"It was an illusion, of course, but I half believed it, and when I said goodbye to that class in the spring, I felt sick with guilt. It was as if I was abandoning you for the second time.

"Then, the following winter, I learned the third grade teacher was retiring. I immediately petitioned the school board for a transfer, and I got it. I would be your teacher again, this time, when you were eight.

"That year, as I watched you mature, I was proud you were becoming your own person, and I felt selfish for trying to hold on to you. At the end of the year, I stopped imagining you were with me. But I always wanted you back. I prayed that one day I would meet you as a man . . ."

"I just sat there, immobilized by my own emotions," Gordon told me. "Slowly she held out her arms and, for the first time in thirty-seven years, we touched."

I was contacted by few mothers who had relinquished babies to Georgia—most, perhaps still burdened by guilt and shame, refrained from responding to my classified ads. I learned of Ruby Burdette as I had Ann Cardell, through her relinquished son. Memphian Solon Freeman found his mother, also of Memphis, through an ad in the classified section of the local newspaper. He was glad he took the initiative; Ruby told him that though she had wanted to, she would never have searched— she feared disrupting his relationship with his adoptive parents.

Reunion has done nothing of the sort, Solon told me. "My adoptive mother and my birth mother get along really well—they go out to eat together all the time—and my daughters love both their grandmothers."

Solon himself sees Ruby almost daily, sometimes helping her with a project that she initiated to give some meaning to her loss. She calls it the Love Home.

It's a small maternity home, operated out of Ruby and her husband's house: when I spoke with her she had cared for 109 young women. "It all began when I watched a movie on unwed pregnancy," she told me. "The Lord laid it on my heart that I needed to help young girls in the trouble I'd been in."

Ruby's maternity home is as different as she can make it from the one Georgia put her in. "My girls get good food; Georgia's women gave us nothing but peanut butter and oatmeal," she said. She charges nothing for her services, relying entirely upon church donations. And Ruby's young women face no pressure to relinquish their babies; most elect to keep them.

"I feel like I'm completing a circle," Ruby said.

11.

Georgia's Children

How we crave arrangement. Often, overwhelmed by the incalculable sadness Georgia had engendered, aware of the many of her direct victims who wished to speak with other birth parents or adoptees, and to form a support group, I would refrain from returning that day's transcribed interviews to their separate folders, leaving them instead in a companionable pile. Then, reaching for a fresh legal pad, I'd list concrete facts about Georgia's story. They would seem so orderly, so neat, so irrelevant.

"I understand your sense of outrage," an elderly Memphis attorney had told me. "But what is the point of writing this book?"

And so blessedly often, as I rooted through the arrangements I'd effected upon the information stored in folders and in my brain for answers that were never where I thought I'd find them, I'd hear from someone who had imposed upon her life patterns more meaningful than any I could create: Ruby Burdette, who had completed a circle with her Love Home; adoptee Heidi Naylor, who had loved and cared for over sixty foster children. Another adoptee, Mary Margolis of St. Louis, Missouri, had begun speaking to small groups about her family's dissolution.

One of four children stolen by Georgia Tann from their mother, Irene Green, Mary Margolis had reunited with her sisters and brother after a separation of sixty years. By then Irene had died, but the siblings had a warm, close relationship. "How your audience must applaud," I told Mary.

She corrected me gently: "They're usually too busy crying."

My comment had been clumsy. But I was often made inarticulate by such evidence of human resilience and common sense. To have transformed a personal tragedy into a vehicle for helping or informing others seemed noble: The recounting of such feats seemed sufficient reason for any book.

I didn't know how many of Georgia's adoptees had managed to use their experience to help others, or even to survive. But I was speaking frequently with one who was desperately trying to survive: my phone companion, Billy Hale.

Upon taking early retirement from his job in Portland, Oregon, shortly after watching the *60 Minutes* episode on Georgia Tann, Billy had returned to Murfreesboro, Tennessee. "Some of the best years of my life were spent there with my adoptive parents," he told me in explanation. I knew, however, that they were now dead.

Billy had had trouble finding employment. But a childhood friend hired him to do carpentry work and let him park his trailer on his estate. From this vantage point Billy visited his birth uncle, aunts, and cousins in nearby Duffield, Virginia. They were friendly, but Billy wasn't able to see them as often as he wished. He sent me pictures of his trailer, and a recent one of himself. When I had met Billy three years earlier he'd had short hair and worn jeans and golf shirts and a small, Native American necklace. Billy's hair was long now, parted in the middle and swept back over his shoulders. He had shaved his moustache. These changes, including a larger silver and turquoise medallion and an unemotional, stoic expression, connoted a stereotypical Native American appearance that, contrasted with how Billy had looked only one year earlier, seemed disconcerting.

Was there one, real Billy? I wasn't sure he thought so. Having been forced to confront memories that he'd been told were false, he was struggling to absorb them. His adult past had disappeared into the void; his dead mother, Mollie, had become more real than any person living.

Given her poverty and proximity to Memphis, Mollie hadn't had a chance. Upon the relocation of her parents and three youngest brothers to Ohio, she too left Virginia for Kingsport, Tennessee, where her sister Frances was a waitress. Mollie waited tables also until a middle-aged, married farmer offered her a more lucrative post.

"He was evil, despicable, a terrible person," Billy told me repeatedly. His own self-image had never been strong. And when I sensed the additional pain of discovery of the character of the man who'd fathered him I understood why Billy had protected himself by writing his own book in the third person.

"When Mollie told the farmer of her pregnancy he threw her out," Billy had written. "She went to a shelter for unwed mothers and on February 10, 1939, delivered a 6-pound, 13-ounce baby boy."

Mollie's prospects were bleak. She was laid off from her job in a laundry, and, unable to find work, brought Billy by bus to visit her parents. But the Depression had hit Ohio almost as hard as Virginia; Mollie not only found no work but discovered her parents to be so poor that she gave them most of her remaining money. Then, unable to afford bus fare back to Kingsport, she got off at a town twenty-five miles outside it, and, carrying eighteen-month-old Billy, walked the rest of the way.

Mollie's sister Frances told Billy how, encountering a storm en route, his mother had taken refuge in an abandoned shed, where she sheltered him from the water pouring through the chinks in the tin roof with a blanket fashioned from her sweater.

Shortly after reaching Kingsport she was offered a housekeeping position with a farming family: a job with prospects greater than its nature or location, on a street called Poor Hollow Road, suggested. The job wasn't located in a particularly poor area, and her employer didn't bother her once. He and his wife and children lived in the black-and-white, two-story main house; Mollie and Billy stayed in a three-room clapboard cottage. (This was the cottage that Billy had visited in 1992. It was shaded by oak trees and willows, accessed by crossing a wooden bridge forging a small stream. When he crossed it, a Rhode Island red hen and her twelve chicks traversed the short span with him. On a nearby dirt road children kicked up dust balls, playing tag.)

The three years Mollie spent here had been her best, he was sure. Her next job was with another farming family who believed the presence of almost-five-year-old Billy would prove distracting. Her sister had moved to Pennsylvania, Mollie had no other relatives close by, and she was forced to board him for six days a week at a small institution called the Faith Home. "It would not be for long, she promised him," Billy wrote. "She searched desperately for other work."

But even a short stay in a Tennessee orphanage tempted fate too much. Billy wasn't sure when he was spotted. In 1993 he spoke with another former Faith Home resident who, eight years older than he, recalled more detail, including having been driven with Billy and several other children to a Memphis church, to sing. Had Georgia arranged this

Above: Georgia Tann's home, the Memphis branch of the Tennessee Children's Home Society, in 1950. (*Press-Scimitar* Photo/Mississippi Valley Collection/Special Collections/University of Memphis Libraries)

Left: Georgia Tann in the Home's reception area in 1943. (*Press-Scimitar* Photo/Mississippi Valley Collection/Special Collections/University of Memphis Libraries)

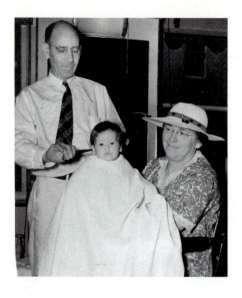

Georgia Tann and a ward, Baby Lucy, who is being groomed before being transported to an adoptive home. (*Press-Scimitar* Photo/Mississippi Valley Collection/Special Collections/ University of Memphis Libraries)

Memphis Juvenile Court Judge Camille Kelley, circa 1941. Judge Kelley's court provided Georgia Tann with 20 percent of the children she placed for adoption. (*Press-Scimitar* Photo/Mississippi Valley Collection/Special Collections/University of Memphis Libraries)

Tennessee political boss Edward Hull Crump (left), with friends. Georgia Tann enjoyed Boss Crump's protection. (*Press-Scimitar* Photo/Mississippi Valley Collection/Special Collections/University of Memphis Libraries)

Wants Home

—Press-Scimitar Photo

A solemn little trick with big, brown eyes, Madge is anxious for a new home and a mother and daddy.

Madge is five years old and "awful lonesome," she told the photographer when he snapped her picture. And if you can help Madge out in this matter of getting a new set of parents and a chance to go to school, Miss Georgia Tann, executive secretary of Tennessee Children's Home Society, wants to hear from you. The little girl is a ward of the society.

Left: This advertisement ran in the Memphis *Press-Scimitar* in 1930. It describes five-year-old Madge as "a solemn little trick with big brown eyes," who is " 'awful lonesome.' " (*Press-Scimitar* Photo/Mississippi Valley Collection/Special Collections/University of Memphis Libraries)

Yours for the Asking!

George Wants to Play Catch But He Needs A Daddy to Complete Team

PS 12-7-35

"Catch this ball, Daddy!"

How would YOU like to have this handsome five-year-old play "catch" with you?

How would you like his chubby arms to slip around your neck and give you a bearlike hug?

His name is George and he may be yours for the asking, if you hurry along your request to the Christmas Baby Editor of The Press-Scimitar. In co-operation with Miss Georgia Tann of the Tennessee Children's Home Society The Press-Scimitar will place 25 babies for

Right: Published in the *Press-Scimitar* in 1935, this advertisement was headlined "Yours for the Asking!" The caption read "How would YOU like this handsome five-year-old to play 'catch' with you? How would you like his chubby arms to slip around your neck and give you a bearlike hug? His name is George and he may be yours for the asking." (*Press-Scimitar* Photo/Mississippi Valley Collection/Special Collections/University of Memphis Libraries)

Paul Isn't One Bit Embarrassed

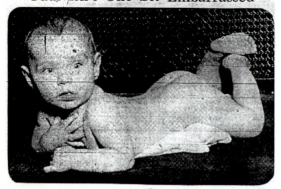

—Press-Scimitar Photo

Our photographer caught Master Paul, above, a la nude, but the young gentleman wasn't the least perturbed. Fact is, he isn't worrying about anything right now except getting a home and a mother and daddy to love him and see that Santa Claus fills his sock brim full this Christmas.

Paul, who is seven months old and a blond, is one of 25 babies to be placed for adoption Christmas Eve by Tennessee Children's Home thru co-operation of Press-Scimitar.

This advertisement ran in the *Press-Scimitar* in 1929. "Our photographer caught Master Paul a la nude, but the young gentleman wasn't the least perturbed. . . . Paul, who is seven months old and a blond, is one of 25 babies to be placed for adoption Christmas Eve by Tennessee Children's Home." (*Press-Scimitar* Photo/Mississippi Valley Collection/Special Collections/University of Memphis Libraries)

They'd Like to Be Your Christmas Gift

—Press-Scimitar Photo

"'Course, we aren't babies, but just the same we want a mother and daddy, too," say these youngsters, Polly, 3, John, 3, and Mary, 4, left to right above, who are among the 15 children and babies to be given away this Christmas by Press-Scimitar and the Tennessee Children's Home Society. Would you like to open your arms to one of them?

This picture, which was published in the *Press-Scimitar* in 1931, was headed "They'd Like to Be Your Christmas Gift." (*Press-Scimitar* Photo/Mississippi Valley Collection/Special Collections/University of Memphis Libraries)

Above: Billy Hale with his mother, Mollie Mae Moore, before he was stolen from her in 1944. Mollie searched for him until she died forty years later but never saw him again. (Billy Hale)

Left: Billy Hale and his wife, Rosetta, at their wedding in 1996. By then, Billy had spent years helping to find children who'd been abducted. Rosetta helped him in his work. (Rosetta Hale)

Above: Barbara Davidson reuniting
with her sister, Mary, in 1986. At
that point, they had been separated
by Georgia Tann for forty-four years.
Barbara described the reunion as
"wonderful, wonderful. It was the
most wonderful night of my life."
(Barbara Davidson)

Left: Barbara Davidson at age six,
one day after her arrival at her
adoptive home in California in
1948. Having already been abused
by a foster father and by Georgia
Tann, she was angry and wondering, "What bad things will
happen next?" She was later abused
by her adoptive father. It is testimony to her strength that she came
out of this whole. (Barbara Davidson)

Cleveland Panell and his sister, Shirley Ann. Cleveland was only fifteen when his five-year-old sister was stolen, but he began searching for her immediately, visiting Georgia Tann, Juvenile Court Judge Camille Kelley, and the Tennessee Department of Vital Statistics, and even calling FBI director J. Edgar Hoover. He found Shirley Ann in 1979, after a search of thirty-seven-and-a-half years. (Cleveland Panell)

Shirley Ann at age five, before she was stolen and placed for adoption with a Hollywood actor and his wife. (Cleveland Panell)

My daughter, Beth Raymond Good (front left), reuniting with her birth family: mother Gail; father Salvatore (Sal); and, from left, brothers Chris, Alex, and Mike. These brothers and the brother Beth was raised with, Tim, were groomsmen at her 2006 wedding. Beth danced two father-daughter dances: one with her adoptive father, Bob, and one with Sal. (Beth Raymond Good)

visit? Were the children auditioning for parts they would never want? Billy would never know. But shortly afterward two of Georgia's workers arrived in a black, chauffeur-driven limousine and told him they were taking him for a ride. Then on to Memphis, where Billy would experience the things he'd spend the rest of his life trying to forget.

Mollie didn't learn of Billy's abduction until seventy-two hours later, when she went to pick him up on Saturday. Setting on the counter of the reception area the basket of eggs that constituted partial payment for his boarding, she asked to see him.

"He's not here," said Belle Hall, the matron.

Mollie stared in surprise.

"He's gone with the social workers." As Mollie began to scream, Belle added, "They had papers. It was legal."

Billy's Aunt Frances told him that Mollie had then assaulted Belle, breaking her nose. Records of his mother's subsequent arrest and imprisonment had been destroyed by the time Billy asked to see them in the 1990s.

Hitting Belle was the last decisive action of Mollie's life. Losing him, Billy wrote in his book, left her "broken, without spirit." On one of her futile visits to orphanages and police stations in Virginia, Kentucky, North Carolina, and eastern Tennessee she met a trucker named Wallace Harper, who "lived on the wild side. Briefly, Mollie lived on the wild side too."

Mollie's life could be considered wild, Billy added, only in comparison to the one she had lived before: after her marriage she wore makeup and drank beer.

She does appear, in a photo taken of the couple in the early 1950s, more worldly than before. Wallace, his greasy hair in a pompadour, his collar spread-eagled over what appears a black lounge suit, resembles a gangster. He saw himself, however, as a Lothario: knowledge of his affairs, both in Kingsport and, after he joined the Air Force in 1952, in San Diego and Los Angeles, devastated Mollie. "But she didn't want a divorce," Billy wrote. "Wallace was all she had."

Even without a divorce she lived a solitary life, remaining in Kingsport during Wallace's tours of duty both because of his desire for freedom and her own reluctance to leave the town in which she had last seen her son.

She gardened and kept pets. She also maintained a scrapbook that, Billy said, allowed him to look straight into her soul. It contains the card she would have given him on his fifth birthday, and a postcard of a little boy perched on a rock in a stream, his head averted—did she pretend it was Billy? And there were newspaper articles, carefully clipped, garnered from different papers over a span of twenty years, but always with the same theme:

"Tyke Survives Snakes, Gators After Being Dumped In Georgia Swamp."

"Police Examine Buried Wooden Box Near Nansemond, Virginia, On The Edge Of Dismal Swamp, Where A Thirteen-Year-Old Boy Was Held Chained For Eight Days. . . ."

"Kelly Is Better—When Sheriff's Deputies In Miami, Florida, Found Kelly Puente, Four, In A Cage He Weighed Only Fourteen Pounds; Now He Is Up To Twenty-Four."

"Doing Fine—Sharla Johnson, Seven Months, Of Fairbanks, Alaska, Is Recovered From Several Hours' Exposure to -40 Degree Temperatures. . . ."

"Knoxville Police Believe Kidnapped Child Still Alive."

The scrapbook also contains pictures of Billy as a toddler, and of Mollie, growing older. One, showing her at age fifty, lifting the edges of her square dancing dress to show a peacock fan, heartened Billy: she is smiling. Another shows her at seventy, her hair white and permed, with her favorite big brother.

She is with Harrison, too, in the last snapshot taken before her death. He hugs her; she is crying: she had been talking, Harrison told Billy, of him.

Mollie was one of an unknowable number of parents who died without learning if their children had survived into adulthood. Many had not. Georgia seemed immune to guilt, and never publicly expressed sorrow about a single child's death. She also denied the accusations of local pediatricans that scores of her children had perished, admitting only to two deaths, which she said had occurred in October of 1945.

She refused even to acknowledge illness in her children, and forbade her boarding mothers from summoning medical help. Faced with desperately sick children, however, some boarding mothers panicked and sent them to the hospital.

The trip was often made too late. The deaths of most of these babies were presumably recorded, and the children buried in the area of Elmwood Cemetery used by her adoption agency. But Georgia disposed of the bodies of children whose deaths she could conceal in less regular ways. A reporter for the *Press-Scimitar* passed Georgia's Home one night in the 1940s and saw someone burying something in the backyard—a child, the reporter believed. Former investigator Robert Taylor told me that Georgia had had the local Thompson Brothers Funeral Home cremate some of the children. "Getting rid of the evidence," Taylor said. "A grave is proof."

No death certificates were issued for many of these children. "There were a lot of deaths nobody knew anything about," pediatrician Clyde Croswell said in 1950.

As terrible as these deaths were, they seem sadder upon consideration of their causes, which were usually heat prostration or a combination of starvation and dehydration caused by gastrointestinal infection—painful ways to die. The deaths could also easily have been prevented, had Georgia respected the children's fragility and medical advice. Charles Carter, a pediatrician who in the 1940s volunteered his services to the Home, was particularly disturbed by Georgia's overriding of his orders regarding a very sick infant. "I had prescribed penicillin, and learned later that she'd ordered her nurses to stop giving it to the baby, but continue to chart it as if they were," he told me.

"Georgia Tann simply would not listen. She would say, 'I'll take your words under advisement,' but she never did. She did what she felt best, regardless of what anyone said. She felt she knew the babies, and what the babies needed."

The common practice in the 1930s and '40s was to hospitalize full-term infants for a week, and premature babies until they weighed over five pounds. Georgia, however, sometimes took children only a few hours after birth, and often quickly transported them to adoptive homes thousands of miles away. Babies arrived at their new homes feverish and dehydrated. Some died shortly after their journey, including an infant girl sent to a New Jersey couple to whom Georgia had previously sent a baby boy with a heart defect. The poor health of many of Georgia's children was such a constant and well-known fact that a Memphis hospital reserved an entire ward for their care. A hospital in Los Angeles also maintained a ward for the many sick babies she sent to local adoptive parents. Physicians in these states and others complained about Georgia to the Department of Public Welfare and the state director of the Tennessee Children's Home Society, but no one curbed her, and she continued to cause child deaths.

By 1932, only eight years after Georgia's arrival in Memphis, the city had the highest recorded infant death rate of any U.S. city of over one hundred thousand residents. Over the next two years, the recorded Memphis infant mortality rate soared even higher. And the true number of babies who died was higher than was ever recorded, since Georgia frequently failed to report her children's deaths.

The reported rate, however, was sufficiently disturbing that in 1935 the U.S. Children's Bureau sent Dr. Ella Oppenheimer to Memphis to investigate the cause.

She found it quickly. "The most striking difference in cause of mortality between Memphis and the cities with which it is compared is mortality from gastrointestinal disease among white infants, which in 1934 was very much higher in Memphis that in any of the other cities except Louisville," she wrote in her report, "Infant Mortality in Memphis."

Georgia Tann dealt only with white children. The most frequent cause of death of the children she boarded was gastrointestinal disease.

Dr. Oppenheimer also noted that many of the Memphis deaths occurred in Memphis General Hospital—the very hospital to which Georgia's boarding home mothers, defying Georgia's orders, frequently sent sick children.

Dr. Oppenheimer's search for facts was hampered by Georgia's lying. "On July 2, 1935, the executive of the [Tennessee Children's Home Society] in Memphis [Georgia Tann] stated that no infant had died since the beginning of the calendar year," Dr. Oppenheimer wrote. But she must have doubted Georgia's truthfulness. In "Infant Mortality in Memphis," the doctor implicitly criticized Georgia for taking babies from hospitals and maternity residences earlier than was medically recommended, and then often placing them in unregulated boarding homes. She strongly urged that these boarding homes be licensed, and that they be supervised by the state.

Dr. Oppenheimer's recommendation had no immediate impact on Georgia, who continued to do whatever she wished. The first real attempt to curb her occurred in 1943, six years after the formation of the Tennessee Department of Public Welfare. The Department's commissioner was, like virtually every politician in the state, intimidated by Georgia and her attorney Abe Waldauer, a major lieutenant in Crump's Machine. Some of the Department's employees collaborated with Georgia. But other social workers were more concerned with the welfare of her children than politics, and they wanted the state licensing of boarding homes that Dr. Oppenheimer had recommended.

In preparation for this, Roberta Miller, director of the Child Welfare Division of the Department of Public Welfare, conducted a study of ten Memphis boarding homes for children. In 1944, one of her caseworkers, Faye Wallis, reported the study's results in the *Tennessee Public Welfare Record*. Nine of the ten boarding homes were overcrowded: one two-room apartment housed ten children. In another, six infants shared a single crib. A third home lacked refrigeration, and newborns were being fed spoiled milk.

One child suffering from syphilis, and another from tuberculosis, lived in two other boarding homes; Georgia had refused to allow them medical treatment. Sixteen more children lived in the attic of a house that the fire department had condemned as a firetrap. And two-year-old twins lived with a seventy-nine-year-old boarding mother who, nearly blind and too senile to remember their names, addressed them as "Old Man" and "Old Lady" and fed them bread scraps.

"Tennessee is one of the few remaining states which has no legislation regulating boarding homes for children," Roberta Miller wrote in "What Do You Know About Tennessee's Adoption Laws?" published in the *Tennessee Public Record* in 1944. "We would not go to a beauty shop or restaurant which is unlicensed, yet by our inertia and lack of interest in safeguarding children, we sit back and wink at the commercial boarding homes operating in Tennessee for babies and small children."

Roberta Miller and Faye Wallis knew that Georgia Tann was the person using most of these commercial boarding homes. In Tennessee's boss-ridden environment, however, they were apparently afraid to say so outright, and their articles never mentioned Georgia's name. Nevertheless, Georgia and her attorney were incensed by both pieces. Abe Waldauer wrote several heated letters of complaint to Miller's boss, Commissioner of Public Welfare William Shoaf.

But Miller, Wallis, and other ethical social workers forged on, drafting an ordinance requiring regulation of children's boarding homes, and persuading local newspapers to publicize the need to safeguard children's health.

The workers must have celebrated when, in 1945, the legislature passed a law mandating the licensing and inspection of every children's boarding home in Tennessee. But while the social workers had toiled Georgia and Abe had worked too, exercising their political clout. A subsection of the new law exempted any boarding homes used by Georgia Tann's agency from compliance.

She had won again, and children in her boarding homes continued to die. So did children in her Home on Poplar Avenue, which had opened in 1943, and where conditions were possibly even worse than in the boarding residences. "In summer, the heat was unbearable," said Mrs. Leon Sims of Philadelphia, Mississippi, who worked in Georgia's Home throughout 1943. "It was particularly hard on the children with fevers." Georgia called her and the other two caretakers nurses, "but none of us were honestly nurses," she told me. "I was the only person on duty at night, and cared for as many as twenty-five children. Every one needed attention, but I simply didn't have enough time. There was a lot of illness—the main problem was diarrhea."

Gastrointestinal illness is, as Dr. Oppenheimer of the U.S. Children's Bureau had noted, a serious problem in babies, whose bodies are so small that they can dehydrate within hours. A particularly severe epidemic of the disease in Georgia's Home in 1945 caused the deaths of forty to fifty children in less than four months. This was despite the efforts of pediatrician Clyde Croswell, who volunteered his services to the Home, and who urged her to hospitalize her sick infants and not admit any more children into her orphanage. "She didn't follow the instructions," he told a Memphis reporter in 1950.

After having remonstrated with Georgia, who insisted that only two children had died, Dr. Croswell met with Abe Waldauer and other members of her board of directors. "I offered to show them a list of the infants who had died—a staggering toll," he said. "They didn't want to see it."

Doctors Croswell and Carter and four other Memphis physicians complained to Probate Court Judge Samuel Bates, whose court had long officiated over Georgia's adoptions. In May of 1946 Judge Bates wrote a six-page, single-spaced letter to the commissioner of the Tennessee Department of Public Welfare, William Shoaf, detailing the doctors' complaints. Some concerned the dysentery epidemic that had killed forty to fifty children, Georgia's failure to properly screen adoptive parents, "the advertisement of particular children for adoption," and her failure to assess the care children received in their adoptive homes. Among the others reported were

- "Dr. C. E. James, who . . . maintains an office in the Methodist Hospital, . . . stated that of the babies released to the Tennessee Children's Home Society that were born at the Methodist Hospital, all would leave there in perfect

health, but in many instances were returned in one or two
months in an emaciated condition and that many of them
died as a result of neglect. He recalled an instance where
a child was given to prospective adoptive parents, but that
it lived only two weeks. . . ."

- " . . . Dr. Croswell stated that he had advised Miss Tann not
to bring the babies out of the hospital before they weighed
at least five pounds, but she continued to disregard this
advice. On an occasion he told her not to bring any children into the Home because of an infection, but she
brought in five and three or four of them died. . . ."

- "Miss Tann, according to Dr. Croswell, had a woman assis-
tant by the name of Flanikan who frequently came on duty
in a drunken condition. She gave castor oil in disregard of
his instructions. . . . Dr. Croswell secured the services of a
registered nurse and tried to put her in charge of the babies,
but Miss Tann would not permit this with the result that
the nurse left. . . . Dr. Croswell said he couldn't be party
to things going on of that type and continue a good citizen,
so he discontinued his connection with the Tennessee
Children's Home Society. . . . 'The mortality rate that is
reported is nothing in comparison to what it actually is.'"

Judge Bates's letter amounted to a show-cause order. Unless his
charges were proven to be untrue, or Georgia Tann was removed from
her position as head of the Memphis branch of the Tennessee Children's
Home Society, he wrote, he would stop approving her adoptions.

Judge Bates wanted Shoaf to investigate Georgia and shut her down. As the Commissioner of the Tennessee Department of Public Welfare, Shoaf had the power to do so (his successor, J. O. McMahon, would close the Home after her death). Shoaf was, however, a politician, and in 1946 Boss Crump still controlled Tennessee. Shoaf handed the responsibility of investigating Georgia Tann over to Georgia's attorney, Abe Waldauer, and other members of her board of directors. They read Georgia's six-page rebuttal, a characteristic mix of deflection, indignation, and lies. ("Dr. James' statement that in many instances babies released to the Tennessee Children's Home Society in perfect health are returned in two or three months in an emaciated condition and that many of them died is not true. Some of our babies died (she admitted to two)—but NOT from neglect on the part of the Tennessee Children's Home Society. This is an infamous attack. . . .")

Abe Waldauer and other board members grilled Doctors Croswell and Carter, then issued a report finding the physicians' charges "groundless," "irresponsible and valueless," and "false from beginning to end."

The Public Welfare Commissioner to whom Judge Bates had appealed, William Shoaf, did nothing. "Mr. Waldauer told me I had no authority in the matter," Shoaf said.

Judge Bates was less intimidated by Georgia and her attorney than Shoaf, and he stopped approving her adoptions. This, however, didn't faze Georgia. She and Waldauer simply spoke to judges in rural Tennessee counties such as Haywood, Hardeman, and Dyer. These small town judges weren't even lawyers, but they were politically savvy, and they signed whatever adoption decrees she wished.

Georgia's ability to operate freely even after Judge Bates's complaints was of course attributable to her connection to Boss Crump. But she was also indirectly enabled by the generally held attitude that adoptable children were expendable.

The author of an article in a 1930 issue of the *Saturday Evening Post* wrote of the plethora of babies to choose from—"beautiful babies, ugly babies; brilliant babies, dull babies; healthy babies, sick, handicapped babies; babies with blue eyes, brown eyes, black eyes; with golden hair, black hair, curly-locked and straight; babies thin and babies fat; babies three days old, three months or years old, and all the way stations in between; babies with full family histories and babies with no family history; without age, name or birth certificate, unknown waifs tossed into alleyways or dumped into garbage cans."

Children in such a market, the article continued, have to sell themselves. Blue eyes were a decided advantage, as was female gender. "Baby girls are more feminine, alluring; they are grand little self-advertisers and they know instinctively how to strut their stuff. . . . They stretch out their dimpled arms; gurgle at some secret baby joke, . . . blow air bubbles from moist cupid's bow mouths . . . and women and strong men grow mad, become besotted with adoration and want to kidnap them on the spot. . . ."

The author contended that males with the wrong hair color were at a distinct disadvantage: "If a boy is red-headed, his chance of finding a new mamma and papa is practically zero. Nobody wants him at all."

The reporter didn't name her sources—she appeared to have had two, one of whom was director of a New York State agency; neither was as successful as Georgia in arranging adoptions.

Much of Georgia's success depended upon her baby ads, which while enjoyed by Memphians appalled many outsiders. "I moved to Memphis in 1936, and was horrified to see on the front page of the paper a picture of a little baby that was going to be given away," former

Press-Scimitar reporter Alfred Andersson told me. "They didn't do things like that in Texas."

When the Christmas baby ads became syndicated in the 1930s they attracted the disapproval of Charles C. Carstens, executive director of the Child Welfare League of America. Georgia ignored his warnings to stop the ads, which his successor, Howard W. Hopkirk, cited in 1941 as a main cause for the expulsion of Georgia and the statewide Tennessee Children's Home Society from the League. (Other reasons cited were Georgia's failure to assess the fitness of adoptive parents and to supervise children in their new homes; Hopkirk was unaware that Georgia was also kidnapping and selling children.) In typical fashion, Georgia and her attorney claimed that she hadn't been ousted from the League, but had voluntarily withdrawn because "of many of their attitudes with which we were not in agreement."

Georgia further commercialized children by making them perform: "Sit on that man's lap and call him 'Daddy,'" she told one little girl. She also demeaned children by excessively catering to her clients, giving children to some adults who wanted, not babies to raise, but objects to give away. "I was bought by a couple and given as a gift to my adoptive family," Wilhelmina Newsome of Memphis told me. "My adoptive mother was depressed over the death of her own mother, and instead of buying her a puppy, her friends gave her me."

Georgia also debased children by using them as bargaining chips, placing them with politicians and social workers whose opposition she hoped to defuse. One of the more blatant instances of such bribery occurred in 1949, when she gave a Tennessee legislator two children to prevent his support of reform adoption legislation.

Georgia sometimes sent couples two or three children "on trial," allowing them a year to decide which child they wanted to keep.

Georgia Tann's attorney frequently referred to children as products.

"It is not often that we have the good luck that we have in your case, namely of having the merchandise in hand and in stock to deliver to you immediately," Abe Waldauer wrote to one of Georgia's prospective clients in 1944.

"This is one business in which we can never tell when we can fill an order," he wrote to a less fortunate applicant that same year.

In 1947 Abe informed a prospective client that Georgia's adoptive parents had "complete custody and control of a child for one year; may submit the child to any physical or mental examination they wish and take any steps they may desire to ascertain they have a healthy and normal child. If it is not, the Tennessee Children's Home takes it back, without question."

And Georgia's clients frequently did send children back, often because they appeared less intellectually gifted than the adoptive parents had been led to expect. The pain experienced by rejected children meant nothing to Georgia, as did the suffering of those not returned but resented, for falling short. Virginia Simmons said, "I was told my adoptive mother ordered me like out of a Sears, Roebuck catalogue." When Virginia developed scoliosis her mother was furious. "She said, 'I spent a lot of money on you, and you're such a disappointment. If I'd known you were going to develop that crooked back I would never have picked you out.'"

While Georgia informed her clients of her liberal merchandise return policy, she presented her usual false face to the public. In a letter to the editor published in the *Press-Scimitar* in 1938 she castigated a White Plains, New York, couple who were considering returning a severely retarded child they had adopted from a New York agency.

"The law is definite and its view of an adoption is final, . . ." she wrote. "If the child has been carried through to the point of legal adoption, to the adoptive parents he is THEIR CHILD. From that point on, the fact that he is adopted should never enter into consideration of his problems. . . .

"If the White Plains couple had borne this child," she continued, "they would have had to cope with his handicap. Whatever their solution would have been, it is the answer to their adopted child's problem. The finality of adoption must be upheld, or the whole structure of the institution, based as it is upon the concept that 'the adoptive parents stand in the place of the birth parents,' is destroyed."

Few other than the initiated would have understood the hypocrisy of Georgia's words.

But as frequently as her children were returned, Georgia knew that she'd stay in business, that the vast majority of her clients had more scruples than she and, even when disappointed by their adoptive children, would keep them. Perhaps it was this insight into human nature that allowed her to risk customer dissatisfaction by misrepresenting her children in the first place.

Falsifying their birth records, she portrayed many as the children of debutants ("Twenty years old, five-feet, three inches tall, 120 pounds, blond, blue-eyed, of English ancestry," was her typical misrepresentation of a birth mother) who had been made pregnant by medical students. The young woman's mother was usually "a society woman," her father, "a prominent physician." Clients' expectations of their adoptive children having the intelligence to eventually attend Harvard must have seemed justified.

Georgia was also consistently unreliable in her representation of her babies' religions. Most of her children were born to Protestant young women. But Abe Waldauer, who was Jewish, had contacts with rabbis across the country, and throughout the 1940s, considerably more than half of her clients were Jewish. They wanted to adopt Jewish babies, so Georgia falsely represented many of her children as Jewish.

Some orthodox Jewish parents were upset to later learn that their children hadn't been born Jewish. Social worker Boo Cravens witnessed a worse consequence of Georgia's lies.

Sent from Nashville to Memphis in 1950 to help close the Home, Boo received letters from social agencies in every state to which Georgia had sent children, requesting information about their birth parents. Discovering an accurate bit of information among the false ones Georgia had recorded, she communicated it to the New York State Department of Public Welfare.

Unknown to her, however, New York law prohibited residents from adopting children of a religion different from their own. Discovering that a boy adopted sixteen years earlier by a local Jewish family had been born Protestant, authorities placed him in a foster home.

Boo didn't want any more children's lives disrupted. So when agencies inquired about other babies adopted by Jewish couples, "we just started lying."

She and other workers changed the children's birth names to Jewish-sounding surnames, she told me, sounding so kind, so truly concerned, that I tried not to consider how such falsifications, heaped upon Georgia's, had hopelessly obscured adoptees' true histories.

Georgia's adoptees, of course, cared less about their adopted parents' religions than their characters. And Georgia placed some children with terrible people. She sold seven-year-old Eugene Calhoun to a farmer so vicious that the child's initiation into his new home consisted of watching his adoptive mother spend three days dying of food poisoning, all the while vainly begging her husband for help.

This beginning was portentous: the farmer was just as cruel to Eugene, keeping him ragged, shoeless, in the fields for eighteen hours a day and in an unheated bedroom at night. He beat him with belts and farm tools; he split his spine with a post-hole digger.

Decades later, Eugene had surgery to remove bone fragments from his spine. But miraculously, he had escaped paralysis, and at age sixteen he escaped the farmer, running away to join the Navy. He later became a printer and a successful, self-taught graphic artist. When I spoke with him in the 1990s he lived in Farmington, Missouri, and was cherishing his relationship with his long-lost mother, brothers, and sister, with whom he'd recently been reunited through search expert Denny Glad after a separation of sixty years.

Another child, adopted through Georgia Tann by a man who hoped adoption might cure his wife of infertility, was left to suffer the consequence of not being curative—would he be resented if the adoptive mother failed to conceive?—or even being so—would he be treated as inferior to the birth child? I know of this boy only from a letter dated in the 1940s; I don't know what happened to him. But I did speak with people adopted for similarly inappropriate reasons, such as to replace a dead birth child.

Although from her earliest years Joy Barner knew she disappointed the people who raised her, she didn't know she was being measured against a ghost, or even that she'd been adopted. Placed with an Arkansas couple as a baby, she grew up believing she was their birth, and only, child. Then at age seven she opened an old trunk to find a first-grade reader inscribed with the name, "Mary Eleanor," a picture of a beautiful little girl with ringlets, and several tiny, dainty dresses. Joy, whose wardrobe was the antithesis of frilly, asked her adoptive mother incredulously, "Were these mine?"

"No!" she shouted. "They were your sister's, and she's dead. Don't ever mention her again."

"But there were ruffly things, like you put on little girls to make them feel partyish," Joy told me. "I asked her why I didn't any have dresses like that. She said, 'Because you are plain.'"

That she was not only a less than adequate replacement but an adopted one was implied throughout her childhood, always in ways that caused pain. When she was fourteen her mother took her to a beauty salon for a permanent wave. Joy loved it, but when they returned home, her adoptive father flew into a rage. "What are you trying to do?" he asked his wife. "Make a whore out of her like her mother?"

Lonely, unloved, Joy cherished her school friends, but her adoptive parents seldom let her socialize. At age fifteen she requested permission to attend a picnic with a male classmate, a doubly risky request, for the boy was Jewish and her father anti-Semitic.

"What's his nickname? Isn't it 'Hymie'?" her father shouted. "He's a Jew!"

"No, no he's not," begged Joy.

Picking up a glass of iced tea, he flung the contents in her face. "If I say he's a Jew, he's a Jew," he said.

When Joy was seventeen she fell in love with another school friend, Jake, who wasn't Jewish, but her father wouldn't allow her to see him either. So on Valentine's Day, 1939, she and Jake drove to Little Rock, Arkansas, were married, and then returned separately to their parents' homes.

Joy hoped to keep her secret from her parents, but she confided in a girlfriend. When she returned home from school several days later her father screamed that he would have the marriage annulled.

"Then I'll just marry him again."

Red-faced, the veins in his neck throbbing, he dragged her to the steel box in which he kept the family's important papers. "You were a mistake," he said. "I want you to know I paid $500 for you, and I could have gotten a good hunting dog for a lot less. You come from the lowest scum on earth."

Joy began to cry.

"Don't bother to cry—that's what you come' from." He threw her adoption papers at her feet. "Now don't go looking for your people," he said. "Don't open Pandora's box."

Her adoptive mother watched, uncomplaining, as he said this.

Joy ran away to the home of Jake's parents, and when he joined the service shortly afterward, moved with him to Florida and then to Augusta, Georgia. Theirs was a wonderful marriage, which when I spoke with her had endured for over sixty years.

During the first years after leaving her adoptive home, Joy tried to ignore what her father had said about her birth family. "I locked it up," she told me. "I closed the door." She bore two wonderful sons, built a life so strong that the news that her adoptive grandfather had left money to every grandchild but her couldn't touch it. "I have what I've worked for," she told herself, "not what somebody gave me."

But she couldn't help wondering about her parents and her older brother, Grady, whose name had been listed in her adoption papers. On June 12, 1943, she had written to Georgia Tann:

"I was brought up completely unaware of the fact that I was an adopted child. When I married a year ago this past February they told me that I wasn't their child. They told me that I was the child of riverboat trash who gave me away because they didn't want me. . . .

"Several months ago I wrote to the Juvenile Court seeking information of my parents or brother. I received an answer from the Chief Probation Officer, F. E. Bradley, advising me to contact you. He said you were the only person who could give me the desired information.

"Miss Tann, surely there is some information you can give me concerning my parents or my brother, Grady. It is very confusing to suddenly realize that you have parents and a brother you've never known. . . .

"You are the only person who can help me, Miss Tann. And I beg of you to give me any information you can that will help me find my people."

Georgia never answered. Joy's attempts to obtain information through the Tennessee Department of Social Services produced no results. And whenever her sons misbehaved she reasoned that her past might be a box best left closed. But when Grady, who after years of effort had obtained a court order releasing his adoption records, contacted her in 1989, she discovered her genealogy to be no cause for shame.

Her parents had been poor, and her father an alcoholic, but he and her mother had loved her and, after she and Grady were stolen from their houseboat in 1925, visited Georgia Tann and Juvenile Court Judge Camille Kelley, begging for their return. They were accompanied by other relatives: the children's uncles and cousins and maternal grandmother, Navada, who never gave up hope of reunion with her grandchildren. She and the children's parents had sent Georgia Tann letters protesting the children's abduction for twenty-five years, until Georgia died. When Joy learned that her own name had originally been Navada, after her grandmother, she felt a connection she'd never felt before.

"She was a full-blooded Cherokee Indian," Joy told me. "Now I know where I got my strong features. She acted as mid-wife when I was born in a two-room log cabin on the bank of the Sunflower River in Mississippi." Joy, who'd long painted miniature scenes on china, had, when I last spoke with her by phone, just finished her first oil painting—a portrait of her grandmother, Navada. "I wish you could see it," she said. "I painted her with her black hair and high, high cheekbones, looking so strong. I would have enjoyed growing up near her."

As is the case of most people strong enough to survive their difficulties, Joy didn't spend an inordinate amount of time regretting something she would never have, preferring to enjoy what she could, the most important of which was spending every possible minute with her brother Grady, who was ill. She was extremely proud of him, for though he'd had a difficult childhood, experiencing several foster and adoptive placements before finding a permanent adoptive home, he hadn't become bitter. "He is a good, good, person," she said.

It was an unsurprising testimonial, given not only the fact of its truth but her joy at having been found by Grady after a separation of sixty-four years. Brothers and sisters reunited after many years don't take their relationship for granted. This was illustrated not only by Joy Barner but by adoptee Barbara Davidson, who in the 1990s told me of her reunion with her sister, whose childhood name was Mary. Barbara's account seemed particularly moving within the context of the suffering they'd shared while in Georgia's custody, and their agonized separation: subjects so painful fifty years after their occurrence that Barbara related them not in linear fashion, but in stream-of-consciousness bursts.

"It was a horrendous thing that Georgia did and only God can help her, I don't know if even God can help her . . ." Barbara was talking, I realized, not only of Georgia's cruelty in parting her from Mary, but in sexually abusing both girls while they were in her custody.

Several people had informed me of Georgia's sexual abuse of children. Among the mail I received in response to my *Good Housekeeping* article on Georgia Tann had been a letter from a fifty-four-year-old man who later told me and another reporter about abuse he and his twin brother had suffered in Memphis in the 1940s.

The twins had been less than eight years old. "We remember being in a big bed, stripped naked; Georgia Tann and some other people were there reaching for us and kissing us and touching us where we shouldn't be touched," one brother told a reporter for *The Daily Pantagraph*.

Taken from their mother at age five, the twins had been placed in the Tennessee Children's Home Society orphanage in Nashville, and then sent to a California adoptive couple. The adoptive mother frequently beat them, often with the cord from an electric iron. The boys ran away, were found and sent to Memphis, where they were put in the Porter Home and Leath Orphanage. The twins later saw a page of its record book that read "Miss Tann wants these twin boys to have institutional training" before being adopted again.

Like other residents, they were viewed every Sunday by prospective adoptive parents, and they were eventually selected by a kind farming couple. But, haunted by memories of separation from their mother, they searched for and in 1987 found her and their two sisters. It was a happy reunion, but did not fully satisfy their need for connection to their past. When I last spoke with them, they were hoping to write a book about their experience with Georgia Tann.

Barbara Davidson and her older sister Mary were abandoned by their mother to Georgia Tann in 1942 and housed in an orphanage that Georgia visited frequently.

Raised until the ages of five and seven by an alcoholic mother so neglectful they had to rummage through neighbors' garbage cans for food, Barbara and Mary had always been close; their devotion intensified when they entered Georgia Tann's custody. "Mary was all I had," Barbara said. "She slept near me at night but it was still frightening; the beds creaked and the floors were cold, so cold, and I would cry for a blanket but no one would give me a blanket."

Rules were strict at the orphanage, Barbara told me, and punishments were illogically applied. Children were denied access to bathrooms at night, but were beaten for wetting their beds. Mary was beaten twice most evenings—once as a warning, and later as punishment. She and other malefactors—children attempting to sneak a drink of water—were caught by women, and occasionally men. "I remember them patrolling, checking our beds—shining a light in our faces—they carried big black flashlights," Barbara told me, nervously. "One night a woman pulled me out of bed by the hair and beat me and beat me—she said I stole a lemon gumdrop and I said I didn't do it. Mary said I didn't either, but the woman hit me in the head, hit me in the head, and hung me in a closet . . ."

Locking residents in closets, I would learn from many other adoptees, was the staff's most frequently used punishment. Barbara and other children were bound with rope around their wrists and suspended by the ropes from coat racks, their feet barely touching the floor. It was while she was bound, Barbara said, that Georgia Tann molested her. "She ran her hands all over me and played with me, that stuff. She said if I cried out she'd hit me in the head."

Georgia Tann assaulted Barbara's sister Mary in the closet, also, and in a bathroom, once using a wooden spoon. "She squatted over me, gouging me," Mary said. "She seemed like a giant. She was sadistic, evil. I thought of her as the devil."

Another adoptee was five years old when assaulted by Georgia in a bedroom. "Yes, sexual abuse at the hands of Georgia Tann was very true and it was presented as your favor," she said. She recalled the bedroom in which she was assaulted as frilly, "a gorgeous room. I remember the shock of the room, so overwhelming and beautiful. I remember being told to come sit in her lap . . .

"I keep trying to block it all out but it keeps coming . . . It's caused me a lot of problems. You won't find," she said, "a whole lot of healthy adults who went through there."

The objects of Georgia's molestation were little girls, but boys in her custody also suffered abuse, usually from male caretakers. Since I spoke with a relatively small percentage of victims I was unable to determine the incidence of abuse, but it seemed high: judging from his own experience, one adoptee said matter-of-factly, "Back then, every boy in an orphanage got molested." I don't really know if Georgia Tann's children suffered more molestation than they would have, then, in any children's institution. (But if Georgia had not stolen many of them, they would not have been institutionalized.)

Residents of orphanages and reformatories have always been vulnerable to pedophiles, and while offenders are still too seldom punished, there is at least recognition today of the existence of child sexual abuse. Such awareness was lacking during the twenty-six years of Georgia's operation in Memphis.

"People didn't talk about child physical or sexual abuse—it was in the closet all over the nation." A physician told me this—a man I greatly respected for having tried diligently but futilely to stop Georgia in the 1940s. Like many elderly Memphians, he asked me not to use his name in this book, and refused to discuss why he had, since the 1970s, worked with abused children. Perhaps he was unaware that what he couldn't prevent in the 1940s had motivated him since then; it's possible it had not. But he spoke eloquently on the subject of mistreated children, telling me that until the publication in 1961 of a study titled "The Battered Child Syndrome," which he described as "a sensation; it woke us all up," physicians assumed that the children they saw whose bones repeatedly broke were simply clumsy.

There was even less awareness, the Memphis doctor said, of sexual abuse than physical abuse of children. And if there was little general recognition of such abuse, I thought, there would be even less among citizens trained by Crump not to notice anything at all. Dr. Clifton Wooley—another pediatrician who was more courageous than the average Memphian of the 1940s—told me of his attempt to obtain help for a year-old baby whose arm had been broken by his mother.

"It was swollen in the middle of the shaft, between the wrist and elbow; the mother's neighbor told me the mother had broken the child's arm because he wouldn't eat his pablum.

"I went to the Juvenile Court, the police department, every agency I could think of—I could get no one to look into the case. I could get no one to pay attention. Things were really lax in those days."

When I asked him if he believed Memphis authorities would be even more reluctant to investigate a woman who, unlike the abusive mother, was known to have Crump's protection, he assented. That greater laxity, I determined from speaking with adoptees who while in Georgia Tann's custody were physically or sexually abused in orphanages, foster homes, and adoptive homes, was extended to any adult with whom she dealt. Judging from descriptions of their boldness, they were well aware of their immunity to punishment.

"I saw it with my own two eyes—no doubt about that—attendants, yard guys taking boys out into the woods. That was just everyday, normal activity—we thought that was life."

I must have betrayed some shock, for the man who said this asked, "What are you doing, living in the Dark Ages?"

His name was Randall Gookin, and he lived in Senatobia, Mississippi; the sense of self he communicated through the phone lines—one I would have found strong in any person—seemed particularly remarkable once I had learned of his past.

Born in Memphis to irresponsible parents in 1937, he was cared for by his grandparents until age four, when his grandmother died and his grandfather married a woman who refused to raise him. His grandfather took him to Georgia Tann, who boarded him at a Tennessee orphanage. It was there that he witnessed the abuse he described to me. Like many of the men who spoke of such things he said that he himself hadn't been abused; the reason wasn't what I heard most frequently—that he fought too hard—but "because of my nature. I was rowdy, dammit, mean and ugly. . . . I'm a harelip, have a cleft palate, I was the ugly duckling of the family and the ugly duckling of the orphanage.

"Oh, [but] I had pictures taken of me lots of times—it ain't nothing."

"Pictures in which you were dressed, or undressed?" I asked.

"Both, yeah, sure, we all had to pose—somebody would line us up naked or pose us in the shower."

The physical features he believed spared him from outright rape may also have prevented his being sold by Georgia Tann. But like other children in her custody he was subject to what he called inspections. "People would come in and look at us like we were dadburned animals in the zoo. A lot of times we were told, 'We want you to meet someone, we may have you a new mamma and papa and we want to see how you get along'—I heard that so damn many times I got sick of it.

"'Course, nobody never wanted me.

"Bear in mind, though, when you get old enough to work, then people want you. They'd say, 'Oh, you're a strong little fella.'" He served in nine different foster homes, beginning when he was eight.

"I waxed floors, washed dishes, vacuumed, mowed lawns, fed the cows, cleaned out barns—I was a little servant. No one ever came to check on me. I was beat with rosebushes, rubber hoses, razor strops, two-by-fours . . ."

The birth children in the foster homes were often as cruel as their parents, he said. "They'd say, 'You're not our brother. You're just here to work, and we don't have to.' I was with one family that had a truck patch out on James Road during tomato picking time, their boys and I were sup-posed to pick tomatoes. They wouldn't work and I had to fill up their bas-kets. I got mad and threw a whole bunch of tomatoes at them—ruined them—and the father beat me with a garden hose. I said, 'I'll fix him,' and unhitched the trailer of tomatoes so it rolled down the road and turned over and squashed everything and he beat me again and I ran away."

He was caught, however, sent back to Georgia Tann, re-placed and placed again until he ran away for good at fifteen. His grandfather got him a job in construction, which he kept for nine years. Visiting an uncle at age sixteen, he fell in love with a girl from a nearby farm. They mar-ried three years later, and, when I spoke with him, he and his wife had recently celebrated their thirty-sixth wedding anniversary.

His years in an orphanage and foster care had, he said, left two marks, one of which he considered a realistic—and some might con-sider unduly pessimistic—view of the foster care system. He was sure that children in foster care in the 1990s were being treated as badly as he was.

When I ventured that conditions might have improved, he said, as if in pity, "You don't know nothing. People don't take these kids because they love them. There oughta be a way to put little cameras on foster kids and see what really happens to them."

Well, I told him, I understand one legacy of having been involved with Georgia—what's the other?

His laugh rang through my phone's earpiece. "Strength."

He must have sensed my skepticism because he chuckled again.

"You have no—" he started over, with patience. "Could you believe me if I told you that being raised in an ugly duckling world and being punished and made to work like a slave made a person out of me—it gave me a lot of determination to fight and do better for myself—I think I learned a lot. I sure as hell don't think kids should be mistreated but it made me independent, made me work for what I want."

I had heard similar protestations, what I'd always considered rationalizations, from other adoptees. One man appended a description of his punishment for refusing to eat breakfast in a Tennessee orphanage—"I got five right across the face"—with "You might think it was brutal but it got my attention; I choked the food down."

He strains to persuade himself, I thought, that his suffering had meaning. I was inclined to think this too of Randall Gookin, but his tone almost convinced me of his words. That suffering could fortify a person had always seemed implausible, but I wanted to believe it; I recorded with more than usual care what he offered as proof of how strong his fires had forged him.

"I traveled around a lot on my first job but when the kids were old enough for school, I promised my wife, we'll settle in one place. In 1962 I bought sixty acres in Senatobia, farmed them and also began working in a factory—I've been supervisor now in three different ones. I have two of the most wonderful daughters in the world—they're grown and settled now, but they live to come home. I have a wonderful wife, four beautiful grandkids, a family. We're closer than close, as close as dirt is to the earth."

The next time I heard from Billy Hale, I couldn't help contrasting his situation with Randall Gookin's. Billy was lonely, I knew, in his trailer and at work, renovating a mansion for a friend who was usually away on business.

But he was making efforts both to connect with his old world and make a new life. He spoke frequently with his adult children, and was thinking of buying some land near Kingsport and building a house. He had run an ad in the personals column and made dates with three women.

He was accepting, finally, that his mother Mollie was dead, and was searching for something constructive to do with his memories of pain and loss. He sent me poems with such titles as, "The Closet," "Who Am I?" and "Why Me, Lord?" Several had been published in an anthology. It didn't seem to be enough. But now, he told me with enthusiasm he hadn't evinced before, he was writing an article about his abduction and molestation for the *Missing Children's Bulletin*, which is published by the Missing Children's Locate Center. In that his story concerned, he wrote, "not the stereotypical type of slime that lurks around playgrounds and public toilets, waiting for the chance to steal and rape children, but a woman of some standing in her community," and that such supposedly respectable molesters still operate today, his tale would serve, he hoped, as a caution. Conscious of his duty as reporter, he had planned to write dispassionately. But from the beginning he risked the first person. "My biggest fear," he wrote, "was being murdered."

The worst abuse occurred in a boarding home to which Georgia Tann sent him upon his arrival in Memphis. Billy didn't know the location of the house, but, judging from the frequency with which Georgia visited, he believed it was near her Home on Poplar Avenue. It housed twelve children and was owned by a thin woman with white hair. A handyman lived in the basement. He was big-boned, and wore overalls, and smoked constantly. His name was Peterson, Billy recalled.

The other children warned Billy to stay away from Peterson, and he hoped to. But when he was playing in the yard several days later he fell into a puddle, and the white-haired lady told him to stay on the porch until he dried. Underneath the porch was an entrance leading to the basement, and Peterson came out and up to Billy. "Come with me," he said.

Billy tried to dodge his big hands, but the man got him. He carried him to the basement.

Decades later, Billy could still see the room—a washing machine stood against one wall, a furnace against another; behind the furnace was a door. The man unlocked it and pushed it open. The room was small and dark; the bed sheets were dirty and he laid Billy on them. He unbuttoned his overalls. "Don't you cry," he told Billy. "I'll kill you if you do."

This was the first of dozens of rapes that so tore Billy's flesh that by the time he was adopted a year later he was at times incontinent, and was eventually forced to undergo surgical repair.

Billy tried to explain how he bore the abuse. "In my head, I built a safe room," he said. "It had thick walls and no windows and big locks on the door. I went in there whenever he touched me and it was like I couldn't feel, like I was just watching a movie involving some other boy."

For the rest of his life, Billy had stored his painful memories—of his mother Mollie, of being stolen and hurt—in the safe room. Only recently had he considered letting them out, and he'd reached that decision by default, through realizing that despite his locks they had been seeping through cracks, provoking rages and behaviors unworthy of Mollie's son.

He had related his past to the members of his survivor-of-sex-abuse support group: "I've drained them of all the help they can give me.

"Maybe"—I believed he was thinking now of his newsletter article—"it's my turn to help."

Through the centuries there have been countless adults who have abused children, but there are apparently only so many abusive techniques.

I realized the archetypal nature of certain punishments before I began my Georgia Tann project, after *Good Housekeeping* published an article I'd written about a young girl who had survived what could well have been fatal abuse. As was often the case when I wrote about people who had suffered hardship, reader response was considerable. Elderly nuns wrote that they had prayed all night for the girl. And several readers sent news clips regarding children in their area who had recently been abused; reading, I was struck by the similarities between their torture and that of the subject of my story. So many of them had been burned, as had she, by cigarettes and scalding water, irons, stove coils. Some had been almost drowned. They had been starved, and imprisoned—in bedrooms, basements, closets; they'd been tethered—to sinks, bedposts, railings; they were forced to stand naked outside in the snow. They had been punished for bedwetting, sneaking food, and, most frequently, general "badness," the exact nature of which was so seldom specified they must have believed it was in their very being. As a result of their torture, many had died.

I don't know exactly whom Georgia killed, other than the forty to fifty babies who perished in her Home during the winter of 1945; four more babies and "many" others mentioned in a letter of complaint written to the Tennessee Department of Public Welfare; the infant who died one week after reaching her New Jersey adoptive home; premature twins who, taken too early from the hospital, died one day after arriving at their boarding home; and the babies left unattended in the broiling sun. It is hard to think of how many must have died. The stories of survivors, alone, are overwhelming.

Of course it's impossible even to gauge the extent of survivors' suffering. Barbara Davidson, who was molested both by Georgia Tann and by her adoptive father, was frequently hit while in Georgia's custody. "The women hit us on the scalp so no one could see the bruises," she told me.

She was so traumatized by this that as an adult she had to be anesthetized to undergo simple procedures like teeth cleaning. She and other adoptees who'd been locked in closets suffered from claustrophobia.

And over and over during my research I spoke with adoptees who were afraid to immerse their heads under water, or to sit in bathtubs—legacies of bathing methods used in a Memphis orphanage Georgia sent them to. Joe Pannell told me of witnessing one of these techniques in 1945, when he was ten.

"Some of the workers had a bad habit of ducking kids underwater and holding them down," he said. Younger children were the workers' most frequent targets, so Joe and another ten-year-old orphanage resident, whose younger sister was also a resident, frequently monitored the little girl's baths.

"And one day we saw a woman holding Gus's sister Barbara Jean underwater," Joe told me. He and Gus shoved the woman and grabbed the little girl. "She was just about drowned," Joe said.

Years after that rescue, he and Barbara Jean married. Speaking with Joe on a day when other interviewees had told me terribly sad stories, I felt revived—more so than was justified. Yet the fortification I took from speaking with him helped me perceive how the next adoptee I spoke with, who was as troubled as any I knew, managed to keep going.

"The bathtubs were some of the most frightening things," Barbara Davidson said. "We'd have to stand in the hallway, naked, boys and girls together. 'Stand in a straight line,' the woman in front would say, and we'd be shaking, seeing the steam coming out from those tubs, the water was hot, so hot, scalding . . ."

In response to my observation that her caretakers must have been sadistic she said quickly, "I can't believe they enjoyed hurting us. They used the water to keep us in control."

She wanted to believe this, wanted to protect herself from realizing she'd been in the hands of people devoid of moral centers; I would have, too, in her place. However, not having been one Georgia's victims, I could both applaud Barbara's struggle to keep from falling into the abyss and sense how hard she had to work to avoid it.

And Barbara was one of the lucky ones. She had survived. The insight her words provided into the amount of energy she and other adoptees expend each day making sense of, repressing the past deepened my appreciation of the truth of what they had believed for decades: something good must come from this mess.

Must come, despite the fact that it will never compensate adoptees for the loss of capacity for sexual pleasure occasioned by repeated sexual abuse. Or their having been hung from coatracks by ropes tied around their wrists, or dangled down laundry chutes.

Nothing will assuage the hunger spasms suffered by infants delivered to their adoptive homes feverish and dehydrated, or by older children who were also underfed while in Georgia's care. During the two years that Heidi Naylor spent in Georgia's network she was fed little but cold oatmeal. When she was adopted at age seven, she had crooked legs caused by rickets, and scars on her back and buttocks from having been whipped with a switch fashioned from a rosebush.

Two of Heidi's younger siblings, Arthur East and Judy Young, who remained in Memphis a year longer than she, were also malnourished. "I was so hungry I'd sneak into the kitchen and swipe cabbage and lettuce—it was the only food they didn't lock up," Arthur said. He shared his bounty with three-year-old Judy, of whom he was particularly protective because of her muteness: since her first day in Georgia Tann's custody, the toddler had refused to talk. Even after her adoption, with Arthur—she refused to part from him, so that the couple from Oxford,

Mississippi, who wanted one child ended up with two—Judy was silent for a year.

Barbara Davidson's sister Mary was so underfed by some of the foster mothers Georgia Tann placed her with that at age seven she still fit in a highchair. One boarding mother, angry that Mary had tasted the butter she was churning, made her sit in the highchair for two days, without eating. Finally the woman gave her a pail containing mashed potatoes, chicken, biscuits, and gravy, and told her to feed it to the dog. Instead, Mary ate the food herself, and was beaten.

During Joe Pannell's years in a Memphis orphanage, he and other children were frequently put on two-week-long fasts of bread and water. During that time "we'd be brought into the cafeteria to watch the other children eat, but not be able to eat ourselves," Joe told me. The workers, he said, wanted to demonstrate "how cruel they could treat you."

Abuse like this "makes you know you're a nothing. It makes you a nothing. And that stays with you all your life."

Another of Georgia's cruelties that will never be assuaged was her callous separation of siblings. Heidi Naylor, who entered Georgia's network at age five with her four siblings, ages two to six, told me that later being separated from them had been more painful than had been any other abuse she'd suffered while in Georgia Tann's custody.

For a time, all five children were housed in the same orphanage. But in October of 1948 Heidi and her older sister, Virginia, were abruptly flown to California.

"I remember it all," Heidi told me, "the plane, and the Biltmore Hotel [in Los Angeles]." She, Virginia, and three other children were taken to a hotel room by one of Georgia's workers, Alma Walton. None of the children knew they were going to be adopted.

"And all of a sudden—with no preliminary—I was taken to an elevator and told I would never see my sister again: 'That was good-bye to your sister,' Alma Walton said."

Heidi was taken to the lobby, which was full of waiting adoptive parents. Alma Walton pointed out one couple. "And she just nonchalantly said, 'Oh, that will be your sister's parents,'" Heidi told me. "Then she pointed to another couple and said, 'Oh, they'll be yours.'"

Heidi mourned the loss of her sisters and brother, and when she turned twenty-one she began looking for them. "But the records were as tight as drums," she told a reporter for the Memphis *Commercial Appeal* in 1980. "It was like hitting your head against a brick wall."

It took over thirty years, but she was eventually reunited with Virginia and their three younger siblings, Arthur East, Judy Young, and Susan Trotter.

Older siblings of children seized by Georgia Tann were sometimes tortured by grief for decades. Cleveland Panell was fifteen when he lost his four-year-old sister, Shirley Ann. Their mother had died on February 16, 1942, prompting the newspaper headline "Mother Dies: Leaves Eight Children."

"Two days after she was buried there was a knock on the door," Cleveland told me. "It was a social worker"—she worked for the Department of Public Welfare, he said, "and under the table for Georgia Tann.

"'Are you taking care of your brothers and sisters?' she asked me. 'Oh you're such a good boy.' She patted me on the head.

"Now it was eight in the morning and we were very poor. I had just made oatmeal for everybody. Of course the beds weren't made, and the oatmeal pan was in the sink.

"And on that little pretence she filled out a report: 'House unkempt, dishes in the sink.' And the court took my sister away from my father. Judge Kelley turned her over to Georgia Tann."

Cleveland went to see Georgia, begging for Shirley Ann's return. "And Georgia Tann was pampering me to death. She said, 'Look at the life your sister's going to have. Don't worry, I'll always let you know where she's at.' And they put my sister temporarily in a little building on Chelsea Avenue. I called Georgia Tann up and said, 'I want to see my sister.'

"She said okay. She took me over there and I visited for half an hour, and then Georgia said we had to go. They had to pull my sister away from me. I mean absolutely she was screaming."

When Cleveland asked to see Shirley Ann the next week, Georgia told him she had a bad cold and couldn't take him. "The following week it was, 'Oh, she went shopping,' and after that 'Blah-blah-blah,' and the next thing you know I never saw my sister again."

For the next thirty-seven years Cleveland searched for Shirley Ann, calling the police and FBI director J. Edgar Hoover, writing letters to the Tennessee Department of Public Welfare, sometimes working as late as 2:00 A.M. He spent his annual two-week vacations driving from his home in Fall River, Massachusetts, to the Memphis City Hall, where he pored through old records. In 1975 he visited the Department of Vital Statistics in Nashville, where he spoke with a worker who, like the Memphis City Hall employees, said she couldn't give him information about his sister, because she'd been adopted.

"I broke down and started crying. It was a big public building and a crowd gathered. And I said, 'Don't you tell me I don't have a sister named Shirley Ann. I was there—she was born at home and I was there!'"

He apologized to the worker afterward and returned home. Several months later the woman sent him a letter: "Somewhere in the future if I can help you, I will."

"That gave me hope," he told me. He sent the worker Christmas cards for four years—he always sent the same card, which had a religious theme.

"A lot of the family said, 'Why don't you give up? She's probably dead by now. She's probably forgotten you,'" he told me. "I said, 'If she's alive I want her to know she has a brother that's been looking for her for thirty-seven years.'"

And in 1979 the Vital Statistics employee wrote him, "I could lose my job, I could lose everything by giving you this information: your sister was adopted by a Hollywood couple in April of 1942."

Cleveland and his wife immediately drove from New England to California, "right to the door of the *L.A. Times* to put an ad in the paper. I had a little picture of my sister and put it next to the ad—it was 1-inch by 2-inch, and it ran on Mother's Day, May 13, 1979."

Georgia Tann had sent large numbers of children to Los Angeles. By 1979 many had long been searching for their families, and "I got a lot of calls from women, crying, saying, 'That's me in that picture!'"

None of the women were Shirley Ann. But the ad also attracted the attention of two other Georgia Tann adoptees who were skilled in searching. Soon he was on the phone with the sister he hadn't seen in almost forty years, and who, he discovered, had also been looking for him.

But she was confused by his name, "Cleveland"—she recalled him by his nickname, "Cleebo." She cried for five minutes when she realized who he was. "And don't I have these other brothers, and a sister: Thomas, Roscoe, Charles, Elmer, Richard, Thelma?"

"Honey, it's 'Velma,'" he told her. Her recall was remarkable, considering the fact that she'd been only four when stolen.

Shirley Ann, who when young had resembled the child star Shirley Temple, had been raised in mansions by a Hollywood actor and his wife

who liked to show her off. She told Cleveland they'd given her everything. "Everything but love."

Georgia splintered so many families and caused so much pain. She
forced some robbed mothers to bear the agony of seeing their children
marketed in the newspaper. Adoptee Barbara Savin's mother kept the
clipping advertising her baby daughter all of her life, always hoping for
reunion with her, but she died before Barbara could find her.

The practices of Georgia and her helpers seemed designed to
inflict the greatest possible psychological damage. When Barbara
Davidson was six years old, she found a kitten and brought it to her
bed. "The women saw it and they drowned it in a rain barrel and they
made me watch," she said. "And they said, 'Absolutely no animals are
allowed, absolutely no animals.'

"Then they put my hand in the water, oh God, my hand in the water
and made me touch that tiny body . . ."

The adoptees I spoke with agreed about what the state of Tennessee
should do as compensation for having allowed Georgia to operate for
twenty-six years. They wanted information that would help them find
their lost relatives. One of the more vocal proponents was Roger
Cleghorne, who while in Georgia's custody endured beatings with switches
he himself was forced to fashion from tree branches. One broke while he
was being beaten with it, and he was struck with terror. "I thought I'd be
killed," he told me in 1993. Seeking not deletion of or even compensation
for his past, but reconnection to it, he had searched for years for his sister
Glenna—unsuccessfully—with no help from the state of Tennessee.

When I spoke with Barbara Davidson, she had long been reunited
with her sister Mary, from whom Georgia Tann had separated her fifty
years earlier. "The last time we were together as children we were in a

big room with tile on the floor and we must have known what was coming because we were clinging and crying," Barbara said. "They wanted to take Mary away. Two women came in and they couldn't get us apart so they drug Mary out of the room by the hair on her head. Mary had such beautiful long blond hair and one of the women just wrapped it around her hand, wrapped it around her hand like a rope and dragged Mary away and she was screaming and I was screaming, 'Mary, come back, don't leave me, come back,' but she never came back."

They remained apart for the next forty-four years, during which Barbara had to deal not only with sexual abuse at the hands of a foster parent and her adoptive father but with what had become of her nature. "I was surprised my adoptive mother didn't send me back," she said. "When I left Memphis I was hateful, mean—I did terrible things to my new brother, hit him every time he turned around. He'd go up and down the alleys digging in trash cans for something pretty to bring me and I'd throw it at him. I pushed him down when he was rollerskating and I broke his glasses.

"I don't know what eventually turned me around, but I realized my adoptive mother loved me. By the time I was ten I started smoothing out, caring more about people and what I was supposed to do . . ."

The years during which the sisters were separated took Mary, who was never adopted, through foster homes and, as she grew older, the Tennessee Industrial Home and the Tullahoma Reform School, from which she escaped three times, only to be caught, returned, and punished.

She was discharged at eighteen, and, wearing the clothes she had worn when she'd been admitted five years earlier, hitchhiked to Chattanooga, where she found work in a beauty shop. She, like Barbara, eventually married and raised a family; the sisters were forty-four and forty-six years old when they reunited in 1986.

"The first time I saw Mary again was at the airport and it was wonderful, wonderful," Barbara told me. "We went to my house and talked about our pasts, lay across the bed and looked at each other's photo albums. We told each other things no one else will ever know; we laughed and we cried. We looked at each other's clothes and asked, 'What size shoe do you wear?'—stupid things sisters should have been doing all these years and we did it in one night, but it was a wonderful, wonderful night. At 4 A.M. my husband woke up and said, 'Aren't you two girls asleep yet?' like we were a couple of thirteen-year-old kids. It was great, it was really, really great. It was the most wonderful night of my life."

When I began talking to the two sisters in the 1990s, they spoke with each other frequently. But their renewed closeness had not exempted them from problems regarding their pasts. Barbara, quieter and more reserved than her older sister, had particular difficulty. "I talked to no one about what happened," she told me. "I wanted to get on with my life. I didn't want to go backward. I thought I'd been through too much already—I didn't need to remember. But I was wrong.

"Eleven years ago I started having flashbacks—it was horrible. For decades I'd been levelheaded and now I fell apart. They'd come at me, flash in front of me, and I'd see myself as a child. Sometimes they'd come out of nowhere, other times they'd have a trigger . . .

"One day I was in a store and a woman grabbed her little boy by the hair and lifted his feet off the floor and hit him so hard—that was me all over again; Georgia's women didn't hit us when we were on the floor, they had to have us up in the air; it went all through me. I dropped my groceries and I looked that mother in the eye and I was crying and I said, 'Don't hit him. Don't you dare hit him.' It made her stop. I guess I had a look on me like I would have killed her.

"I'm only letting myself remember some things," she said. "There's lots more that wants to come out. A lot of people say it would help to talk about it. But I don't have anyone to talk to about it."

"Not even," I asked, "your sister, your husband?"

"I can't bother Mary with it—her past was harder than mine." As for her husband, she'd told him some things, but out of embarrassment or shame could not get out the rest. Psychiatrists, she feared, wouldn't believe her stories.

And for the first time I realized there had been a consequence of the passage of the 1951 law legalizing Georgia Tann's illegal adoptions that was almost as harmful as the continued separation of adoptees from their kin. By covering up the scandal, legislators had denied its magnitude, even its very existence. And if Georgia's crimes had been unimportant enough to ignore, adoptees must have felt, how insignificant must be the pain they had caused? Did this account for the stoicism I'd sensed in so many of Georgia's adoptees? Was it fear of being considered exaggerators that caused some to justify abuse: to say—as had the former orphanage resident who'd gotten "five across the face" for refusing his breakfast—"[I]t got my attention; I choked the food down"?

I feared that Barbara Davidson was ashamed, that she believed she was weak.

Remedying this, I thought, would require the same change as would the reunification of separated family members: the release of adoptees' original birth certificates and adoption records. This would be no panacea for adoptees seeking reunion, since the information in Georgia's records was often false. But the opening of Tennessee's adoption records would be an admission that they should never have been closed. *A terrible wrong has been done to you*, it would state; *you have a right to be angry and sad.*

By the 1990s, Georgia's victims' fight for access to their original birth certificates and adoption records was led by the Tennessee Coalition for Adoption Reform, a three-thousand-member group headed by Memphis search expert Denny Glad and adoptee Caprice East. (Caprice, who'd been born after Georgia's death and hadn't been directly affected by her, was nevertheless appalled by her crimes.) One of my informants regarding possible changes in Tennessee adoption law was Billy Hale, who sent me copies of letters he'd written to the governor and other elected officials, pressing for legislative change.

The next time Billy called he spoke of having attended several committee meetings chaired by Denny Glad. He sounded animated, strong; our former roles seemed reversed, for I had just spoken with Barbara Davidson, who had cried, and I sounded sad.

"What's wrong?" he asked. I explained how I, having never undergone experiences such as Barbara's, couldn't adequately talk to her, and that she didn't want to bother her sister Mary who, having never been chosen by an adoptive family, had been worse off than she.

Billy asked for her number.

It doesn't comfort adoptees like Billy and Barbara to know that Georgia Tann was never happy. She was unhappy despite the approximately $1 million she made from her black-market business, and all that it bought her: cars; furs; homes in Memphis's best residential section; several rental properties; a tourist court; two hundred acres of timberland; a vacation home in Biloxi, Mississippi; and a small motel in California. And from 1938 to 1943 she owned Tannwood, a seven-acre rural estate on the border between Memphis and Mississippi. Tannwood had cedar, persimmon, magnolia, and dozens of other kinds of trees, as well as hollows, hills, and greenery-enclosed paths upon which she and Ann rode their horses every morning.

Tannwood was the setting of the only photograph I've ever seen in which Georgia, dressed in a plaid shirt and trousers and astride her horse, looks comfortable. But she couldn't relax, even at Tannwood. Instead of using the farm as a respite, she worked it. With the precision with which she spoke on matters unrelated to her Home, she told a Memphis reporter of canning 1,815 jars of strawberries, grapes, peaches, pears, plums, apples, figs, blackberries, butter beans, string beans, corn, okra, peppers, peas, beets, pimentos, tomatoes, and squash.

She tended and named every one of her twelve hens, twenty-three turkeys, twenty-six ducks, forty-two guineas, five calves, four hogs, three horses, and two dogs. She even found time to force parenthood on one of her animals, slipping newborn ducklings beneath a sleeping and infertile duck named Mrs. Goo Goo, who woke to find herself the mother of quintuplets.

Georgia's obsession with manipulating human families—and frustration at her inability to control every one—may have contributed to her chronic bad temper. "She became high strung and blew off steam at the slightest excuse," said a Memphis taxi driver in 1950. Her most frequent targets were birth parents and the reform-minded social workers she called "that bunch." Her anger also affected adoptees and, occasionally, even her clients. While she fawned over most adoptive parents, particularly those of great wealth and social prominence, she hounded others, extorting large "donations."

"She terrified people," said former social worker Mildred Stoves, whose friend had adopted through Georgia. "He was a teacher and didn't make much money, and Georgia would ask for $2,000, $3,000. His wife would tell me, 'Miss Tann's threatening us; the threat is veiled, but . . .'"

With the stakes this high, Mildred assured me, adoptive parents "scraped up what they could."

Mildred's friends were fortunate in being able to satisfy Georgia's demands. When another couple was unable to pay the $1,500 she demanded of them, she took back their adopted child.

Georgia's withholding of medical information about her children also hurt adoptive parents—and the children. In 1949 a pediatrician at Vanderbilt University Hospital in Nashville spoke of several "tragedies that could have been prevented" if the adoptive parents "had had full social and medical information before them at the time of the adoptions.

"One concerned a child who had been irreparably damaged in eyes, heart and mind by a case of German measles which his mother had during pregnancy. . . ."

He told of another case regarding the adoptive placement of four children, all born to the same mother. "As fast as the children were born, there was someone [Georgia Tann] taking the children out of her hands and handling adoptions of them," he said. "She [the mother] had syphilis at the time the last child was born—and that child was adopted by a clergyman, who knew nothing of the background."

Georgia also sometimes reneged on her promises to prospective clients. In March of 1947 Mrs. W. A. Hachmeister of Memphis arrived at the Home to pick up the infant girl she'd been promised, only to discover that Georgia had changed her mind about the placement. It was to have been an unusually open adoption for the time: the baby's mother had chosen Mrs. Hachmeister and her husband as adoptive parents. Georgia had also agreed to this, two months before the baby's birth.

Once the child was born, however, Georgia refused to let Mrs. Hachmeister adopt her; Georgia's purported reason was that Mrs. Hachmeister and the baby's mother were of different religions. It was an odd justification, considering the many non-Jewish children Georgia placed with Jewish clients, but she felt no need for logic, or kindness.

She ignored Mrs. Hachmeister as she pled for the baby, promising to have her baptized and raised in the Catholic religion of her birth. Georgia kept the infant. Shortly afterward, the child "was removed from the Home to the Methodist Hospital, where she expired, death resulting from dysentery evidently contracted at the Home," Mrs. Hachmeister wrote to her attorney in 1949. "[T]his little soul's physical form lies in a nameless grave, a symbol of sacrifice."

Georgia's cruelty extended even to her own family members, whom she played off against each other by giving her current favorite expensive gifts. She caused such jealousy between her adopted daughter June and her partner Ann that years later June refused to let her son and daughter play with children who, although unrelated to Ann, happened to bear her surname, Hollinsworth.

Georgia was cruel to June even on the occasion of her marriage, to a man Georgia didn't like. Georgia boycotted the wedding and, during June's honeymoon, destroyed the clothing she'd left at home.

Georgia was a successful businesswoman, but she wasn't emotionally steady. In 1928 she suffered such a nervous upset that, wrote Ann, "she can't attend to business matters." In 1933 and 1934, Ann described Georgia as "near a nervous breakdown" and "almost to the breaking point." Georgia herself told a Memphis reporter that in 1941 she had been "tired, worn out, on the verge of a nervous breakdown." She dealt with this by buying Tannwood.

June's daughter Vicci Finn described another way in which her grandmother dealt with tension. Temporarily leaving the running of her Home to her attorney and several of her workers, "Georgia would disappear into her house with Ann for a few weeks and emerge as if everything was all right." Vicci also said that Georgia could be very impulsive.

"On the spur of the moment she would just take off for Cuba. My mother and father [June's second husband, whom Georgia liked] wouldn't even know she was gone. Georgia would call and say, 'Get down here right now, drop everything—I want you to come down and keep me company. Let's go swimming, let's party, let's gamble.'"

Georgia's ability to summon the energy to be so vicious and lively seems particularly remarkable considering her physical problems, which besides severe arthritis and a limp caused by a car accident, included heart attacks suffered in 1941 and 1943. In 1945 doctors at the Mayo Clinic diagnosed her with cancer. She refused surgery, and until her death in 1950 relied upon narcotics for pain.

Georgia had other difficulties as well, for not even Crump could stop the letters of complaint about her that poured in from all over the country. Georgia and her attorney received angry letters from lawyers in Mississippi, Maryland, Missouri, Arkansas, Alabama, Indiana, New York, New Jersey, Ohio, Pennsylvania, Texas, and California. Many demanded information about the children Georgia planned to place with their clients.

Abe Waldauer dealt with these complaints by threatening Georgia's cancellation of the proposed adoption, at which point most prospective adoptive parents probably muzzled their lawyers. Fighting with the Tennessee legislature took more muscle. By 1945, Georgia's practices were widely criticized by ethical social workers and others in Tennessee, and a bill that would have required her to assess the qualifications of adoptive parents reached the legislature. Georgia worked furiously, blackmailing clients into sending telegrams opposing the bill, and using her political contacts, particularly her attorney. Without the knowledge of the bill's sponsor, Abe Waldauer gathered a quorum of Crump-appointed legislators to a secret meeting held before the state senate's regular session, and had the bill defeated.

In 1947 Tennessee adoption reformers drafted a bill authorizing the State Welfare Department to investigate adoption proceedings. Again utilizing their Crump connections, Georgia and Abe had the bill buried in committee.

Georgia's biggest legislative challenge occurred in 1949. By then the adoption reform group included Judge Samuel Bates and the Memphis pediatricians who three years earlier had complained about Georgia; members of the clergy; and civic groups like the Junior League and the League of Women Voters. Some adoptive parents were also involved, motivated in part by her blackmailing of them. Adoptive father Jesse Jackson, a Memphis florist, told a reporter in 1950, "I found that I was being used by Miss Tann as a tool. I finally told her I was through being used in such fashion." He described how Georgia would address a telegram to state legislators, urging them to vote against adoption reform, and "demand" that it be sent over his signature. "She used many other [adoptive] parents in the same way until they rebelled as I did," he said.

Even more threatening to Georgia was the fact that Boss Crump had lost his statewide power with the 1948 election of political outsiders Gordon Browning and Estes Kefauver as governor and senator. Georgia worked furiously, bribing a pivotal legislator with the gift of two adopted children and getting the support of as many adoptive parents as possible.

But after twenty-four years of suffering under Georgia Tann, Memphians were fed up. During heated legislative fighting in Nashville the former Children's Bureau social worker who'd objected to Georgia's adoption methods in 1925 but who, because of Georgia's stranglehold on Tennessee adoptions, had later been forced to adopt through her, gave a speech supporting adoption reform. Afterward she walked into the capitol lobby, where she saw Georgia Tann and Georgia Robinson, superintendent of the Porter Home and Leath Orphanage, in tense conversation.

"I hope you understand how I felt," the adoptive mother said.

"I certainly do understand how you felt," Georgia Tann retorted. Then in a hostile tone she added, "I think you ought to know that I recently had a letter from the mother of your child."

The adoptive mother considered this a threat to tell her son's mother where he was living. Like most adoptive parents of the time she didn't want her child to meet the mother who'd borne him, and she burst into tears.

The reform bill passed both houses anyway, inspiring Georgia and her attorney to a desperate move. The pro- and anti-reform camps had agreed upon an amendment excluding the bill's second paragraph, which had nothing to do with Georgia Tann. The amendment directed the "striking [of] the entire second paragraph of section 5." Secretly gaining access to the bill's rough draft, Abe Waldauer inserted a carat between "second" and "paragraph," added the words "and third," and then crowded an "s" at the end of "paragraph." The amendment now directed the exclusion of not only the second paragraph but the third one, which contained the reform measures aimed at curbing Georgia. The governor signed the botched bill, and it became law.

It would be Georgia's last success, and she must have known it. For while Crump maintained control of Memphis until his death in 1954, his influence in the state capitol had lessened. In 1950 three prominent Memphis adoptive fathers complained to Governor Gordon Browning about Georgia's blackmailing of them, and that fall he determined to close down her Home.

No hero, he apparently meant to delay announcement of Georgia's crimes until after her death, and dealt with her in response to the complaints, not of long-suffering adoptees and birth parents, but of adoptive parents who had, in the main, profited from her. Browning so hamstrung investigator Robert Taylor as to ensure the superficiality of the idealistic young attorney's probe. Georgia, of course, may not have anticipated the shallowness of the investigation of her crimes. And the prospect of even the most cursory inspection would have appalled her.

Death may have been a relief; it was certainly at hand. Increasingly debilitated by cancer, she was confined to her bed by August 12, 1950, and attended by a nurse. For the past few years, knowing death was near, she had spent money madly, on cars, furs, and the refurbishing of her residences. She sent her daughter June and her husband on trips all over the country, urging them to stay in the most elegant hotels.

Her last purchases, made a month later, were strictly utilitarian: syringes, catheters, a hospital bed. At the end, she left her home on Stonewall Court only for medical treatment, including almost daily trips by ambulance between August 29 and September 7 for X-ray treatments to the pelvis. On September 11 she was too ill to make the trip.

She died at home in her four-poster bed at 4:20 A.M. on September 15, surrounded by her family and a few friends. Her death came just three days after she had been exposed in news articles, and some Memphians speculated that she had killed herself from shame. Her mother, who survived her, bridled at the rumor: "Sissy [her name for Georgia] didn't do that," she said frequently afterward.

Other citizens implied that Georgia's death had been encouraged by her helpers. And its timing was convenient for people beside herself. Dead women can't rat on their confederates.

But it's much more likely that she died naturally, of cancer. Services were held in Memphis the day after her death; she was buried in the local cemetery in Hickory, Mississippi, on September 17. "She had on a beautiful orchid negligee with a great big orchid pinned on her," a resident told me.

Georgia may finally have been at peace, but her collaborators were not. A few days after the funeral "men in suits came in a big Ford," a Hickory woman told me. "They asked my husband and me if we knew Georgia Tann.

"'My wife was at the graveside,' my husband told them.

"'Was it an open casket?' they asked me. 'Yes,' I said.

"'Was it *her*?'

"'Yes.'

"'Really?'

"'Truly.'"

Georgia was really dead.

Of course her collaborators continued to worry, until even the most skittish realized the limited scope of Browning's investigation. And adoptive parents across the country were terrified. Actor Dick Powell, who with wife June Allyson had adopted a baby through Georgia, vowed to fight any effort to make him return his child. "If they come to get my daughter, they will have to bring a large cannon," he said. He and other adoptive parents were quickly mollified by the passage of the Tennessee law that legalized Georgia's illegal adoptions.

As for Georgia herself, she had won again, slipping away without being held accountable for her crimes. She bequeathed little but embarrassment to her family members, who, accustomed to wealth, were left in relative poverty. Of the $1 million she'd made, only $80,000 worth of stocks and property remained. By the time the lawsuit against her was settled nine years later, her estate had dwindled to $45,000, and the state attached two-thirds of that.

She left no money for children's causes, or for the institution that had consumed her. But she had left adoption a terrible legacy.

The law must be consonant with life. . . . Mankind is possessed of no greater urge than to try to understand the age-old question: "Who am I?"

—Judge Wade S. Weatherford Jr., SC, Seventh Judicial Circuit Court, ruling on an adoptee's petition to gain access to adoption records

Part Three

Georgia's Secrets

12.

Georgia's Lies

When my daughter was four and beginning to understand what having been adopted meant, she reeled: she'd lost her place on earth. "Whose tummy did I grow in?" she demanded, near panic. "Was it Lynn's, Jean's, Susie's, Kathy's, Kappy's . . . ?" She named relatives, neighbors, friends. She seemed prepared to interrogate strangers. And by the fall of her sophomore year in college she was ready to learn the answer to her question. "I've spent nineteen years not knowing my birth mother. I don't want to spend more," she said.

Finding her mother would have been difficult, maybe impossible, if Beth had been a typical American adoptee, since American adoptees are legally forbidden knowledge of their birth parents' names. In all fifty states, adoptees' birth certificates—which list the children's birth names and the names of their birth mothers and, often, fathers—are sealed upon finalization of their adoptions. Their adoption records are also sealed.

Adoptees are then issued false birth certificates that portray their adoptive parents as their birth parents.

And in 1996, when my daughter was nineteen and ready to search, all states but Alaska and Kansas—which have always allowed adoptees copies of their original birth certificates once they come of age—continued to deny adoptees knowledge of their identities even after they became adults.

Adult adoptees in the other forty-eight states could learn their birth parents' names only through the help of private investigators, search groups, or attorneys. And there was no assurance that any of these would be successful—not even the lawyers, who had to convince judges that the adoptees had "good cause" for knowledge of their roots. "Good cause" is a vague term that many judges deemed inapplicable even to grave reasons, such as the need for biologically compatible bone marrow. A Georgia Tann adoptee living in California told me of appearing before a Tennessee judge who ruled that her leukemia was insufficient reason to justify access to her health history. The adoptee later discovered that this judge had rubber-stamped many of Georgia's illegal transactions.

The reasons that other judges withhold adoptees' records are hopefully less self-serving than the Tennessee jurist's, based solely upon their interpretation of their states' adoption laws.

The reason for laws denying adoptees knowledge of their birth names and identities is said, by legislators across the country, to be to protect all members of the adoption triad: adoptees, birth parents, and adoptive parents. Issuing false birth certificates to adoptees and sealing their true ones protects them, it's claimed, from the traumatic realization that they had been conceived out of wedlock.

Maintaining the anonymity of birth mothers is said to help them preserve their privacy and prevent them from being intruded upon years later by the children they relinquished.

Adoptive parents are depicted as needing the strongest possible assurance that their children and their birth parents will never meet.

Adoptees have long understood the speciousness of these arguments. Most assume they were born out of wedlock; few are shocked by that supposition, or would be devastated to learn it was true. Few single mothers are unduly embarrassed by their status, and 88.5 percent of birth mothers, according to a study published in 1989, support adult adoptees' access to their birth parents' names.

Many adoptive parents not only appreciate their children's need to know their origins but help them search.

Beth was lucky, for although she may never see her original birth certificate she had long known what I believed was her mother's last name. The word "Garvey" had been typed in the margin of a court paper sent to my husband Bob and me after the finalization of Beth's adoption in 1978. Eighteen years later she procured through the Internet the phone numbers and addresses of every Western New York state resident named Garvey.

She wouldn't call all of them; she didn't want to embarrass her mother by speaking with a relative who might not know she'd relinquished a child. Instead Beth would seek the help of a local support group, Adoption Network Cleveland, in determining which female Garvey, if any, was her mother, and contact her.

I had long understood that American adoption is particularly closed and secretive. But it wasn't until I began studying Georgia Tann's impact on the institution that I realized that European countries like Germany, England, Scotland, Wales, Belgium, Holland, Sweden, Norway, Denmark, Iceland, and Finland allow adoptees access to their original birth certificates. Australia, New Zealand, provinces of Canada, Israel, Taiwan, China, Japan, and Korea give adoptees access. The United

States is one of very few countries that legally forbids adopted adults knowledge of their birth names.

American adoptees have long been furious at being denied a right enjoyed by every other American citizen. Adoptee Caprice East, who with Denny Glad headed the Tennessee Coalition for Adoption Reform, pointed out the unfairness: "Serial killers can know where they came from, but I can't."

For decades Georgia Tann's adoptees and their relatives fought individually to escape her influence and to find their birth families. Then, after finding a sister placed for adoption by Georgia Tann, Memphian Carolyn Mitchell began helping members of other separated families find lost relatives. In 1978 Denny Glad founded Tennessee's The Right To Know, a search group that also fights for adoptees' access to their original birth certificates and adoption records.

Throughout the decades, Georgia Tann's indirect victims, who although they never met her suffered from her legacy of secrecy, have mounted similar campaigns. Their names are well known in adoption circles:

> Jean Paton, who after locating her birth mother in 1942 created an organization called Orphan Voyage. "In the soul of every adoptee is an eternal flame of hope for reunion and reconciliation with those he has lost through private or public disaster," she wrote.

> Florence Ladden Fisher of New York, who in 1971 founded the Adoptees' Liberty Movement Association (ALMA), which now has branches across the country, and called withholding birth information from adoptees an "affront to human dignity."

Betty Jean Lifton, also of New York City, whose 1998 memoir, *Twice Born: Memoirs of an Adopted Daughter*, eloquently espouses adoptees' right to knowledge.

And there are countless other adoptees who describe the blankness regarding their pasts as "a constant gnawing." It creates "a hole that can't be filled," a "vacuum for which there is no substitute"; it is "a piece of my soul that is gone." Not knowing who they are is like being "a jigsaw puzzle with pieces missing," "the center of a wheel missing two spokes." "No one has the power to deny me my birthright."

Fairness alone would seem to dictate that adoptees should be allowed to know who bore them. But most Americans, including me, had long assumed that the falsification of adoptees' birth certificates had at least sprung from the motives of well-meaning social workers anxious to relieve adoptees of the stigma of illegitimacy. Typical was the reasoning of the author of a popular book on adoption published in 1940 who wrote that withholding information about adoptees would help prevent "reporters nosing about for news" coming upon something really juicy and publishing it, "causing untold suffering and permanent damage. Unscrupulous birth relatives could trace a child if they wished, and use their knowledge to upset a well established adoptive relationship. . . ."

The same rationale had been expressed several years earlier, however, by someone less well meaning. In a 1937 letter to her attorney, Abe Waldauer, Georgia Tann justified her refusal to tell the Tennessee Department of Public Welfare or the Departments of Public Welfare in other states anything about her children, including their birth names. Disclosing information, she wrote, would result in adoptive information being leaked to social workers in the counties where the adoptive parents lived, and the child's adoption becoming "a very tempting morsel of gossip."

Georgia's attorney was as dedicated as she to secrecy in adoption, not only out of disinclination for providing food for gossip, but, as Abe wrote her on April 25, 1940, to avoid placing "an effective instrument of blackmail in the hands of unscrupulous [birth] parents and open[ing] the way for them to prey upon real [adoptive] parents whose fine impulses have impelled them to accept children for adoption."

Needless to say, Departments of Public Welfare in states across the country, including Tennessee, resented being denied information about the children Georgia placed with local citizens, and in 1944 a Tennessee adoption law was proposed that would have made her adoptions less secretive. On October 6, 1944, Abe Waldauer wrote on Georgia's behalf to the Chairman of the Committee on Social Legislation in Nashville:

"The proposed statute regarding adoption is atrocious, and should not be accepted.

"We object to the requirement of Section 1 that the [adoption] petition must be filed in the county where the [adoptive] parents reside. In order to be secure in the position of adopting children, anonymity is essential. The first place one [a birth parent] would look in seeking to find a child would be in the records of the county of residence of the adoptive parents.

"Section 3, requiring natural parents to be made defendants [i.e. informed that their child was being adopted] is contrary to all advanced thinking of correct social service. This places in the hands of the real [birth] parents of the child an effective instrument of blackmail. Only backward states require service of process on the real parents of the child."

The proposed reform law, he continued, "is just an attempt to make adoptions difficult, and to surround the entire procedure with the sort of intrusive inquisitiveness of social workers that will have the effect of reducing adoptions in Tennessee. We are unalterably opposed to the State Department of Public Welfare becoming an investigative agency of this character. This would inject the State Department into adoptions, and would mean that information respecting adoptions would be available as choice morsels of gossip for inquisitive women in a political set-up. . . ."

A desire to cater to adoptive parents anxious to prevent their children's birth parents from finding their children wasn't the only reason Georgia kept her adoptions secret, but it was a large one. "We never tell the natural [birth] mother or reveal to others where the child is and where it is being placed for adoption," Georgia told a reporter for the *Commercial Appeal* in 1948. "Adoptive parents want to take the children and love them as their own, and they do not wish to be subject later to interference and confusion."

But while Georgia refused to let birth mothers know who had adopted their children, she frequently let adoptive parents know whose children they'd adopted, by giving them adoption decrees that listed the name of the child's birth mother. She may have done this to satisfy adoptive parents' curiosity. And she apparently wasn't worried that her clients would share this information with their adopted children, leading to an adoptee and birth mother reunion that might lead to exposure of her child stealing.

She was correct in her assumption. Most adoptive parents of the time were as loathe to have their children find their birth parents as they were to have the birth parents find their child. In an attempt to prevent the child's searching, many adoptive parents didn't even tell adopted children that they'd been adopted. I know of only four Georgia Tann clients who gave their children information about their backgrounds. Three did it out of kindness. The other was Joy Barner's adoptive father. After telling her, "I paid $500 for you, and I could have gotten a good hunting dog for a lot less," he threw her adoption papers at her feet, shouting, "You come from the lowest scum on earth."

Contemporary adoptive parents, like Bob and me, are also often given the names of their adopted child's birth parents. There have been no studies of how frequently this happens, or of why it occurs. But the fact that adoptive parents are sometimes given birth parents' names, and that, except in cases of open adoption, birth parents are never given the names of adoptive parents indicates which party courts and some adoption agencies consider important. This continues to be the party Georgia favored, the adoptive parents. Today's adoptive parents, however, are more likely to give their adopted children their birth parents' names.

Of course Georgia and her lawyer had reasons for secrecy other than to placate and coddle adoptive parents. To a great extent, Georgia operated in plain sight. But absolute openness regarding her adoption practices, which would have been tantamount to an admission of kidnapping, would have taxed even Boss Crump's tolerance. Georgia and her attorney's need for concealment was so specific that their argument that openness would provide "an effective instrument of blackmail . . ." might never have been used again. But over five decades later, in 1996, a lawyer defending secrecy in adoption paraphrased Abe Waldauer's words: "[Openness] could be easily used as blackmail or the threat of blackmail."

The use of wording so similar to Georgia's was no coincidence, but rather evidence of the endurance of her legacy of secrecy in adoption.

Considering her general proclivity for deception, her need to cover her tracks, and her energy, it was perhaps inevitable that she would be the person to begin the practice of falsifying adoptees' birth certificates. What is remarkable is that until I began my research neither I nor anyone else knew that she had originated this identity theft. One reason for this, of course, is her escape from historical notice. Another is that the first state to pass a law "amending" adoptees' birth certificates, in 1931, was Alabama, not Tennessee.

Adoptees and their advocates, however, have long suspected a link between falsified birth certificates and baby selling. "Secrecy in adoption does cover a multitude of crimes," Hal Aigner wrote in *Adoption in America Coming of Age*, published in 1992.

The instincts of adoptees and their advocates are correct. In 1928, three years before the passage of the Alabama law calling for the "amendment" of adoptees' birth certificates, Georgia Tann had, extra-legally, begun having the Tennessee Department of Vital Statistics issue phony birth certificates for her adoptees. Nine years later, in 1937, she used her political connections to have a law passed legalizing the practice in Tennessee.

Within twenty years all forty-eight states were issuing adoptees falsified birth certificates, and upon admission of Alaska and Hawaii as states, the number rose to fifty. And in the vast majority of states, legislators and social workers deny adoptees knowledge of their identities forever—for far longer than they did when states first began falsifying birth certificates. Georgia's inducement of legislators and social workers across the country into becoming almost as secretive as she was is one of her most terrible, and extraordinary, accomplishments—one that required her, once again, to stand previous adoption practice on its head.

Until her influence upon adoption hardened in the late 1950s, the prevailing theme regarding it was one of openness. Despite the falsification of adoptees' birth certificates, almost all adult adoptees but Georgia's were given information that would help them find their parents.

They were given this information by reputable social workers who understood the importance of family ties. As late as 1946, the supervisor of the State Charities Aid Association of New York stressed, "The identity of a child is his sacred right, and he should not be deprived of it . . . ," a sentiment shared by the Child Welfare League of America.

Established in 1921, the League had quickly become the most renowned national organization of child welfare agencies. In the 1930s, the League formulated adoption standards protecting all members of the adoption triad, and emphasizing the rights of adopted children to know their roots.

By publicizing these standards, the League hoped to curtail the practices of the many unregulated adoption arrangers who were capitalizing upon adoption's sudden rise in popularity. Some of these arrangers were well meaning but lacked training in arranging adoptions. The League's executive director, Charles C. Carstens, was particularly disturbed by the lawyers, doctors, and others who profited financially from adoption.

One of these black market arrangers, of course, was Georgia Tann. But Carstens was unaware of her unethical practices until 1936, when he began the investigation that culminated in her agency's expulsion from the League for advertising children in newspapers and failing to properly assess the qualifications of adoptive parents. And since neither he nor most other social workers outside Tennessee knew that she stole and sold children, they also didn't know that she falsified birth certificates, in part, to cover her crimes. But her purported reason—to spare adoptees the embarrassment occasioned by the letters "O.W." (out of wedlock), or the word "Illegitimate"—must have sounded good.

Why indeed, reputable social workers had long wondered, should adoptees be stigmatized by birth certificates highlighting their out-of-wedlock status? By 1920, laws forbidding the inclusion of this fact had been passed in Minnesota and New York. But these didn't solve the problem, since adoptees' birth certificates, which often included the names only of their mothers, not fathers, continued to imply their status. Ethical social workers in several states considered eliminating all information but babies' names on birth certificates, but determined that birth parents' names had to be included for historical purposes.

Georgia's practice of issuing amended birth certificates that portrayed adoptees' adoptive parents as their biological parents seemed the perfect solution to a long-standing problem.

But while ethical professionals supported state laws that falsified birth certificates and kept the original ones confidential, they interpreted the word "confidential" differently from Georgia. She kept original birth certificates secret even from her adoptees. Ethical social workers and vital statisticians, who wished only to keep adoptees' origins from the prying eyes of reporters and neighbors, allowed adult adoptees copies of their original birth certificates. Workers like Maud Morlock, consultant in the Services for Unmarried Mothers for the U.S. Children's Bureau, stressed the importance of giving adoptees information about their pasts, "for every person has a right to know who he is and who his parents were."

Throughout most of the 1940s the Child Welfare League of America and other prominent social service organizations understood and sympathized with adoptees' need to search. Many adoption agencies helped adult adoptees find their parents. Then everything changed.

Ethical agencies' evolution from the sharing of information with adult adoptees to the secretiveness practiced by Georgia was gradual enough to make identifying the date of its change difficult. But by 1960

211

virtually all social workers denied adoptees information that would help them find their families.

Georgia's role in corrupting virtually all of American adoption with secrecy was less direct than were her roles in popularizing the institution, commercializing it, and forcing single mothers to relinquish their babies. She couldn't coerce social workers outside Tennessee through* blackmail, as she had the Memphis workers she had provided with adopted babies, and had controlled ever after by threatening to reclaim the children. She couldn't threaten to ruin the reputations of ethical social workers, as she'd done with the rural single mothers she'd silenced by threatening to accuse them of promiscuity to everyone in their home towns. But she could, by her existence and those of her imitators, force ethical social workers to make a terrible choice.

In 1955 and 1956 Senate subcommittee hearings were held that focused upon illegal adoption practices in an ultimately futile attempt to secure passage of a federal law against baby selling. The hearings were chaired by the U.S. senator from Tennessee, Estes Kefauver, one of the political outsiders who in 1948 had been instrumental in Crump's statewide fall from power, which in turn led to the unmasking of Georgia Tann. Her crimes had in fact inspired Kefauver's Washington efforts.

When I had first read the Senate hearings' transcript, I'd concentrated on former investigator Robert Taylor's deposition regarding the deceased Georgia Tann. But once I began seeking a reason for ethical social workers' reversal, I recalled testimony regarding black-market adoption arrangers who were then still alive. Although they operated on a small scale and didn't usually steal children but instead coerced parents into relinquishing them, they profited financially from adoption.

The Kefauver Committee studied the tactics of brokers who had begun operating after Georgia, and were clearly following her lead. A team very similar to that of Georgia and Juvenile Court Judge Camille Kelley worked in Augusta, Georgia, where a probation officer reported the names of babies born to poor parents to a juvenile court judge who terminated the rights of the birth parents. The two then sold the children to couples in California and New York. The probation officer, Elizabeth B. Hamilton, acquired some newborns by telling mothers their babies had been stillborn.

Another baby seller, operating in Wichita, Kansas, kept pregnant women on cots in her basement and allowed clients to choose the woman whose child they would buy.

"Runners," who scouted single pregnant women, operated in cities like Chicago. The runners worked for brokers who paid young women small fees for their children. One scout frequented a parking lot used by truckers from all over the country, asking, "Is there any babes you know that are in trouble that I could take over and give them a few bucks?"

Operators of a Fort Worth, Texas, maternity home fed pregnant women little but cake and water and tricked them into relinquishing their children.

If their babies had physical or intellectual problems, however, the mothers were enjoined to raise them. One young woman testifying before the committee pointed out the irony that she was considered unqualified to raise a nondisabled child, but capable of raising a disabled one who might require greater care.

The committee also heard testimony regarding less organized, ad hoc transactions, such as that of the father in Long Beach, California, who traded his unborn daughter for a poker debt.

A Chicago woman sold her baby to a milkman for $1.

An undercover social worker in New Orleans paid a midwife $30 for an infant girl and received a baby boy as bonus.

A child was sold twice during a train ride from Los Angeles to El Paso.

Fewer than one-third of the estimated 75,000 adoptions that occurred in the United States in 1949 were handled by accredited agencies. I recalled reading articles printed in the 1950s in the popular press, in which reputable social workers agonized over how to keep children from falling into the hands of baby sellers. I recalled their conclusions, and that of Ernest Mitler, special counsel to Kefauver's subcommittee, who investigated black-market placements in New York City; Chicago; Duluth, Minnesota; Norman, Oklahoma; Texarkana, Texas; and Montreal, Canada. Ethical workers, these experts agreed, had to persuade the independent brokers' adult victims—single mothers—and the brokers' customers—adoptive parents—to work with reputable agencies. Doing so required understanding why so many pregnant women and adoptive parents worked with brokers.

The reasons were self-evident. Pregnant women who relinquished their children through legitimate agencies were responsible for their pregnancy-related medical and living expenses. Unmarried women availing themselves of the services of independent operators and baby sellers received free room, board, and medical care. To Katherine B. Oettinger, head of the Children's Bureau, the repercussions were obvious. "The unmistakable fact is that the unwed mother needs help. . . . And until she can get it . . . the black and grey market placements of children for adoption will continue," she wrote in 1958.

Ten years earlier, the prescient social worker Leontine Young had told her colleagues, "Because we cannot give adequate services to the unwed mother, we do not have enough children to place for adoption. Because we do not have enough children to place for adoption, the public grows impatient and ignores us. Caught between public prejudice and ignorance about the unmarried mother and public demand for adoptable children, we can protect neither the unwed mother nor the child. . . . The black market steps in without knowledge or scruples to fill the vacuum we have left."

And the black market operators were fast: according to the Kefauver committee, they approached some pregnant young women within five minutes of their arrival in a new town.

Black-market operators also served prospective adoptive parents quickly and with little red tape—practices that were greatly appreciated. Some clients wouldn't have met the requirements of more careful agencies. And many were comforted by the secretiveness common among black-market transactions, of which few records were kept. Threatened by the prospect of their children's reunion with their birth parents, few adoptive parents realized they might feel secure enough to want to help their children find their roots.

Ethical social workers' concerns weren't entirely altruistic; some feared that brokers would force them out of business, or sully the reputations of all social workers. But their main concern was preventing children from being exploited and sold.

Ethical professionals could conceive of only one way of competing with baby sellers: by imitating them. Ernest Mitler, special counsel to Kefauver's subcommittee, suggested that cities adopt the "Washington Plan" begun by the Washington Children's Home Society in Seattle in 1949. Disturbed by the success of unethical owners of maternity homes whose newspaper ads seemed "like a beam from heaven" to desperate, financially strapped young women, the Home ran its own ad: "Maternity care for unmarried mothers. Including doctors, hospital and living arrangements."

The Washington Home induced fourteen doctors to work for nominal fees, and two hospitals to make special arrangements. "[A]nd a girl can stay home, board out or live in a private home where she is paid for easy work," Mitler wrote in an article for *Look* magazine. By 1953, the agency had handled 103 cases from twenty states, and the unethical maternity homes in Seattle had closed.

Social workers in many other areas continued to be hobbled by lack of funding, and by state laws that frequently required one-year residency for single pregnant women needing financial help. But the Traveler's Aid Society managed to get more flexible treatment of nonresident mothers in Texas. And funds other than those already afforded by Aid to Dependent Children became available for the medical expenses of unmarried women in northern California and other areas.

Ethical social workers also began streamlining their services to pregnant women, allowing them to be followed by a single worker throughout their pregnancy, rather than making them work with several different people. To lure away black marketers' customers, social workers streamlined services to prospective adoptive parents, too, easing restrictive requirements regarding age and religion. And to mollify adoptive parents fearful of "losing" their children to birth parents, social workers began refusing to give adult adoptees information about their roots.

To save children, ethical social workers denied them their pasts. To help them, they hurt them.

Ethical social workers didn't always own up to their capitulation. They rationalized that keeping adoptees' identities secret allowed them to "make a clean break" with their pasts. Secrecy protected adoptive parents from intrusion by birth relatives, they said, and protected the privacy of single mothers.

Some reputable social workers, however, understood the hollowness of these excuses. Annette Baran and Reuben Pannor began their careers in social work in California in the late 1940s. They were then unaware of Georgia's influence upon adoption, which may have been particularly strong near Los Angeles, the site of her sole branch office and of an organization called the Adopted Children's Association.

Composed of one thousand parents who had adopted through Georgia, the Adopted Children's Association was headed by Mrs. Ernest Debs, the wife of a prominent state legislator. During the 1940s Georgia persuaded Mrs. Debs to chair a committee that rewrote California adoption law. Georgia also addressed the California legislature herself.

Passed in 1949, the new law required California courts to recognize the decisions of Tennessee courts regarding adoptions, and made the relinquishments of birth mothers immediately binding. Formerly, California mothers had had a period of time before their children's adoption during which they could reclaim them. The new law reduced the rights of birth parents in California to the level of those in Tennessee—virtually none at all.

Georgia Tann died one year after the passage of the California law. But Annette Baran and Reuben Pannor, and thousands of other social workers, began their careers in environments heavy with her legacy. "I bought into the whole system," Annette Baran told me. "I believed closed adoption worked.

"I accepted that a social worker's effectiveness was measured by how many unmarried mothers she could persuade to surrender their children. That the goal was to persuade all of them to give their children up.

"I also believed mothers could go on with their lives as if nothing had happened, and that 'normal, healthy' adoptees would have no curiosity about their roots."

Through the years, however, these supposed truisms rang more and more hollow. In 1971 a twenty-one-year-old man who had been adopted through Annette's agency said, "I don't expect you to give me any information. But could you call my birth father and ask if he's willing to meet me?"

"No one had ever asked me that," said Baran. But the young man was reasonable and intelligent, nothing like the then-supposed sick and obsessed searcher. "His request made sense," she said. Shortly afterward she hosted a seminar titled "Is Anonymity in Adoption Necessary?" and began research which led to the publication in 1978 of a book by her, Reuben Pannor, and Arthur Sorosky, *The Adoption Triangle*. It was a groundbreaking event that sparked the adoption rights movement.

But by the 1970s the secretiveness Georgia had insinuated into adoption was well entrenched. Virtually no adoptees were allowed knowledge of their origins. "Doesn't this remind anybody of how we treated slaves?" asked an adoptee in a letter to the *New York Times*.

13.

The Fallout

The endurance of Georgia's legacy of secrecy has allowed her to harm many more than the thousands she directly touched. She has hurt every American adopted since the beginning of the falsification of adoptees' birth certificates. She's hurt their birth parents. And she continues to hurt most of the 6 million adoptees and approximately 12 million birth parents alive today.

She hurts them by keeping them apart, causing pain difficult for most of us to imagine. Elderly women speak of having thought of their relinquished children every single day. They cry when they talk of their missing children.

Adoptees suffer too, and spend enormous energy imagining the parents who bore them.

"I remember looking at faces in the crowds, wondering if I might be looking at my mother without knowing it," recalled an adoptee interviewed, as were the next five adoptees quoted, by Annette Baran and Reuben Pannor for *The Adoption Triangle*:

> "I was forever running into people who would start conversations with, 'Do you have relatives in Rochester, or Duluth, or Denver? You look just like someone I know there.' I'd answer as calmly as possible, 'Not that I know of, but who is it?'"

> "I wonder if my natural mother thinks about me. I occasionally look at people driving by. If anyone looks like me I wonder if it might be a brother or sister. I once thought that my mother's best friend was my birth mother because of a resemblance to her. . . ."

> "I used to cry and look in the mirror and wonder if my mother looked like me. When I tried to visualize her, I did not picture her as a princess, nor did I picture her as a streetwalker. I did not care who she was. All I knew was that I had to find her. . . ."

> "I used to fantasize about my birth mother being a whore or an alcoholic and telling me to get lost. [T]hen I'd think about her being rich and prominent and explaining it all to me, taking me in her arms and holding me. I suppose it was natural that I would look at it from all angles."

> "I pictured my birth mother as an earthy, sensuous, laughing, affectionate person, in contrast to my adoptive mother, who was confident, practical, matter-of-fact, but not

very warm. In actuality, I believe, I wanted to be like my birth
mother fantasy."

Briefly enamored of the soap opera *General Hospital*, my daughter
once asked if her favorite actor might be her birth father.

When she said this, I thought of one of our former neighbors, thirteen-
year-old Martha, who lived directly across the street from us in Grand
Island, New York. Martha, too, had been adopted, and, like Beth, then
an infant, had pale skin, light eyes, and dark hair. Martha remarked upon
their resemblance and, during her second visit, ventured that she and
Beth might be biological sisters. I knew that Beth's mother was too
young to have borne Martha, but I couldn't bring myself to say so.
Martha wanted to believe it, wanted what we who haven't been adopted
take for granted.

Of course, Georgia's legacy deprives adoptees not only of the sense
of connection Martha craved, but knowledge of their medical histories.
"There are over 3000 illnesses that are passed through the genes," I read
in a book on adoption. "Regarding their own futures, adoptees can rule
none out."

The following four adoptees spoke of their concern to the authors of
The Adoption Triangle.

". . . I worried about my health. I had no idea what diseases I might have inherited from my biological parents. . . ."

"I have an intense fear of dying at a young age. I wish I
knew the lifespan of my biological relatives. . . ."

Adoptees also worry about unknowingly passing on genetically based diseases to their children:

> "I am very interested in my family heritage. I feel quite deprived not knowing my true ancestry, and I feel that in the future my children have the right to know their heritages. My husband is also adopted. Thus, both of us have no lineage. . . ."

> "I have discovered that I have myoclonic epilepsy and I am very concerned about bringing any more children into the world and what I may have passed on to the children I already have. Had I known when I married that I am epileptic or that there was epilepsy in my family, I might have chosen never to have children rather than run the risk of passing it on to future generations."

Testifying before a legislative committee in 2006, attorney and reunited birth father Fred Greenman asked committee members to "remember what happens when you visit a new doctor. You are questioned about your family's health history, either orally or by a questionnaire. Is your father alive? If so, what is the state of his health? If he died, how old was he? And what caused his death? The same questions for your mother and siblings. Typically, the doctor will also ask you whether any of your blood relatives had any number of specific illnesses such as diabetes, heart disease, cancer, stroke, kidney disease, allergies, thyroid disease; it's a long list.

"Doctors don't ask these questions out of idle curiosity. They know the answers may be crucial to both diagnosis and treatment.

"When a typical adoptee is asked these important questions, his only answer is 'I don't know.'"

Greenman cited the effect of this lack of knowledge on an adoptee in his twenties who had a "persistent stomachache for several days, which he ignored until his wife prevailed upon him to go to the hospital. The 'stomachache' was a coronary attack. He dropped dead on the steps to the hospital. The cardiologist concluded that his coronary weakness was probably genetic. Had he known his family history he might well still be alive."

Depriving adoptees of knowledge of their health histories seems particularly criminal today, when prophylactic measures are available to people who have inherited genetic variations predisposing them to serious diseases such as cancer.

But no matter how important knowledge of their pasts is for adoptees, it is frequently denied them—a fact that they learn very young. "Some of the kids at school used to make a big production out of it . . .," said a twelve-year-old boy interviewed for *How It Feels to Be Adopted*, by Jill Krementz. "They'd ask me a lot of questions like, 'Are you adopted?' And I'd say, 'Yes.' Then they'd ask me if I'd like to know who my real parents are and I'd say, 'Sure.' Then they'd say, 'Well, you can't!' I'd ask them why and they'd tell me, 'You're not allowed to, that's why.' So that's when I really found out about the law and the adoption records being sealed.

"I think kids who are adopted should be allowed to know who their original parents are."

Sadly, relatively few of the adoptees who want to search for their pasts do so. Some are deterred by the difficulty of searching in a country with sealed records. And many are reluctant to upset their adoptive parents, who directly or indirectly often make adoptees aware that they don't want them to search. Some adoptive parents even threaten to disown adoptees who search for their birth parents. Adoptees often delay searching until their adoptive parents have died, only to find that their birth parents are by then dead, too.

Fortunately, increasing numbers of adoptive parents are beginning to respect their children's needs. Understanding them requires little but thought. I recall telling a friend about Beth's desire to find her mother. As was often the case he was hurt for me, assuming Beth's search to be a criticism of my parenting. A relative of his, he said, had adopted two children. The girl was fine, and "had absolutely no need to search." The boy, who needed to, rebelled, ran away, and was now estranged from his adoptive parents.

"Beth and I have a good relationship," I said. "She simply needs to know."

"It's a separate issue, then," he said.

One reason given by adoptees for seeking their birth parents is to assure them that they are alive, happy, and accomplished. When Beth was very young, she fantasized about her mother viewing her. (Beth was not ready to see her mother herself; she would be behind a one-way mirror such as those used in police stations so that she could be viewed, but could not see her mother. Beth would be performing gymnastics.) "I want her to know how strong I am," she said.

Years later, I heard a similar wish from a Georgia Tann adoptee interviewed by Mike Wallace for *60 Minutes*. Stolen along with her sister and two brothers when she was four, Pat Schlothauer had searched for her parents as an adult, only to find they'd died. "She had no chance," said Mike Wallace, "to show her mother and father what kind of person she grew up to be."

"It was really important to me," Pat said, "to let our parents know that I turned out okay, because I felt like, as much as I have hurt, I feel like they've hurt, too.

"So my gift to them would be," she continued, fighting back tears, "I'm a very successful businesswoman, I feel, something to be proud of . . ." I was told that, during the taping, Mike Wallace's eyes were moist, too.

Some of the difficulties regarding adoption are inherent; a child is separated from her birth parents, parents from their child—that will always hurt. Adoptions that aren't necessary, such as many of those arranged by Georgia Tann, and many involving her indirect victims in the 1950s and '60s and even today, should not occur. Adoptions that are necessary should be as painless as possible. Much of the anguish of American adoptees could be alleviated by knowledge. Their right to this seems obvious. As the twelve-year-old boy interviewed for *How It Feels to Be Adopted* said, laws sealing adoptees' records are "ridiculous."

They seem ridiculous to many who have researched the issue. But adoptees are, despite their number, a minority: few members of the general public are aware that adoption records are closed.

"Closed? Like, 'locked up?'" people have asked me at parties. "Didn't that change long ago?"

I was a novice at activism, and felt a fraud. I'd always understood my daughter's need to search for her mother, and once I discovered Georgia Tann's role in adoption I became even more aware of the rightness of Beth's search. But the mind and the heart are not always in sync. Like Georgia's clients, I feared that if my daughter found her mother I would lose her.

But I knew Beth loved me. And I'd seen her mother in her hospital room, two days after she'd given birth: young, embarrassed, and so sad I'd had to look away. Her lawyer had told me she'd be "moving on"—as if she'd be able to forget Beth.

And I'd tried to comfort Beth during her early childhood when she'd cried, and asked, "How can I know she loved me?"

I knew I'd try to reunite Beth with her mother. And so I was grateful to members of a local support group, Adoption Network Cleveland, and to the thousands of other people across the country who were fighting to make such reunions possible.

A critical battle regarding this—one I'd been following for several years—was being waged in Tennessee. By the time my daughter decided to search for her mother, in 1996, adoptees and their advocates were taking their fight to the Tennessee legislature.

Three years earlier the Tennessee Coalition for Adoption Reform headed by Denny Glad and adoptee Caprice East had persuaded the Tennessee governor and legislature to appoint an eleven-member commission to study the state's adoption laws. Its most prominent member was Bob Tuke, an adoption attorney and adoptive father; Caprice East and Denny Glad were also members. The Study Commission held town meetings across Tennessee. Scores of Georgia Tann adoptees, and scores of her indirect victims, testified to their need to know their identities and pasts.

14.

The Beginning of the End

As activists across the country worked to dispel Georgia Tann's power over adoptees, Billy Hale was also shaking off her influence. He was energized by his frequent correspondence with Tennessee politicians regarding possible changes in the state's adoption law. And he was writing poems, which, read in the order of their composition, mapped his journey from a troubled to a less-troubled man.

His earliest writings had been inhabited by two people only:

> The shadow looms over his bed;
> He knows it's time . . .
> ("Under the Porch")

> Dark time drags slowly for a child in fear.
> Sleep is a place where someone finds you.
> ("Someone Listen Please")

"Someone Listen Please" was as bleak as his earlier poetry. But its title acknowledged the existence of someone other than abuser and victim. And in his next poems he moved further beyond, writing first of his mother, Mollie, and then of children suffering today. "A child is crying, can you help her?" he asked in one poem. In another, he wrote, "It's up to me to make some sense of it all."

The first person he had reached out to had been Barbara Davidson. "He called me, and he listened," she told me. "He understood—he'd been through the same thing."

They became friends, and began calling each other in the middle of the night when they couldn't sleep. Billy had set out to help Barbara, but he was soon being helped, too.

"One night he called me and he was upset—his memories were bothering him bad," Barbara said. "And I told him, 'Just pretend my hand is in yours, and I'm squeezing tight.' Billy later said the same thing to Barbara. Separated by hundreds of miles, they never met. But "Pretend your hand is in mine," spoken over the phone, became a comforting catch phrase: one that gave each more comfort than people who haven't been so hurt can probably ever appreciate. Billy's support helped Barbara cope with the flashbacks that had so disturbed her. And Barbara's support eventually helped Billy symbolically assuage his mother Mollie's sorrow.

What he found saddest was her scrapbook full of clippings of rescued children, and that she'd never learned whether he had survived his abduction. After the publication of his article for the Missing Children's Locate Center, he received letters from mothers forced to live in the same terrible limbo.

"I relate to these women," he told me. "They miss their children, and there's a hole in their lives." Anxious to help them, he joined the Locate Center, which searches for missing children and supports their families. Converting most of his trailer into an office, Billy wrote more newsletter pieces and began contributing to a cable television series regarding child safety.

He was inspired, spending forty hours a week on volunteer work while renovating the home of the friend on whose grounds he lived. Officials for the Center appointed him field investigator for Tennessee, and later for the entire southeastern United States.

Assisting the police and members of the FBI, Billy searched for missing children. Some were found alive. Billy was particularly elated by the location of a thirteen-year-old girl who'd been abducted by the leader of a youth group. Speaking later to her joyous parents, Billy felt he was giving his own mother a gift.

Comforting parents less fortunate was difficult, but his empathy helped him do it. "Billy is a constant friend," said the mother of a nine-year-old girl who was found dead. Billy wrote a poem about the child, from which her parents derived some comfort. And when they expressed interest in also doing volunteer work for the Locate Center, Billy persuaded a local businessman to give them a computer, fax machine, and printer. "Our work gives us reason to go on," the father said.

In 1995 Billy began feeling symptoms of the cancer that, misdiagnosed until 2000, would prove fatal in 2003. But for as long as he could, he searched for ways to help parents and children. A lifelong fan of country music, he asked singers to record personal service announcements related to missing children. Willie Nelson, Charlie Daniels, Naomi Judd, and others obliged. Billy considered his newfound sense of purpose sufficient payment. But one of his public service announcements won an international award. And there was more.

Among the singers who had taped television spots for Billy was a young woman named Deborah Allen. When he visited her one evening in 1996 to pick up a videotape, her mother Rosetta opened the door, and Billy fell in love. Within three months, Billy and Rosetta married.

Rosetta was a slim, dark-haired, elegant-appearing interior designer. Billy had a rougher look. "But inside, we're soul mates," he told me.

"When you marry after a certain age, it's so special," Rosetta said in 2004. "We were inseparable. He called me 'Precious.' He gave me joy, and I gave him joy, too. At the end, he said, 'The years with you have been the best years of my life.'"

By the time Billy died his life had come full circle, from early happiness with his mother, to the abuse he had suffered while in Georgia Tann's custody, to joy with Rosetta and the rewards he'd derived from his volunteer work.

He had also lived to see the fruit of his and other adoption activists' labors—a victory that had been achieved with great effort. The three-thousand-member Coalition for Adoption Reform led by Denny Glad and Caprice East had insisted upon helping not simply people who'd been adopted through Georgia Tann, but everyone who'd been adopted in Tennessee.

They had known that persuading legislators to vote for a law opening original birth certificates and adoption records solely for Georgia Tann's direct victims would be relatively easy. The state had been embarrassed by the publicity generated by my magazine article and the *60 Minutes* program on Georgia Tann. The ranks of Georgia's abettors had thinned through the years, and some younger politicians were openly critical of her crimes.

But Coalition members knew that Georgia had hurt all adoptees—both her five thousand direct victims, and millions of indirect ones. Since adoption is regulated by the states, Coalition members could immediately address the needs of only the indirect victims who had been adopted in

Tennessee. But the Coalition persuaded the Study Commission that was writing the proposed new adoption law to give as much credence to the rights of these indirect victims—the "post-1951 adoptees"—as to those who had passed through Georgia's Home. The law would, if passed, grant both groups access to their original birth certificates and adoption records.

Coalition members lobbied strenuously for the new law, buoyed partly by the responses they'd received from the town meetings they had held across the state. Hundreds of adoptees, birth parents, and adoptive parents testified to adoptees' need for knowledge, often so movingly that they reduced their audiences to tears.

One speaker was Eugene Calhoun, who'd undergone surgery to remove bone fragments in his spine after being beaten with a post-hole digger by the farmer Georgia Tann sold him to for $700 in 1933. Eugene had driven five hours from his home in Farmington, Missouri, to the town meeting in Jackson, Tennessee. He described being treated as a slave and denied schooling in his adoptive home, and mourning the loss of the mother Georgia stole him from.

"You people don't know what it's like to be deprived of a family," he said. "Anything you can do to see that this doesn't happen to another child will be wonderful. Don't let it happen to anyone like it happened to me."

Referring to the fact that he was still forbidden access to his original birth certificate and adoption records, he said, "It's heartbreaking to know that my own state where I was born won't even recognize me. That's what I've had for sixty years—no family, no parents, no nothing."

Georgia Tann's indirect victims were also angry. Adoptee Caprice East described adoptees' inability to know their birth names as "being in a witness protection program we didn't ask to be in."

Co-chair of the Tennessee Coalition for Adoption Reform, Caprice lobbied strenuously for the new law, tracing and retracing the corridors of the Capitol Building in Nashville. Pushing a dolly stacked with research, she visited all 133 members of the Tennessee Senate and House of Representatives. Far from shy, she followed one legislator into the men's room, and impressed virtually every legislator with her drive. Caprice "has worked harder on this bill than I've ever seen anybody work a piece of legislation, harder maybe than anybody ever in the history of Tennessee," said Representative Joe Fowlkes.

On May 18, 1995, the Tennessee Senate approved the new adoption law, 32 to 2. The House approved the law, 99 to 0. Then the legislators gave Caprice a standing ovation.

Records would be opened for Georgia Tann's direct victims, the pre-1951 adoptees, on July 1, 1995, and a year later for Georgia's indirect victims. When the pre-1951 adoptees were granted access, one said, "It was the biggest Christmas of my life."

Adoptee Carolyn Godeau received more than she could ever have hoped. She had been told that her mother had died in childbirth, and upon receipt of her original birth certificate and adoption records expected, at best, to meet half-siblings or aunts and uncles. She did find those relatives—as well as Kathryn Trammell, her mother. Meeting Kathryn, she said, was "the most wonderful thing in the world. I lived with a very loving, kind, generous mother and father. . . . But knowing you have a family and roots with somebody is so important.

"I found the most wonderful mother and sister and brother anyone could ask for."

Kathryn, who had been told that her daughter had died at birth, was as ecstatic as Carolyn.

"I went into shock," Kathryn told a Memphis reporter in 1996. "We met and it was like a dream. I still can't believe at my age, eighty-three years old, and having a baby!"

The widely read newspaper article about Kathryn and Carolyn's reunion seemed both uplifting and sad to Georgia Tann's indirect victims. Many of them also hoped to receive their original birth certificates and to reunite with their birth families. But by the time the piece ran the hopes of the post-1951 adoptees had been dashed. While the part of Tennessee's new adoption law regarding Georgia Tann's direct victims remained unchallenged, the section pertaining to her indirect victims had been challenged in court. On June 24, 1996, six days before the second phase of the new law was to go into effect, a suit was filed in the federal district court in Nashville to block it.

The challenge was led by televangelist Pat Robertson, who claimed that openness in adoption would result in a decrease in adoptions and an increase in abortions. Women threatened by the prospect of being contacted by their relinquished children would abort their children rather than place them for adoption, he claimed.

He and other advocates of secrecy in adoption were opposed by the American Adoption Congress, which had been founded in 1978 to promote openness in adoption.

Advocates of openness and their opponents had sparred in court several times earlier. The adoptees consistently lost: the courts held that the federal and state constitutions didn't prevent states from sealing records. If adoptees' records were to be unsealed, it would have to be done by the state legislatures.

The Tennessee legislature's passage of an open records law—and the possibility of a chain reaction—had alarmed Pat Robertson and his allies, and prompted the filing of the Tennessee class action suit. The lawsuit was brought by Small World Ministries, the only adoption agency in the state affiliated with the National Council for Adoption (NCFA). A Washington, D.C.–based lobbying organization, NCFA gets its funding largely from adoption agencies who try to placate insecure adoptive parents by trying to keep adoptees and birth parents apart. The lawsuit was also brought on behalf of three of Small World Ministry's clients: an anonymous birth mother and two anonymous adoptive parents. Another anonymous birth mother joined them in the suit a few days after the complaint was filed.

The plaintiffs were represented by the American Center for Law and Justice (ACLJ), a law firm founded and funded by Pat Robertson. ACLJ attorneys apparently understood the futility of challenging the section of Tennessee's new law pertaining to the direct victims of a baby seller. But in their suit before the U.S. District Court for the Middle District of Tennessee, they argued that the second phase of the new law, which opened the records of Georgia Tann's indirect victims, violated federal and state constitutional rights of birth parents to privacy.

Denny Glad, Caprice East, and other Tennessee Coalition members had anticipated this argument. They had tried to defuse it by including in the new law something to which they were philosophically opposed: a contact veto which could be filed by any birth parents who didn't want to meet or speak with their relinquished children. Inclusion of a similar veto had helped ensure passage of open adoption records legislation in 1990 in New South Wales, Australia. The veto had been invoked by only 2 percent of birth parents in New South Wales, and Coalition members hoped that few birth parents affected by the new Tennessee law would utilize the veto as well.

Tennessee's contact veto didn't apply to the direct victims of Georgia Tann, but only to the post-1951 adoptees. Those whose birth parents filed a contact veto would, like Georgia's direct victims, receive their original birth certificates and adoption papers. But they would be subject to civil and criminal penalties if they attempted to contact their parents.

In writing the new law, Coalition members had also accepted another compromise, this time on behalf of the small number of birth mothers who had relinquished children conceived as the result of rape or incest. Adoptees whose records revealed that they had been conceived in this way would not be given their adoption files, original birth certificates, or the names of their birth parents.

ACLJ attorneys insisted that neither the nondisclosure of information regarding this vulnerable subcategory of mothers, nor the contact veto, provided sufficient protection. Birth parents, the ACLJ attorneys insisted, were terrified of being contacted by their children. Unsealing birth records would "open the way for adoptees or others to blackmail the natural [birth] parents by threatening to disclose embarrassing circumstances surrounding the birth," ACLJ lawyers said, quoting an opinion of the New York Court of Appeals.

This claim echoed Abe Waldauer's attorney's assertion fifty-six years earlier that openness would place "an effective instrument of blackmail in the hands of unscrupulous [birth] parents and open the way for them to prey upon real [adoptive] parents. . . ."

The supposed victims and victimizers differed in the telling, but the ACLJ lawyers' language was more similar to Georgia Tann's attorney's than they realized. Georgia had instituted secrecy in adoption partially to appease her clients, adoptive parents who didn't want their children to reunite with their birth parents. NCFA and its member adoption agencies were primarily concerned with the wishes of adoptive parents as well. But, realizing that obvious bias toward the most privileged members of the adoption triad might make judges unsympathetic to their cause, NCFA and the ACLJ attorneys feigned concern for birth mothers—the women no one had ever really cared about.

The ACLJ attorneys also argued that the opening of adoption records would result in an increase in the number of abortions, and a decrease in the number of adoptions. The National Council for Adoption joined the ACLJ in the lawsuit, as friend of the court.

The lawsuit challenging Tennessee's new adoption law had been brought against the governor, the attorney general, and the commissioner of Human Services of Tennessee, who were represented in the lawsuit by the Tennessee Attorney General's Office. Sixty-nine triad members—thirty-three adult adoptees, seventeen birth parents, and nineteen adoptive parents—supported the Tennessee Attorney General's Office as friends of the court in defending the new adoption law. So did attorney and adoptive father Bob Tuke and adoptee Caprice East, on behalf of the Study Commission.

Fred Greenman of New York City, the American Adoption Congress's legal advisor and a reunited birth father, volunteered his services pro bono. The AAC also retained the services of three Nashville attorneys, Harlan Dodson III, Anne Martin, and Julie Sandine, who worked for reduced fees.

Members of the Tennessee Coalition and the AAC attorneys submitted to the court affidavits, statistics, and results of studies regarding adoptees' medical and psychological need for knowledge of their birth families.

And, countering one of their opponents' main arguments, the AAC lawyers insisted that their opponents' use of the word "privacy" regarding birth parents' wishes was misleading. Privacy, they asked, from whom? Most birth mothers, like most people, desired privacy from the public regarding their pregnancies. But "very few, if any, asked for 'privacy' from the children they surrendered for adoption," attorney Fred Greenman wrote later. "You may have an unlisted phone number for privacy, but you still give it to your children so they can call home."

Lawyers for Georgia Tann's victims also insisted that their opponents' claim that birth mothers had a "reasonable expectation of secrecy" from their children was false. No such written promise was ever made to them. (Birth mothers were, however, sometimes promised that their children would later be able to contact them. Birth mothers were also often required to sign papers promising not to contact their children—hardly a sign that agencies really believed the mothers desired "privacy.")

Oral assurances to birth mothers of secrecy from their offspring, if they were ever made, were fraudulent. State laws sealing adoptees' original birth certificates had always been subject to change. Even under closed records laws, adoptees had long been allowed access to their records at the discretion of the courts. Today, with the help of adoption search groups and the Internet, adoptees unable to see their records are still sometimes able to find their families. And adoptive parents who receive the names of their children's birth parents sometimes share this information with their children. How could any relinquishing mother be assured she would never be found?

The lawyers for Georgia Tann's victims also refuted their opponents' claims that openness in adoption would result in a decrease in adoptions and an increase in abortions. The very opposite, Fred Greenman had discovered, was true. The only two states that had always allowed adult adoptees access to their original birth certificates were Alaska and Kansas. A comparison of adoption and abortion rates throughout the country revealed that adoption rates in Alaska and Kansas were higher than those in the United States as a whole, and that the adoption rate in Kansas was higher than in all four surrounding states. A comparison of resident abortion rates in the different states showed that abortion rates in Alaska and Kansas were lower than those in the country as a whole, and that the rate in Kansas was lower than in any of the four states that surrounded it. If openness in adoption had any impact on the rates of abortion and adoption, it was to decrease the number of abortions, and to increase the number of adoptions.

On August 23, 1996, the federal district court in Nashville ruled in favor of Georgia Tann's victims, lifting a temporary restraining order that had thus far prevented them from accessing their records.

But ACLJ attorneys quickly appealed to the U.S. Court of Appeals for the Sixth Circuit, and obtained a stay that once again prevented the second phase of Tennessee's new law from going into effect. Plaintiffs and the defense made their arguments all over again. Then on February 11, 1997, the Court of Appeals affirmed the District Court's finding, dissolving the stay. To adoptees' further joy, the Court of Appeals also took the unusual step of dismissing the entire case and rejecting all federal constitutional claims.

Writing for the court, Judge Albert J. Engel said, "[W]e note our skepticism that information concerning a birth might be protected from disclosure by the Constitution. A birth is simultaneously an intimate occasion and a public event—the government has long kept records of when, where, and by whom babies are born."

Judge Engel also praised the Tennessee law. "The statute appears to be a serious attempt to weigh and balance two frequently conflicting interests: the interest of a child adopted at an early age to know who that child's birth parents were, an interest entitled to a good deal of respect and sympathy, and the interest of birth parents in the protection of the integrity of a sound adoption system."

ACLJ attorneys asked the U.S. Supreme Court to review the decision, but the court refused.

Georgia Tann's victims were jubilant. But more work lay ahead. Having exhausted their possibilities in federal courts, ACLJ attorneys began an action in Tennessee state court, arguing that the new adoption law violated the state constitutional rights of birth and adoptive parents to privacy. On March 26, 1997, ACLJ attorneys requested a restraining order barring implementation of the second phase of the law from the State Circuit Court in Davidson County, Tennessee. The order was granted. But after both sides presented their arguments Georgia Tann's victims won again. On May 2 the court vacated the restraining order, finding that a "birth parent has no constitutional rights to nondisclosure of his or her identity."

ACLJ lawyers then appealed to the Tennessee Court of Appeals, which issued another stay, and, after reviewing arguments, reversed the state circuit's ruling, finding that the new adoption law did in fact violate state constitutional law. (The court had been persuaded by ACLJ attorneys' assertion that birth parents had had a "reasonable expectation" of having their identities kept secret from their children.)

After having experienced four previous court victories, Georgia Tann's indirect victims and their advocates were chilled—and aware that more than Tennessee's new law was at stake.

"This court battle has the potential to make or break the case for open adoption records. . . . If the court finds in favor of the Tennessee law, the case will become a millstone around the necks of those who oppose giving American adoptees the same records to which all other Americans are entitled by law. If it goes against us, we will have little hope of having open adoption records anywhere in the United States, because this case will come back to haunt us again and again," an AAC member had written in 1996.

On October 2, 1998, the AAC attorneys filed a motion to appeal the decision of the Tennessee Court of Appeals to the Tennessee Supreme Court. The motion was granted, and the opposing sides presented their arguments on June 3, 1999.

The courtroom was packed. Many of those present were members of Denny Glad and Caprice East's Tennessee Coalition, which had kept the pressure on during the grueling three-year fight. Most Coalition members wore identifying labels: "Adoptee," "Birth Parent," "Adoptive Parent."

"The Law's ultimate fate is now in the hands of the five Supreme Court Justices. . . ." wrote a reporter for the Coalition newsletter.

The wait for the Justices' decision seemed excruciatingly long, but it was definitely worthwhile. Issued on September 27, 1999, the decision was both unanimous and an enormous victory for open records. The Justices had determined that Tennessee's new adoption law did not violate the constitutional rights of birth parents. It did not violate the rights of adoptive parents. The new law could stand.

No longer, said Representative Joe Fowlkes, would Tennessee adoptees be treated like "cattle or property."

"Victory in Tennessee!" exulted a reporter for an adoption newsletter. Across the state of Tennessee, and, in adoption circles, throughout the entire country, the mood was euphoric.

Finally, justice. And, as AAC and Coalition members had predicted, and Pat Robertson and NCFA had feared, justice was also coming for the indirect victims of Georgia Tann who had been adopted outside Tennessee.

In 1999 a group of advocates led by Carolyn Hoard, a birth mother and member of the American Adoption Congress, caused Delaware to change its law to allow adult adoptees copies of their original birth certificates.

From 1998 to 2000 Helen Hill and other adoptees from a group called Bastard Nation successfully fought for the right of Oregon adoptees to have access to their original birth certificates.

Bastard Nation caused original birth certificates to be opened to Alabama adoptees in 2000 as well.

In 2004, a successful campaign by Paul Schibbelhutte, a reunited birth father and member of the American Adoption Congress; Janet Allen, a state senator, an adoptee, and a member of Bastard Nation; and Lou D'Alessandro, a state senator and an adoptive father, opened original birth certificates to adoptees in New Hampshire.

Nine other states—Colorado, Hawaii, Indiana, Montana, Michigan, Ohio, Oklahoma, Washington, and Vermont—allow adoptees born before or after certain dates access to their original birth certificates.

In each state, adoptees and their advocates relied heavily on arguments made in the Tennessee case. As of January of 2007, open records bills were pending in six more states.

Epilogue

"The evil that men do lives after them. . . ." Change the gender of the protagonist, and Shakespeare could have been anticipating the pain caused by Georgia Tann. I saw it in the faces of her direct victims for over a decade. And I saw it in my daughter's face when, during the winter of her sophomore college year, she spoke of a need to know her birth mother that was so intense she wanted to leave school to find her.

She met her mother the following fall. Aided by the knowledge of her mother's surname, hospital records indicating her first name, and old city directories for Niagara Falls, New York, I'd found it easy to locate her.

"Oh my God!" Gail cried when, at Beth's request, I phoned her. "I've been waiting for this call! Tell Beth I married her father—she has three younger brothers!"

Ten days later Beth drove with her boyfriend from her college campus in Bowling Green, Ohio, to Niagara Falls to meet her family: parents Gail and Salvatore (Sal), three birth brothers, four grandparents, aunts, uncles, and cousins. It was a wonderful reunion. Like most reunited adoptees she reveled in the similarities between herself and her birth relatives. She looks like both of her parents, uses the same gestures as her mother, and shares the family's love of cards and board games. Like her, they're confident, resilient, and thrive on competition. She learned her health history and received a family tree—an album full of pictures of distant relatives and of the home in which her ancestors had lived in Italy.

And she received gifts her excited family had quickly assembled. An aunt gave her a photo album of Gail and Sal's wedding, and of Beth's three brothers as babies. Another aunt had knitted an afghan bearing Beth's name and birth date. Her uncle Keith, an artist, had painted her portrait. She received sweatshirts with Niagara Falls logos, a Buffalo Bills jacket, jewelry, flowers.

Living with her family the following summer, and continuing to visit them frequently afterward, Beth filled the gap that had always pained her. Her family got the chance to know and love her. And I, who'd felt threatened by Beth's search, learned that love isn't finite, and that adoptive parents who help their children search sometimes become even closer to them than before.

All four of Beth's brothers—the brother she'd been raised with, Tim; and her birth brothers Christopher, Michael, and Alex—were groomsmen at her wedding in May 2006. Gail, Sal, and Beth's birth grandmother sat in the front of the church with Bob, my mother, and me. When it came time for the traditional father–daughter dance, Beth danced twice—first with Bob, and then with Sal. There were over three hundred guests at the wedding; virtually every one teared up during the second dance.

It will be some time before all American adoptees who want to find their birth mothers will have the necessary tool—their mother's name—that allowed Beth to locate Gail. Despite the progress made since the 1999 Tennessee court victory, adoptees' original birth certificates remain sealed in thirty-four states. The obstacles to access remain the same as those faced by the Tennessee Coalition for Adoption Reform: the National Council for Adoption; insecure adoptive parents; and people who believe that birth mothers don't want contact with their children, and that openness in adoption leads to abortion.

NCFA and its allies are much better funded than the grassroots organizations fighting for openness. But adoptees will win. And, I hope, right will also triumph over another of Georgia's legacies: the sale of children whose mothers were robbed of them, or unduly coerced into relinquishment.

The outright theft of children is relatively uncommon now in the United States: the availability of contraceptives and the virtual erasure of the stigma of single parenting have made single pregnant young women much less vulnerable than during Georgia's time. Most raise their children. Those who relinquish their babies often enter into open adoptions, in which they select the adoptive parents and afterward maintain some degree of contact with their children.

Today, most child stealing occurs in poor countries like Guatemala, India, Indonesia, Thailand, Cambodia, Samoa, and China. The brokered children are both the benefactors and victims of the fact that adoptive parents are now eager to adopt children of all races. Children whose parents can't care for them are more likely than before to get the adoptive homes they desperately need. But poor children who don't need adoptive homes are vulnerable to baby brokers anxious to feed the growing international market for children.

Many of these current-day brokers are Georgia Tann clones. Typical is an American broker, Lauryn Galindo. Between 1997 and 2001 she made $8 million by arranging eight hundred adoptions of Cambodian children by unwitting Americans, including the actress Angelina Jolie, who adopted a son through Galindo in 2003.

Like Georgia's birth mothers, Galindo's were impoverished. And like Georgia, Galindo used spotters: "baby recruiters" who located vulnerable women in destitute rural areas. The recruiters passed the mothers' names on to "baby buyers," usually orphanage directors or taxicab drivers, who offered the mothers small amounts of rice or money for their children. The buyers often told the mothers that they could have their children back at any time, or that when the children became adults they could petition for their mothers to immigrate to the United States.

The children were then tested for hepatitis and AIDS. Children who tested positive were returned to their birth families. If the tests were negative, the child was taken to an orphanage or "stash house." Investigating agents found conditions in these facilities "horrendous": naked, filthy babies lay in hammocks covered with feces.

The children were then assigned to prospective American adoptive parents who paid Galindo between $10,500 and $11,500 in adoption "fees." With the children stored and purchased, Galindo furnished them with Cambodian passports by passing them off as orphans. She erased their identities, falsifying their names and histories and giving them phony birth certificates.

Galindo differed from Georgia in being sentenced by an American court to prison, if only for eighteen months. Her justification for her crimes was, "It was always my intention to save children from desperate circumstances, and I feel like I was always acting with the highest integrity." Georgia Tann would have said the same thing, if she'd ever felt the need to defend herself.

Other Georgia Tann imitators operate in China. "China has a growing black market in babies, often girls, who are abducted or bought from poor families or unwed mothers and sold to parents who want another child, a servant, or a future bride for their son," a reporter for *China Daily* wrote in 2006.

Relatively few Chinese brokers are caught and prosecuted. But in 2004 over twenty people were arrested after twenty-eight baby girls were found at a highway toll gate in Binyang, Guangzi province, stuffed into nylon tote bags stacked on the luggage rack of a long-distance bus. The infants, aged three days to three months, had been drugged and bound. One, whose face was mottled red and blue with cold, had died.

"Most of the people arrested were middle-aged women from Binyang," a policeman told news agency AFP. "They probably wanted to make some money." The baby-selling ring was larger than was immediately apparent; fifty-two people were eventually convicted of this crime.

The source and the intended destination of the babies were unknown. "It's possible the parents gave the babies away. Family planning policy is very strict and they probably had exceeded their birth limit and wanted to give the babies away to avoid fines," a police officer said.

"Perhaps some of them were born to unwed mothers or migrant workers."

It's also possible that some of the children had been stolen. "China often balks at releasing embarrassing statistics, including the number of its young citizens abducted in front of schools, on streets and in busy markets," Mark Magnier wrote for the *Los Angeles Times* in January of 2006. "But experts say the problem is growing, despite repeated efforts by the government to crack down on traffickers. China has disclosed that it rescued 3,488 children in 2004, according to the official New China News Agency. Experts say those children are only a fraction of those lost."

One of those lost is six-year-old Chen Ying, whose parents last saw her in 2005 as she set off to school, dressed in a black-and-white checkered coat. Her father, Cheng Zu, had made a pencil drawing of her one night before she went to sleep. After she disappeared he and his grieving wife showed it to reporter Magnier. "You can see why someone would want to abduct her," Cheng Zu said. "She's so pretty."

He and Cheng Ying's mother were unable to get any help from her school. The police wouldn't help either, and refused even to fill out a missing person's report. And when a witness later reported seeing a man with someone matching the little girl's description, the police refused to follow up the lead.

Cheng Ying's parents earned only $200 a month, but they had done everything possible for their daughter, sacrificing to send her to a special "Hope Primary School." After she disappeared they touched her face in her father's drawing of her, and in snapshots, trying to connect with her.

They were numb with sorrow, her father even thinking of suicide. "I just hope, wherever she is, they're taking care of her," he said.

Most adoptions of foreign children are legitimate rescues of children who would otherwise be warehoused in institutions, or suffer a worse fate. But some children have been taken wrongly from their families. It's not known how many of the children placed with unsuspecting American adoptive parents have been abducted or obtained through fraud. But international adoption can cost as much as $40,000—and even a fraction of this can seem an enormous sum to brokers in countries where the average annual income is $1,800. And Americans are adopting increasing numbers of children from very poor countries.

"Last year, nearly 23,000 children born abroad were adopted into American families," a reporter for the *New York Sun* wrote in 2006. "China is currently by far the most common go-to country for adoptive parents, with nearly 8,000 orphan visas granted from that country last year. Russia comes in a distant second, followed by Guatemala, South Korea, Ukraine, and Kazakhstan.

"But adoption counselors say would-be parents are increasingly turning an eye to African countries."

With celebrities like Angelina Jolie and Madonna adopting babies from Africa, the number of Americans seeking to adopt from that continent is likely to grow.

There are often many middlemen involved in foreign adoption transactions, and abuses can creep in all along the line. "Brokers seek out pregnant women and offer them money for their babies who are then advertised on the Internet; notaries and agents take a slice to produce medical documentation which is sometimes falsified; other officials take a cut to issue passports and other papers," wrote a Reuters reporter in 2001.

"Adoptive parents are sometimes instructed to set out for a foreign country with large amounts of cash in their pockets for under-the-table transactions. One terrified prospective mother found herself in the dead of night handing over $8,000 to a bunch of Russian gangsters in a parking lot," the Reuters report continued.

Such criminal operations also occur in Malaysia, where baby-selling rings are "thriving, fueled by a shortage of babies available for adoption," reported ABC Radio Australia in 2005. "Police say the gangs have been employing mostly Indonesian women as prostitutes, denying them contraception so they can conceive, and then selling the babies. . . ."

Baby stealing is less frequent in developed countries, but it does occur. According to Interpol, brokering is being investigated in such countries as Greece, Italy, France, and Portugal, where the ringleaders are Bulgarian thugs. Criminal gangs dupe poor, pregnant Bulgarian women into moving to Greece to secure what the women believe will be lucrative jobs.

"But there was no job," twenty-three-year-old Yanna Dobrena Yordanova told reporters for the *Belfast Telegraph* in July 2006. Instead of being given employment, she was expected to surrender the child she was carrying. Rescued by an Athens, Greece, organized police crime unit, Yanna escaped this fate. But babies of other young women are sometimes sold to adoptive parents before their mothers even leave the hospital.

"What you have is too much money changing hands and too many people trying to get that money by producing babies for adoption," said Fred Greenman, legal counsel to the American Adoption Congress. Greenman is also the attorney who helped ensure the 1999 legal victory that gave people adopted in Tennessee access to their original birth certificates. He's well aware of Georgia Tann, and of the fact that the past is not yet past.

It lives on in another Georgia Tann legacy that leaves adopted children vulnerable: the cursoriness of preadoption home studies. While the qualifications of some prospective adoptive parents are thoroughly examined, those of others are not—a fact that had terrible consequence for a five-year-old Russian girl adopted by an American in 1998.

Even a perfunctory study of Masha's new father, Matthew Mancuso, would have revealed that he had neither a bedroom nor bed for Masha, who was forced to sleep with him. For five years he raped her and sold pornographic pictures of her on the Internet.

In 2003 Masha, then eleven, testified against him at trial. And on May 3, 2006, she testified before the House Energy and Commerce Committee regarding the need for adoption reform.

"A lot of people ask how anyone could let a pedophile adopt a little girl," she said. Referring to the three agencies involved in her adoption, she continued, "I found out after I was adopted that none of these agencies asked Matthew many questions. They never really checked him out. They showed him pictures of me, probably on the Internet, before he had a home study to adopt me. In some of the pictures they showed him of me from the orphanage I was naked.

"He told them he was divorced and had a daughter he wasn't close to. I found out later that the reason his daughter didn't talk to him is that he molested her, too.

"While I lived with Matthew no one ever came to check on me even though the Russian government requires it. Since my story came out we found out that two other kids—a boy from Romania and a girl from Russia—were adopted by pedophiles, too. . . . Just so you know, fourteen other Russian kids have actually been murdered by their adoptive parents in America. I'm sure there are other kids in trouble. But no one seems to care about any of this."

The Hague Convention on Intercountry Adoption, a multilateral treaty that covers all adoptions between countries that ratify it, is trying to reform international adoption. Under the Convention, agencies that perform adoptions in Hague countries will be required to meet standards meant to protect all members of the adoption triad. In particular, governments of adoptees' countries of origin must determine if adoptees are legitimately eligible for adoption because they were orphaned, or were relinquished by parents who were not robbed, deceived, or bribed. Other provisions include more stringent investigation of prospective adoptive parents; full disclosure to adoptive parents regarding agencies' policies and fees; the preservation and disclosure of all information on adopted children; the paying of agency employees on a salary or fee-for-service, rather than contingency, basis; and prohibition of child-buying.

The Convention's proposed requirements are admirable. But, according to Trish Maskew, president of Ethica, a Tennessee-based nonprofit organization promoting ethics in adoption, they are not enough. The Hague regulations will only cover adoptions between two Hague countries. This would involve 11 percent of all foreign adoptions, the State Department estimated in 2003.

Legislation to cover non-Convention adoptions must also be passed. A crucial need is a law making the sale of, or traffic in, children for the purpose of adoption illegal. Such a law, advocated in the 1950s by Estes Kefauver, the Tennessee senator appalled by the crimes of Georgia Tann, is needed for all adoptions, both international and domestic. And information regarding adoptees' birth names and backgrounds has to be preserved and made available to adoptees, whether their adoptions have occurred in the United States or overseas.

If knowledge of the long-buried story of Georgia Tann teaches us anything, it is the importance of ridding adoption of lies and secrets. Until we do, she and her imitators will continue to corrupt adoption.

Notes

Prologue

x: ". . . over five thousand adoptions": In 1946, Georgia Tann reported having arranged five thousand adoptions—*Press-Scimitar*, December 6, 1946, "Years Ago She Found a Career: Now Miss Tann Completes 5000th Adoption Case." She continued to arrange adoptions for almost four more years, until her death on September 15, 1950. She arranged 223 adoptions in 1949: *Press-Scimitar*, March 10, 1950, "Marked Increase in the Number of Children Offered for Adoption." She placed "more than 100" children for adoption between January 1, 1950, and September 1, 1950. Figures for 1947 and 1948 are unavailable, but she is reputed to have placed over 250 children per year during that time: Neill, October 1978, p. 38. The true number of adoptions arranged by Georgia Tann is probably closer to six thousand than five thousand.

x: "She had molested . . . in her care": Interviews with Barbara Davidson, 1992 and 1993; interviews with June Jardin, 1992.

x: "by the 1930s . . . highest in the country": Oppenheimer, p. 1.

x: "And the actual . . . former Memphian told me": Interview with Robert Taylor, 1992.

xi: "She had been . . . to Tennessee": Interview with Vallie Miller, 1992; interview with Regina Hines, 1993; interview with Hickory, Mississippi resident, 1993.

xi: "and agencies like . . . adoptions a year": A Report of the Children's Aid Association of Boston, "Our 1937 Children," May 1938.

xi: "In 1928 . . . arranged 206": *Press-Scimitar*, March 11, 1929, "Clearing House of City's Orphans Always Busy."

xii: "Since the passage . . . twelve other states": See notes to pp. 240-241. Michigan granted limited access before Tennessee granted full access.

1. Georgia's Home

2: "Georgia's orphanage at . . . the wide front porch": *The Commercial Appeal*, November 28, 1942, photograph of Home; *Press-Scimitar*, April 13, 1943, "Babies Smile Thru Dark War Clouds: Spacious New Home for Tots on Poplar"; interviews with May Hindman, 1992.

2: "three nurseries were . . . sleeping babies": *Press-Scimitar*, April 13, 1943, "Babies Smile Thru Dark War Clouds."

2: "But . . . the women weren't nurses": Interview with Mrs. Leon Sims, 1994.

2: "the head caretaker . . . while drunk": Taylor, p. 10.

2: "And the outfits . . . hardest to sell": Interview with Vallie Miller, 1992.

2: "Two of Georgia's . . . of the main building": Miller, V., p. 48.

3: "'I picked you out' . . . told them": Interview with Jimmye Pidgeon, 1992.

3: "When she was . . . stern telegrams": *The Commercial Appeal*, January 28, 1948; *The Commercial Appeal*, September 14, 1950, "Tennessee Action on Report of Black Market Babies Climaxes Bitter Controversy."

3: "futile habeas corpus suits . . . local press": *Press-Scimitar*, November 20, 1937, "Dad Who 'Gave Away' Children Wants Them Back — Court Says No"; *Press-Scimitar*, April 29, 1940, "Claims Society Misled Her and Took Child"; *Press-Scimitar*, 1947, "Unwed Mother Asks Return of Baby"; *The Commercial Appeal*, August 30, 1947, "Unwed Mother Plans New Fight for Child"; *Press-Scimitar*, March 24, 1951, "Child Placement Illegal, Welfare Chief Asserts"; *Press-Scimitar*, March 25, 1951, "Placing Children Described as Illegal"; *Press-Scimitar*, March 26, 1951, "Seeking Custody of Three Children"; *Nashville Tennessean*, April 3, 1951, "Couple Opens Fight to Regain Three Children"; *Nashville Tennessean*, April 4, 1951, "Court Delays Adoption Fight"; *Associated Press*, March 19, 1952, "Tann Victim Seeks Children's Return."

3: "expulsion from the Child Welfare League of America": Miller, V., p. 85; Taylor, p. 7.

2. Georgia's Disappearance

5: "It wasn't until . . . her crimes": *Nashville Tennessean*, September 12, 1950, "Black Market in Babies Probed at Shelby Home."

5: "And this reference . . . seller in print": Interview with Robert Taylor, 1992.

6: "At a press . . . 'Society,' Browning said": *Nashville Tennessean*, September 12, 1950, "Black Market in Babies Probed at Shelby Home."

6: "it was a token . . . or her helpers": Interview with Robert Taylor, 1992.

6: "Taylor was also . . . children for Georgia": Interviews with Robert Taylor, 1992, 1993; *Press-Scimitar*, November 17, 1950, "Taylor, Gianotti Tangle in Tann Investigation."

6: "Robert Taylor as investigator": Taylor was the brother of Peter Taylor, who wrote for the *New Yorker, Southern Review, Kenyon Review, Sewanee Review,* and *Partisan Review.* His novels include *Summons to Memphis,* published in 1985, for which he was awarded the Pulitzer Prize.

6: "Even worse, Georgia's . . . by her attorney": Taylor, p. 15; Neill, "Adoption for Profit, Part I," October 1978, p. 51; Interviews with Robert Taylor, 1992, 1993; interview with Ben Goodman, 1993; interview with Vallie Miller, 1993; *The Nashville Tennessean,* September 12, 1950, "State Prober Charges Baby Records Moved"; *Press-Scimitar,* November 17, 1950, "Taylor, Gianotti Tangle in Tann Investigation."

6: "and, of course . . . he wished": Interview with Hazel Fath, 1993; *Press-Scimitar,* June 27, 1951, "Others Figure in Tann Case."

6: "In 1951 the . . . die in committee": Neill, "Adoption for Profit, Part I," October 1978, p. 57; interview with Denny Glad, 1990; interview with Robert Taylor, 1993; *Press-Scimitar,* March 7, 1951.

6: "A proposed federal . . . was quashed": *Press-Scimitar,* October 22, 1950, "New Angles Develop in Probe of Children's Home"; *The Commercial Appeal,* September 25, 1950.

6: "The sole result . . . should never have made": *State ex rel. Heiskell v. Tennessee Children's Home Society,* No. 53339 R.D. CCh. Ct. (Shelby Co., TN), Consent Decree (n.d.).

7: "keeping the babies . . . suffocating heat": Interview with Mrs. Leon Sims, 1994.

7: "Georgia had refused . . . for the disease": *Press-Scimitar,* October 19, 1950, "Tells of Keeping Unmarried Mothers for Miss Tann."

7: "virtual prisoners . . . their frantic parents": *Press-Scimitar,* October 19, 1950, "Tells of Keeping Unmarried Mothers for Miss Tann"; Miller, V., p. 68.

7: "they demanded their . . . children remained alive": Browning papers, Letter from Governor Gordon Browning to Mr. R. B. Kylie, September 16, 1950; Letter from Governor Browning to Alice Decanter, September 16, 1950; Letter from Governor Browning to Mae L. Day, October 25, 1950; Miller, V., p. 52.

7: "Only two of . . . their birth parents": *The Commercial Appeal,* May 17, 1951, "What About Adoption Here?"

8: "Twenty-three-year . . . to Massachusetts": *Press-Scimitar,* October 8, 1950, "Mother Kidnaps Baby at Children's Home Society"; interview with Josie Statler, 1992.

8: "But other parents . . . got them back": *Nashville Tennessean* (AP), August 4, 1952, "Tennessee Mother Weeps as Court Takes Three Children."

8: "'The children will be . . . for the others'": *The Commercial Appeal,* October 5, 1950, "Trio Comes Here to Study Children."

8–9: "But state workers disposed . . . three oldest in an adoptive home": Miller, V., pp. 64-69.

9: "Georgia had violated . . . Tennessee": Georgia and her agency lacked the required state license to place children. Georgia also frequently violated a state law requiring that adoptive parents appear before a Tennessee court for the finalization of their child's adoption. See *Nashville Tennessean*, September 17, 1950, "Baby Placing Termed Invalid"; *Press-Scimitar*, March 24, 1951, "Child Placement Illegal, Welfare Chief Asserts."

9: "and other states": Letter from Mississippi State Children's Bureau to Abe Waldauer, May 4, 1936; Letter from the New Jersey Department of Institutions and Agencies to Fannie B. Elrod, September 24, 1950; *The Commercial Appeal*, September 22, 1950; *Press-Scimitar*, October 22, 1950, "New Angles Develop in Probe of Children's Home."

9: "But several politicians . . . through her": Neill, "Adoption for Profit, Part II," November 1978, p. 74; interview with Jimmye Pidgeon, 1992.

9: "they quickly passed . . . her illegal placements": Tennessee Public Acts 1951, ch. 202, sec. 33.

9: "But several adoptive . . . had been illegal": *Nashville Tennessean*, April 1, 1951, "State to Insure Coast Adoptions"; Miller, V., pp. 59-60.

9: "Some adoptive couples . . . adoptions annulled": *The Commercial Appeal*, September 30, 1950, "California Couple Want to Nullify Adoptions"; *Press-Scimitar*, March 26, 1951, "Seeking Custody of Three Children," Miller, V., p. 72.

9: "In contrast, adoptees . . . had been legal": Interview with Earlene Phillips, 1992.

9: "Yet one of . . . a 'blood heir'": Interview with Joy Barner, 1993.

10: "But I understood . . . ever returned home": Miller, V., pp. 55-56.

10: "I also learned . . . California and New York": Neill, "Adoption for Profit, Part II," November 1978, p. 75.

10–12: "When Georgia Tann . . . 'felt like she belonged'": Interview with Elizabeth Huber, 1992.

12: "Soon after meeting . . . told me, crying": Interview with Barbara Davidson, 1992.

13: "Having conducted largely . . . oblige Barbara": Interviews with May Hindman, 1992.

3. Billy

Sources for this chapter are personal and phone interviews with Billy Hale; Billy Hale's unpublished manuscript; and Billy Hale's unpublished journals.

18: "*60 Minutes* had produced a segment about her": CBS News, *60 Minutes*, originally aired January 12, 1992, "Black Market Babies."

4. The Plague

21: "a city that . . . seemed blessed": *The Commercial Appeal*, August 24, 1958, "The Time Memphis Died"; Allen 1947, p. 213; Weisberger, p. 57.

21: "Established in 1819": Allen, pp. 212-213.

21: "Memphis was strategically . . . century commerce": Weisberger, p. 57.

21: "The city emerged . . . relatively unscathed": *The Commercial Appeal*, August 24, 1958, "The Time Memphis Died."

22: "Trading in wartime contraband . . . the citizenry," Allen, p. 213.

22: "But while Memphis . . . was medieval": Capers 1966, p. 188.

22: "Six thousand privies . . . business section": Weisberger, p. 59.

22: "composed of . . . human excrement": *Press-Scimitar*, July 14, 1975, "So New York Thinks It Has a Problem? Ask Memphis About Yellow Fever Epidemic."

22: "sloughs of manure . . . hogs and goats": Weisberger, p. 59.

22: "Standing water is . . . breeding ground": Weisberger, p. 58.

22: "*Aedes aegypti* . . . of Yellow Fever": Capers 1966, p. 190.

22: "Yellow fever, which . . . of New Orleans": White, p. 2A.

22: "vicious cycle that . . . killed the insects": Weisberger, p. 58.

22: "Memphis had suffered . . . 1850 and 1870": White, p. 2A.

22: "During the torrid . . . 2,500 died": White, p. 6A.

22: "For the next several years . . . display of fireworks": White p. 6A.

23: "But by the time . . . across the Atlantic": *Ibid*; Crosby, p. 13.

23: "'Yellow Fever here . . . 36 cases'": *Ibid*.

23: "quarantines": Capers 1966, p. 194; White, p. 7A; Robbins, p. 52.

23: "cleansed streets and . . . carbolic acid": White, p. 7A.

23: "Barrels of . . . on street corners": White, p. 7A; Robbins, p. 43; Weisberger, p. 61.

23: "cannons were fired . . . clear the air": Finger, p. 84; *The Commercial Appeal*, September 6, 1878, "Guns Brought Here from Helena to Fight the Fever."

23: "Desperate citizens invoked . . . evil-smelling plant, asafetida": White, p. 7A; Robbins, p. 43.

23: "On July 29 . . . infected mosquito": White, p. 7A.

23: "couldn't prevent . . . through the woods": Robbins, p. 43.

23: "In late July . . . by yellow fever": White, p. 7A.

23–24: "On August 13 . . . a bloody pool": Kate Bionda's illness was the first publicized case of Yellow Fever in Memphis, but there were several previous cases that were not immediately reported: Keating, p. 107.

23–24: I have ascribed to Kate Bionda the typical symptoms of yellow fever: Finger, p. 84; Capers 1966, p. 191; Weisberger, pp. 61, 85; Robbins, pp. 39-40; *Press-Scimitar*, August 7, 1978, "Yellow Fever's Horror Recalled 100 Years After Its Departure." For a comprehensive and chilling firsthand account of symptoms by a physician who during the 1878 Memphis epidemic treated 280 patients before contracting the disease himself, see Collins, S. H., Dr., "Original Communications," *The Cincinnati Lancet and Clinic, A Weekly Journal of Medicine and Surgery*, New Series, Vol. 1, Whole Vol. XL, 1878, pp. 265-268. See also the J. M. Keating account, *A History of the Yellow Fever Epidemic of 1878 in Memphis, Tennessee*, printed for the Howard Association, 1879. Further information can be found in the Yellow Fever Collection in the Memphis Library; in the Mississippi Valley Collection at the University of Memphis; and in the Memphis History Exhibit in the Pink Palace Museum in Memphis, Tennessee.

24: "Some thought it . . . a 'miasma'": Weisberger, p. 58.

24: "Physicians of Kate's . . . and calomel": Robbins, p. 44.

24: "leeches": Finger, p. 84.

24: "A doctor from . . . 'cures that killed'": Robbins, p. 44.

24–25: "They assumed incorrectly . . . vomit or bedding": Weisberger, pp. 58-59.

25: "Within two days . . . residents fled": Wiesberger, p. 60.

25: "to places as . . . New York": White, p. 7A.

25: "families escaped in . . . and on foot": Robbins, p. 39; Capers 1966, p. 195.

25: "Men shoved aside . . . crowded trains": White, p. 7A.

25: "'The ordinary courtesies . . . an inexpressible terror'": Weisberger, p. 60.

25: "Terror was also . . . offering them supplies": *Press-Scimitar*, August 7, 1978, "Yellow Fever's Horrors Recalled 100 Years After Its Departure."

25: "This resulted in . . . from cracked lips": *Evening Appeal*, December 27, 1932, "Horrors of Plague Live on Through Years."

25: "Yellow fever plagued . . . more than twenty thousand people": Finger, p. 96; Weisberger, p. 58.

25: "But Memphis, with . . . other towns combined": White, p. 7A.

25: "and soon garnered financial . . . over the country": Robbins, p. 43.

25–26: "But as Sister . . . 'hands to wash'": Finger, p. 84.

26: "All but two hundred . . . of them died": Capers 1966, p. 198.

26: "and suffered a 7 percent mortality rate": *Ibid*.

26: "Between deaths and . . . forty-one to seven": Finger, p. 84.

26: "the staff of . . . and Colonel Keating": *Memphis Appeal*, September 7, 1978. *The Memphis Appeal* is now called *The Commercial Appeal*.

26: "For a while funeral bells were . . . became too frightening": Weisberger, p. 61.

26: "with a silence": Finger, p. 84.

26: "the rumble of death wagons": White, p. 7A.

26: "and the call . . . 'your dead'": *Press-Scimitar*, April 7, 1932, "'Bring Out Your Dead,' Called Yellow Fever."

26: "booming cannons": Weisberger, p. 61.

26: "Of course some . . . of the sick": Weisberger, pp. 62-63.

27: "babies found coated . . . their dead mothers": Weisberger, p. 61.

27: "A madam named . . . for the dying": Weisberger, p. 62; *Memphis Appeal*, August 29, 1878.

27: "Relief efforts were . . . 'our only hope'": the Charles G. Fisher Papers, the Mississippi Valley Collection, the University of Memphis, telegram sent September 20, 1878.

27: "as was Sister Ruth . . . had been 'Sunbeam'": Finger, p. 87.

27: "Annie Cook had also succumbed": *Press-Scimitar*, August 7, 1978, "Yellow Fever's Horror Recalled 100 Years After Its Departure."

27: "Charles Fisher died . . . in New York": the Charles G. Fisher Papers, the Mississippi Valley Collection, the University of Memphis, telegram to his sister Susie from Luke E. Wright, September 26, 1878; *Memphis Daily Appeal*, September 27, 1878.

27: "Colonel Keating, who . . . 'about to dawn'": Weisberger, p. 60.

27: "Finally on October . . . epidemic was over": Weisberger, p. 63.

27: "Memphis had lost . . . citizens to death": *The Commercial Appeal*, December 8, 1963, "Letter Is Picture of Fear, Death."

27: "Most of the . . . St. Louis never returned": *The Commercial Appeal*, August 24, 1958; Robbins, p. 46.

27: "Among those who . . . theater, and industry": *The Commercial Appeal*, August 24, 1958.

27: "Almost all of . . . of the plague": Miller, W. 1957, p. 6.

28: "the population dropped . . . to 33,000": Weisberger, p. 64.

28: "plunging the city . . . in national rank": Capers 1966, p. 207.

28: "for the replacements . . . were poor": Miller, W. 1957, p. 8.

28: "They couldn't afford to pay taxes": Capers 1966, p. 200.

28: "civic leaders were . . . the city bankrupt": Robbins, p. 46.

28: "Across the country . . . to the ground": McIlwaine, p. 175.

28: "Memphians began replacing . . . with pavement": Weisberger, p. 64.

28: "wells and cisterns . . . modern waterworks": *Press-Scimitar*, September 14, 1975, "So New York Thinks It Has a Problem?"

28: "But yellow fever returned in 1879": White, p. 8A.

28: "Five hundred eighty-three people died": Weisberger, p. 64.

28: "So although Memphis . . . in 1893": *Press-Scimitar*, September 14, 1975, "So New York Thinks It Has a Problem?"

28: "Then yellow fever . . . in 1897": *The Yellow Fever Epidemic of Memphis*, by Mildred Hicks, Memphis/Shelby County Library and Information Center.

28–29: "and hundreds of . . . cared for them": *Gordonsville* (Tennessee) *Gazette*, January 27, 1879 (Memphis Correspondent of *New York World*), "The City Swarms With Helpless Children Whose Parents Are Dead"; interview with Barbara Nikulski, 1993.

29: "Georgia would also . . . hid from her in attics": interview with Memphis resident who requested anonymity.

29: "sixty thousand rural émigrés": Miller, W. 1957, p. 7.

29: "he was born in 1874": *The Commercial Appeal*, October 17, 1954, "Young Mississippian Worked as Printer and Store Clerk, Then Came to Memphis at 18."

29: "plague spread from . . . killing his father": *Press-Scimitar*, August 7, 1978, "Yellow Fever's Horrors Recalled 100 Years After Its Departure"; Miller, W. 1964, p. 12.

29: "into poverty so . . . at Christmas": *Time* Magazine, "Memphis' Boss Crump: Ring-Tailed Tooter," May 27, 1946; Miller, W. 1964, p. 14.

29: "At eighteen he moved to Memphis": *The Commercial Appeal*, October 17, 1954, "Young Mississippian Worked as Printer and Store Clerk, Then Came to Memphis at 18."

29: "the pungent odor . . . raw whiskey": Street, p. 16.

29: "sweetly scented lilacs": Ibid.

29: "giant wharf rats": Coppock 1967, p. 2.

29: "bagnio girls": Coppock 1980, p. 101.

30: "Crump had . . . school education": Leake, p. 7.

30: "assaulted several men": Interview with Jerry Gardener, 1992. Crump assaulted her father in a barbershop. See Miller, W. 1964, p. 40 for account of Crump thrashing his boss.

30: "standing on tables . . . shaking his fist": Miller, W. 1964, p. 69.

30: "By 1910 Crump was mayor": Gunther, p. 69.

5. Mollie

Sources for this chapter are interviews with Mollie's son, Billy Hale; Mollie's sister, Frances Sylvie; Mollie's brother, Harrison Moore; and Mollie's sister-in-law, Stella Moore.

6. Georgia's Youth

37: "She was contemptuous . . . as 'cows'": Interview with Vallie Miller, 1992.

39: "Being in a comparative . . . 'sleuthing' for me": Interview with Hickory resident whom I call "Maisie." For reasons that will be apparent, I have given her a pseudonym, and have omitted the names of other sources living in or near Hickory, Mississippi.

39: "She also sent . . . by a local reporter": *Meridian Star*, March 25, 1993, "Film Depicts Hickory Native's Scandal."

46: "Her mother, Beulah Yates Tann . . . Second Chancery District Court": Rowland, p. 545. Bibliographical sketch written by George C. Tann, undated. Mississippi State Archives, Jackson, Mississippi.

46: "became known for finding homes for orphans": Interview with Hickory, Mississippi resident.

46: "The poor, rural . . . with their care": Williams, pp. 5-6.

46: "'I wish I had a' . . . for temporary care": *Press-Scimitar*, July 2, 1935, "Miss Tann Started Early at Home-Finding Career; She's Given Happiness, Security to 3,000 Children."

47: "Rob was born three years before Georgia": Results of 1920 Census; interview with Hickory, Mississippi resident.

47: "He was thin; they were heavyset": Interview with Hickory, Mississippi resident.

47: "Rob was also . . . 'he thanked her,' she said": Interview with Hickory, Mississippi resident.

47: "wide brow and . . . resembled him": Comparison of pictures of Georgia Tann, published in Memphis newspapers, with a picture of George C. Tann, undated, from Mississippi State Archives; interview with Hickory, Mississippi resident.

48: "Big-boned and . . . clothing for women": Interview with Hickory, Mississippi resident.

48: "She wore her hair . . . as a man's": Pictures of Georgia Tann that were published in Memphis newspapers; interview with Hickory, Mississippi resident.

48: "She evinced . . . in marriage": Interview with May Hindman, 1992; interviews with residents of Hickory, Mississippi, 1993.

48–49: "George, however, forced . . . 'girl in the family'": *Press-Scimitar*, July 2, 1935, "Miss Tann Started Early at Home-Finding Career: She's Given Happiness, Security to 3,000 Children"; *Nashville Tennessean*, October 22, 1950, "Father Favored Music, She Saw Greater Need."

49: "Some married, homosexual . . . and considered ennobling": Faderman, pp. 2-3, 17.

49: "The first such school was Mt. Holyoke College . . . in 1837": Faderman, p. 13.

49: "Martha Washington College . . . would graduate": *Press-Scimitar*, July 2, 1935, "Miss Tann Started Early in Home-Finding Career."

49: "By 1880 forty thousand . . . colleges and universities": Faderman, p. 13.

49–50: "A study cited . . . women in general": Faderman, p. 14.

50: "Many female professors . . . partnerships with other women": Faderman, pp. 21-22.

50: "What were considered . . . were ubiquitous": Faderman, p. 19.

50: "after graduating in 1913": Records of Martha Washington College, Abingdon, Virginia.

50–51: "taught school briefly in Columbus, Mississippi": George C. Tann, handwritten note, Mississippi State Archives; Rowland, p. 545, bibliographical sketch written by George C. Tann, undated, Mississippi State Archives, Jackson, Mississippi.

51: "Charity work was . . . local poor": *Nashville Tennessean*, October 22, 1950, "Father Favored Music, She Saw Greater Need."

51: "'Hours later,' Georgia . . . the baby home": *Press-Scimitar*, July 2, 1935, "Miss Tann Started Early at Home-Finding Career; She's Given Happiness, Security to 3,000 Children."

52: "This incident . . . young, neglected children": *Ibid.*

53: "mothers she called 'cows'": Interview with Vallie Miller, 1992.

53: "An incident that . . . maintain his composure": *Press-Scimitar*, July 2, 1935, "Miss Tann Started Early at Home-Finding Career; She's Given Happiness, Security to 3,000 Children."

53–54: "Around 1906, when . . . 'made the most of it'": *Ibid.*

54: "Referring to this . . . 'her life's work'": *Press-Scimitar*, December 6, 1946, "Years Ago She Found a Career."

55: "When a young mother . . . 'good homes [and] splendid educations'": Probate Court of Shelby County, No. 41796-R45, *Petition for Writ of Habeas Corpus, Grace Gribble, Petitioner, vs. Tennessee Children's Home Society and Miss Georgia Tann.*

55: "In a May 1935 . . . 'wealth can give'": Letter from Abe Waldauer to the Honorable G. C. Moreland, May 23, 1935.

56: "Over 460 orphanages . . . between 1890 and 1910": Nelson, p. 96.

57: "Georgia obtained employment . . . as field agent": http://freepages. genealogy.rootsweb.com/gpakt/pamsfamily/MamawR/mamaws.htm.

57: "Mississippi residents, however . . . inherit from them": Williams, p. 7.

58: "One spring morning . . . Rufus's brother, Clyde": Interview with Helen Greer, 1992; interview with Regina Hines, 1992; interview with Andre Bond, 1992; *Mississippi Press*, July 22, 1992, "Adoption Scandal: Answers to Family Ties May Be In Moss Point."

58: "Georgia's father, George . . . an abandoned child": Interview with Helen Greer, 1992; interview with Regina Hines, 1992; *Mississippi Press*, July 22, 1992, "Adoption Scandal: Answers to Family Ties May Be In Moss Point."

58: "She was run out of town": Interview with Vallie Miller, 1992; interview with Hickory, Mississippi resident, 1993.

58: "Her father had friends in Memphis": *Nashville Tennessean*, October 23, 1950, "Miss Tann Played for Political Favors."

58: "After working briefly for a Texas orphanage": *Press-Scimitar*, December 6, 1946, "Years Ago She Found a Career"; *Press-Scimitar*, July 2, 1935, "Miss Tann Started Early at Home-Finding Career; She's Given Happiness, Security to 3,000 Children."

7. Georgia's Memphis

Page 59: "He didn't rid . . . stay in business": *The Commercial Appeal*, August 1, 1976, "How Crump Lost a Round with the Private."

Page 59: "providing black residents . . . and athletic fields": *St. Louis Post-Dispatch*, July 3, 1938, "Ed Crump The Boss of Memphis."

59: "free milk": Biles, pp. 44-45.

59: "young professionals with political positions": Biles, p. 46.

60: "money collected into . . . by city workers": Interview with Alfred Andersson, 1992.

60: "provided a . . . slush fund": Leake, p. 51.

60: "The fund . . . from city workers": Gunther, p. 71.

60: "Within hours he . . . citizen had voted": Aspero, pp. 21-22; Daniels, p. 50; Street, pp. 16, 28.

61: "even by night . . . quickly having it repaired": Leake, p. 66.

61: "And those who . . . lives so easy": Leake, p. 82.

61–62: "When a young attorney . . . 'whole bigger world'": Interviews with Roswell Stratton, 1995; *Press-Scimitar*, May 15, 1941, "Stratton, County Court Clerk, Breaks with Crump"; *Press-Scimitar*, May 16, 1941, "It Can Happen Here"; *Press-Scimitar*, May 26, 1941, "Story Behind Break with Crump"; *Press-Scimitar*, July 31, 1942, "Stratton Forced by Ill Health To Step Out of Race."

62: "The Machine's base . . . municipal workers": Leake, p. 69.

62: "attend nightly rallies": Interview with Robert Taylor, 1992.

62: "young attorneys who . . . speeches for Crump": Leake, pp. 69-70.

62: "For thirty years": Leake, p. 68.

62: "bloc of state . . . however he wished": *The Commercial Appeal*, October 17, 1954, "Influence of Crump in State Had Waned." "Mr. Crump's power extended into the Legislature, enabling him to name speakers and leaders and to decide what bills should be enacted. His trusted lieutenants were on the scene in the halls calling the signals dictated by telephone from the man in Memphis."

62: "like the union . . . in the Mississippi": Interview with Jenny Gardner, 1992.

62: "legislation passed by . . . office of mayor": Daniels, p. 22.

63: "He resigned instead contests elected county trustee": *St. Louis Post-Dispatch*, July 2, 1938, "Ed Crump the Big Boss of Memphis."

63: "mastermind 102 political contests without defeat": Hinton, p. 15; *Newsweek*, October 25, 1954, Crump obituary.

63: "In 1922 he . . . power was confirmed": Street, p. 28.

63: "With elections this . . . needed to campaign": Leake, p. 63.

63: "But Crump's hold . . . than physical": Daniels, p. 50.

63: "So even during . . . raising money": *The Economist*, p. 236.

63: "Crump also capitalized . . . for his candidates": *St. Louis Post-Dispatch*, July 2, 1938, "Ed Crump the Big Boss of Memphis."

63: "Local reporters attempting . . . not post bail": *St. Louis Post-Dispatch*, July 2, 1938, "Ed Crump the Big Boss of Memphis"; *The Commercial Appeal*, August 3, 1928, "Picture of a Memphis Election"; "Ed Crump: Public Enemy No. One," published by the Loyal Tennesseans League, undated.

64: "asleep even when they were awake": Daniels, p. 23.

64: "Crump fire a . . . with a jury": "Ed Crump: Public Enemy No. One," published by the Loyal Tennesseans League, undated, p. 8.

64: "'It always was a Crump man'": Leake, p. 45.

8. The Little Wanderers

66: "Infanticide was practiced . . . and Plato": Brace, p. 14.

66: "'exposed,' abandoned . . . on hillsides": *Ibid.*

66: "forced into slavery or maimed for exhibition": *Ibid.*

66: "by the Middle . . . in Zittau, Germany": Forman, p. 43.

67: "According to Rachel . . . the eighteenth century": Forman, p. 44.

67: "An orphan asylum . . . the sixth century": Brace, p. 21.

67: "The first orphanage . . . in 1727": Olsen, p. 89.

67: "But such institutions were rare": *New York Times*, August 6, 1874.

67: "including legislation . . . born outside marriage": Acts of North Carolina, 1741, Ch. 14, Sec. 10, as quoted in Scott Edward, Laws of the State of Tennessee Including Those of North Carolina Now in Force in This State from the Year 1715 to the Year 1820 Inclusive. Knoxville: Heiskell and Brown, 1921, I, 55-57.

67: "Several states passed . . . from their mothers": Kunzel, p. 127.

67: "With trepidation I read of . . . in 1793": Holt, p. 24.

67: "the murder of . . . on the hand": Shannon, pp. 47-48; Holloran, p. 20.

68: "Indentured children worked . . . or any land": Sory, p. 8.

68: "Four indentured youngsters . . . Plymouth winter": Patrick et al., p. 27.

68: "Lacking sufficient employees . . . with neglect": O'Hagan, p. 313.

68: "Those discovered alive . . . religions and names": O'Hagan, pp. 311-312.

68–69: "An infant found . . . Cherry Hill": O'Hagan, p. 312.

69: "Infants whose discovery . . . witnesses, or perpetrators": *Ibid.*

69: "sent to poorhouses": *New York Times*, April 9, 1922, "Bargains in Babies."

69: "with infant mortality . . . on average": Reports of State Board of Charities of New York, "The Review of Reviews", July 1929, p. 50.

69: "and, in places . . . 124 babies died": O'Hagan, p. 313.

69: "Baby farms were . . . to raise them": Coulter, p. 1.

69: "some farmers starved": *New York Times*, "The Baby-Farming Case," August 4, 1878.

69: "baby farms whose . . . of their charges": Zelizer, p. 119.

69: "an 1895 *New York* . . . 'to inhuman crimes'": *New York Times*, October 15, 1895.

69–70: "exposing babies . . . skin blackened": *New York Times*, September 16, 1873.

70: "cracking their skulls against walls": *New York Times*, July 16, 1925.

70: "One baby farmer . . . seven-year sentence": *New York Times*, July 23, 1925.

70: "the number of . . . in Boston": Holt, p. 74.

70: "on steps, in filthy cellars": Brace, p. 91.

70: "the iron tubes . . . in Harlem": Brace, p. 100.

70: "or jostle for . . . underground presses": *Ibid.*

72: "'feeble-minded' . . . 'depraved' morals": Kammerer, p. 235.

72: "The author of . . . and 'misshapen'": *Ibid.*

72: "A physician writing . . . 'equipped sexually'": *Mental Hygiene* 4. October 1927. "The Unmarried Mother: A Sociopsychiatric Viewpoint," Henry C. Schumacher, M.D., p. 777.

72: "a 1918 study . . . or epileptic": Kammerer, pp. 235-237.

72: "'probable epileptics'": *Ibid.*

72: "Their babies . . . their worst traits": Kaplan, p. 35.

72: "'It is well known . . . an insane condition'": Brace, p. 43.

72: "Referring to . . . 'irresistible effects . . .'": *Ibid.*

72: "who he believed . . . all of society": Brace, p. 92.

73: "Between 1853 and . . . were 'resettled'": O'Conner, p. 149.

73: "Notices were posted": Holt, p. 103.

73: "Brace, who believed . . . ride the Train": Brace, p. 266.

73–74: "'On a given . . . in comfortable homes'": Holt, p. 55.

74: "Most were headed . . . heard of": Patrick, *et al.*, p. 53.

74: "the Train made several stops": Holt, p. 49.

74: "church, or opera house": O'Conner, p. xvi.

74: "Farmers examined . . . their muscles": *Ibid.*

74: "to tell . . . acrobatic stunts": Holt, p. 49.

74: "Robert Petersen . . . quasi-legal son": Patrick, *et al.*, p. 128.

74: "Interviewed in the . . . remain their maid": Patrick, *et al.*, p. 53.

75: "One little girl . . . 'see my mother'": *The Orphan Trains*, documentary, produced by the American Experience and PBS by Janet Graham and Edward Gray, aired in the fall of 1995.

75: "Reformers took note . . . child workers": Zelizer, p. 64.

75: "Child labor . . . seem wrong": Zelizer, p. 210.

75: "With less emphasis . . . valued as children": for a thorough discussion of the changing attitude toward children, see *Pricing the Priceless Child*, Viviana A. Zelizer, New York, Basic Books, 1985.

75: "Between 1850 and . . . a century before": Zelizer, p. 11.

75: "Some contemporary accounts . . . to tight corseting": Foreman-Peck, p. 6.

76: "The earliest such . . . 'wrath of God')": Sorosky, *et al.*, pp. 28-29.

76: "Over the previous . . . 'an infernal lie'": *New York Times*, February 5, 1921, "Adopts 'Triplets', Calls Them Her Own: Fooled Even Her Husband."

77: "article published in . . . 'order for a child'": *Sunset, the Pacific Monthly*, February 1921, "Adopting a Baby," p. 83.

77: "But in 1926 . . . 'break in life'": *New York Times*, May 21, 1925, "Wife Admits Child 'Born' at Baby Farm Was Bought for $75."

78: "that the number . . . 1934 and 1944": Zelizer, p. 190.

78: "and if you adopt . . . and culture": Interview with Karen Wickham.

78: "Even as she . . . 'more than inheritance'": *Nashville Tennessean*, October 23, 1950, "Miss Tann Played for Political Favors."

78: "she falsified children's records": Kefauver Hearings, pp. 195-196; interviews with Christine Nilan; Linda Meyers; Joe Wilkerson; and Robert Taylor; *Press-Scimitar*, March 25, 1951, "Placing of Children Described as Illegal."

79: "And Georgia virtually . . . 'select the home'": *Press-Scimitar*, July 2, 1935, "Miss Tann Started Early at Home-Finding Career."

79: "But by 1935 . . . and South America": *Press-Scimitar*, December 2, 1937, "A Christmas Gift for You—A Baby."

83: "And I'd read an article in the . . . 'the trouble begins'": "The Life of An Adopted Child," Martha Vansant, *American Mercury*, February 1933.

84: "Writing to Georgia . . . 'her own unworthiness'": Letter from Abe Waldauer to Mrs. Thorne Deuel, March 9, 1943.

84–85: "There were 1,700 . . . had been only 200": Solinger, p. 170.

85: "'With tears in . . . child be placed'": Solinger, p. 173.

85: "'Please help me . . . to try to live'": Letter from Mary Owens to Mrs. O'Conner, May 21, 1940, letter in possession of author.

9. Georgia's Methods

90: "she visited merchants . . . benefits of adoption": Interview with Virginia Simmons, 1992.

90: "She mentioned the tax . . . arranging two thousand adoptions'": *The Commercial Appeal*, September 29, 1939, "TCHS — Memphis Recognized As Legal Adoption Agency by the State."

90: "heading a national child-placing monopoly . . . 'available for adoption'": *Press-Scimitar*, May 21, 1949, "Miss Tann Says Public Orphanages Support Black Market in Babies."

90: "But she had realized . . . in the country": *Press-Scimitar*, September 15, 1950, "Miss Tann Dies During Inquiry."

91: "Georgia delivered speeches . . . major cities": *Press-Scimitar*, June 15, 1947, "A Caution from Miss Tann": AP, December 21, 1948, "Memphis Woman to Head Children's Association"; *Press-Scimitar*, June 5, 1947, "Weigh Adoption Bill Carefully."

91: "lauded by a national . . . 'in adoption laws'": *Press-Scimitar*, September 15, 1950, "Miss Tann Dies During Inquiry."

91: "Eleanor Roosevelt sought . . . child welfare": Denny Glad, 1991, pp. 4-5.

91: "President Truman invited her to his inauguration": Letter from Abe Waldauer to Phillip W. Haberman, January 18, 1949.

91: "Pearl Buck asked . . . book about adoption": *Press-Scimitar*, September 15, 1950, "Miss Tann Dies During Inquiry."

91: "Georgia garnered national notice . . . 'boarding school at the same time'": *New York Times*, September 19, 1929, "Says Orphanage Put Negroes on Hot Stoves."

91: "collecting boarding money . . . she had already sold": Interview with Louise Loop, 1993.

92: "'Her narrowed eyes . . . warning ringing in their ears'": *Nashville Tennessean*, October 26, 1950, "Georgia Tann Campaigned Against Baby Rackets."

92: "She had won Crump's support": *Nashville Tennessean*, October 23, 1950, "Miss Tann Played for Political Favors"; *Nashville Tennessean*, September 26, 1950, "Injunction Halts All Adoptions at Shelby Home." See also pp. 100–101 of text, which discuss laws supported by Crump-affiliated legislators that enabled Georgia. See pp. 154–155 of text, which describe a law passed at the insistence of reputable social workers that required boarding homes for children to be licensed and regulated, but that exempted boarding homes used by Georgia's adoption agency. A further indication that Georgia had Crump's support is that a judge he consistently backed for election provided children to Georgia. Other judges supported by Crump uniformly ruled for Georgia in *habeas corpus* suits. Another indication of Crump's support is that one of his lieutenants served as the attorney for Georgia's Home. Perhaps the most important indication of Crump's support is that Georgia, who after a brief period as social worker in Mississippi was run out of the state for her child-placing practices, was able to operate her black-market baby ring in Memphis for twenty-six years, until her death.

92: "constantly reminded citizens . . . to her wishes to him": *Nashville Tennessean*, October 23, 1950, "Miss Tann Played for Political Favors"; Bates, p. 6; letter from Abe Waldauer to William Shoaf, undated (c. 1944).

92: "Police officers . . . she had stolen": See Prologue for discussion of Alma Sipple's futile attempt to get police officers to help her find her kidnapped child.

92: "Judges also approved . . . sixteen in a single day": Taylor, p. 2.

92: "But the judge most useful . . . of their children to Georgia": *Nashville Tennessean*, September 24, 1950, "State Investigator Says Force, Persuasion Used in Memphis Baby Racket"; for discussion of Camille Kelley's collusion with Georgia Tann, see Neill, October 1978, p. 52; interview with Robert Taylor, 1992.

92: "Kelley provided Georgia . . . Georgia placed for adoption": Neill, November 1978, p. 74.

92: "A former court worker . . . 'vulture' in Kelley's courtroom": Neill, October 1978, p. 38, p. 52.

92–93: "Marie Long witnessed . . . 'to be adopted'": Interview with Marie Long, 1992.

93: "'Her business . . . campaign coffers'": Interview with Dr. Charles Carter, 1993.

93: "And it's true that Crump extorted kickbacks": Interview with Roswell Stratton, 1993.

94: "An elderly social worker . . . of the substitution": Interview with Mildred Stoves, 1992.

94: "'Miss Tann did for' . . . adopted through her": Neill, October 1978, pp. 50-51.

94: "But she spent her . . . across the country": *Press-Scimitar*, September 12, 1951, "Tann Heirs Target of State Suit."

94: "Ann's 'love for Miss Tann . . . she called 'Sister'": *Nashville Tennessean*, October 25, 1950, "Georgia Tann Campaigned Against Baby Rackets."

94–95: "when the two fought . . . candy and flowers": Interview with Robert Taylor, 1992.

95: "She was about . . . weighed about 155 pounds": Interview with Hickory, Mississippi, resident.

95: "'Her ability to make those . . . point was commanding'": *Press-Scimitar*, September 15, 1950, "Miss Tann Dies During Inquiry."

95: "'Her word was law'": *Nashville Tennessean*, October 24, 1950, "Adoption Home Head's Power Fostered Domineering Attitude."

96: "'Miss Tann put her . . . private life as well'": *Press-Scimitar*, September 15, 1950, "Miss Tann Dies During Inquiry."

96: "one of her legs to be shorter": *Nashville Tennessean*, October 27, 1950, "Charity Forgotten in Miss Tann's Will."

96: "'dope'": Nashville Tennessean, October 27, 1950, "Charity Forgotten in Miss Tann's Will."

96: "probably morphine": Interview with Hilda Deane, 1992.

97: "She wore tailored suits . . . print blouses": Newspaper photographs of Georgia Tann.

97: "black shoes with low Cuban heels": Interview with Christine Nilan, 1992; newspaper photographs of Georgia Tann.

97: "Her nails were manicured . . . no other cosmetics": Interview with Mary Hindman, 1992.

97: "She wore one piece of jewelry . . . worn off her face": Interview with Mary Hindman, 1992; newspaper photographs of Georgia Tann.

97: "Her eyes were blue . . . willpower and resolve": Interview with Hickory, Mississippi, residents.

97: "Her fearlessness was best . . . 'I wasn't afraid'": *Nashville Tennessean*, October 24, 1950, "Adoption Home Head's Power Fostered Domineering Attitude."

97: "And at least twice . . . was unperturbed": Interview with Louise Loop, 1993; *The Commercial Appeal*, December 6, 1979, "Helping Hands Guide Mother, Son to Reunion."

97: "Ann had grown . . . Georgia's hometown": Interview with Maureen Wood, 2007.

97: "Her parents and Georgia's were good friends": Interview with Hickory, Mississippi, resident, 1993.

97–98: "But by 1920 . . . the Receiving Home": Fourteenth Census of the United States: 1920—Population Jackson City, Hinds County, Mississippi.

98: "Letterhead for the . . . 'Miss George Tann'": Letterhead for the Mississippi Children's Home Society; interview with Maureen Wood, 2007.

98: "U.S. Census records . . . as 'George Tann'": Fourteenth Census of the United States: 1920—Population Jackson City, Hinds County, Mississippi.

99: "When he died . . . for several weeks": Interview with May Hindman, 1992.

99: "as did Ann . . . Georgia's mother, Beulah": Interview with Lorene Cole, 1992; Interviews with Hickory, Mississippi residents.

99: "Beulah frequently boarded . . . home in Hickory": Interviews with Hickory, Mississippi, residents.

99: "After June graduated . . . children to adoptive homes": Interview with Lorene Cole, 1992.

99: "Passed in 1852 . . . action of a court": General Assembly—Public Acts of Tennessee 1851-52, ch. 338, sec. 2.

100: "She didn't investigate . . . adopt a child": Interview with Vallie Miller, 1992; interviews with Robert Taylor, 1992, 1993; interview with former Children's Bureau social worker, 1992.

100: "Fortunately for Georgia, Boss Crump controlled the state legislature": See *The Commercial Appeal*, October 17, 1954, "Influence of Crump in State Had Waned": "Mr. Crump's power extended into the Legislature, enabling him to name speakers and leaders and to decide what bills should be enacted. His trusted lieutenants were on the scene in the halls calling the signals dictated by telephone from the man in Memphis." For further evidence of Crump's control within Memphis and the entire state, see *The Economist*, "Manipulation in Memphis," August 21, 1943, p. 236. "Crump controls the Bar Association. Crump has named most of the judges in Shelby County. He named the federal judge. For the first time, he has named a member of the Tennessee Supreme Court. . . . Crump controls the schools, the American Legion, the civic clubs."

100: "in 1937 a law . . . out-of-state residents": Public Acts of Tennessee, ch. no. 310, House Bill no. 1712.

100: "The new legislation . . . a notary public": Public Acts of Tennessee, ch. no. 151, House Bill no. 964.

100: "The statewide director . . . bullied by Georgia": Georgia's agency was a branch of the Tennessee Children's Home Society. But she ran it as an independent unit, under a separate charter, which she obtained in 1941, and she had her own, self-perpetuating board of directors: *Nashville Banner*, September 29, 1950, "End of Memphis Agency's Independence is Urged"; Charter Book Misc. Y, p. 105, June 28, 1941, State Attorney General's Office.

101: "A provision added to . . . by the state": Public Acts of Tennessee 1917, ch. 120, House Bill no. 1276.

101: "For some reason, representatives of . . . apply for a license": Miller, V., p. 43.

101: "a fact that made every adoption . . . illegal": *The Commercial Appeal*, September 26, 1950, "Suit By State Ties Up Adoption Home Here," interview with Robert Taylor, 1992.

101: "Secrecy would be . . . Tennessee Department of Public Welfare": October 6, 1944, letter from Abe Waldauer to E. W. McGovern; March 7, 1949, letter from Abe Waldauer to Charles Cornelius.

101: "to Welfare Departments . . . she placed children": Letter from Abe Waldauer to Jack R. Aron, July 14, 1947; letter from Abe Waldauer to Jack R. Aron, July 16, 1947; letter from Abe Waldauer to Jack R. Aron, July 18, 1947; letter from Abe Waldauer to Jerome Steiner, July 23, 1947; letter from Abe Waldauer to Irving Goldfarb, January 5, 1948.

101: "Georgia wished to . . . adoptions that occurred": Interview with a former Children's Bureau social worker who requested anonymity.

101–102: "A social worker . . . adopt one through Georgia": *Ibid.*

103: "Georgia was vague . . . in February of 1921": Letter from Georgia Tann to Abe Waldauer, June 6, 1934.

104: "But it's patently . . . reduced the children's age": Interview with Robert Taylor, 1992; interview with Vallie Miller, 1992; interview with Roy Dickson, 1992; interview with Betty Jo Mitchell, 1992; interview with Janeice Lambert, 2006.

104–105: "That Georgia and Ann were . . . 'as if born to her'": *Petition In Re Adoption of Ann Atwood Hollinsworth in the Probate Court of Dyer County*, Tennessee, to the Honorable Robert D. Jones, Judge of the County Court, Dyer County, Tennessee, August 2, 1943, Minute Book 10, pp. 39–40.

105: "And it was more critical . . . have been before": Faderman, p. 35.

105: "'Intimacy between two girls . . . her feminine counterpart'": *Ibid.*

105: "Romantic friendships . . . deemed lesbian partnerships": *Ibid.*

106: "'Even in her earliest . . . a woman's body'": Evans, pp. 177-178.

108: "Joan Crawford" (adopted through Georgia Tann): *New York Post*, September 13, 1950, "Bare $1,000: Tennessee Baby Mill."

108: "June Allyson, Dick Powell" (adopted through Georgia Tann): *Nashville Tennessean*, September 13, 1950, "Shelby Lawyer To Head Probe of Baby Market."

108: "Pearl Buck (adopted through Georgia Tann): Interview with Robert Taylor, 1992.

108: "Lana Turner (adopted through Georgia Tann)": *Nashville Banner*, September 13, 1950, "Board Calls for Facts."

108: "New York Governor Herbert Lehman (adopted through Georgia)": Neill, Oct. 1978, p. 39.

108: "'high type'": undated, c. 1938, rebuttal by Georgia Tann of complaints regarding her adoption methods.

108: "There were more . . . Tennessee in 1929": Door, p. 3.

109: "After the children . . . of her office": *The Commercial Appeal*, September 29, 1939, "TCHS-Memphis Recognized as Legal Adoption Agency by the State."

109: "Her own adopted . . . blue-eyed baby, too": Interview with Vicci Finn, 1993.

109–110: "Judge Camille Kelley . . . 'children from her'": Interview with a Memphis resident who requested anonymity, 1993.

110: "One, which ran . . . 'and awful lonesome'": *Press-Scimitar*, November 21, 1930, "Wants Home."

110: "Another ad, published . . . 'Yours for the Asking!'": *Press-Scimitar*, December 7, 1935, "Yours For the Asking!"

112: "I read a nationally . . . 'Richard Practice-House'": AP, December 13, 1929, "Co-Ed Mothers May Lose Baby."

112: "According to an . . . making ends meet": *Press-Scimitar*, December 2, 1937, "Christmas Presents."

113: "'Want a real . . . to place these babies'": *Press-Scimitar*, December 9, 1929, "25 Babies Will Be Christmas Gifts."

113: "A variation of the ad . . . 'are in the majority'": *Press-Scimitar*, December 10, 1929, "Christmas Presents."

113: "Within ten minutes . . . of the children": *Press-Scimitar*, December 2, 1937, "We Have a Christmas Gift for You—A Baby."

114: "'Could YOU Use a Christmas Baby'": *Press-Scimitar*, 1929.

114: "'Which [of three infant boys] Will You Have for Christmas?'": *Press-Scimitar*, December 4, 1930.

114: "'Are You in the Market for a 14-Month-Old Boy?'": *Press-Scimitar*, December 11, 1930, "Eddie is Ready To Move."

114: "'Put Your Orders in Early'": *Press-Scimitar*, December 14, 1932, "Another Baby Christmas Gift."

114: "'Dan, Jimmy, Ray . . . Want One of Them?'": *Press-Scimitar*, December 11, 1931.

114: "They resulted not only in . . . list of sorts": *Press-Scimitar*, December 4, 1930, "25 Tots Ready To Make Tri-State Homes Happy": *Press-Scimitar*, December 11, 1930, "Begin Choosing Babies' Homes: 200 Persons Want 25 'Gifts' From Society."

115: "bouncing in a baby swing": *Press-Scimitar*, December 11, 1931, "Dan, Jimmy, Ray—Want One of Them?"

115: "teething on a crib rail": *Press-Scimitar*, December 15, 1931, "Three Yule 'Packages' Hunting For Home."

115: "cuddling a doll": *Press-Scimitar*, December 9, 1932, "Christmas Means a Lot to Patsy."

115: "porcelain figurine": *Press-Scimitar*, December 16, 1930, "Looking for a Mother, Dad."

115: "as was Master Paul . . . 'seven months old and blond'": *Press-Scimitar*, December 14, 1929, "Paul Isn't One Bit Embarrassed."

115: "Georgia's ads made . . . of their family": *Press-Scimitar*, December 14, 1929, "Christmas Babies Make Hit."

115: "By 1935, she . . . Canada, and England": *Press-Scimitar*, December 2, 1937, "A Christmas Gift for You—A Baby."

115: "Her intention was . . . by selling babies": Berebitsky, pp. 50-74.

116: "She spent no time . . . child was advertised": *Press-Scimitar*, December 9, 1930, "Christmas Baby Is Given Home."

116: "In 1928, Georgia . . . handled 206 adoptions": *Press-Scimitar*, March 11, 1928, "Clearing House of City's Orphans Always Busy."

116: "That same year . . . arranged only eighty-three": Annual Reports of the Spence Alumnae Society, 1938, and of the Alice Chapin Nursery, 1928.

116: "the Boston Children's . . . was five": A Report of the Children's Aid Association of Boston, "Our 1937 Children," May 1938.

117: "Three times more . . . sturdy field hands": Zelizer, p. 149.

117: "But when the Christmas baby series was syndicated": Interview with Betty Jo Mitchell, 1992; interview with Barbara Sabin, 1993; letter from Georgia Tann to C. C. Carstens, January 20, 1937.

118: "When Georgia received . . . a total of $766": Source for financial figures, *Press-Scimitar*, February 19, 1950, "Heiskill Files Bill Charging Miss Tann with 'Unlawful' Use of Funds."

119: "Instead, Georgia or . . . to their new parents": One adoptee described seeing several waiting, prospective adoptive parents in the Biltmore Hotel in Los Angeles:

Interview with Heidi Naylor; *The Commercial Appeal*, January 28, 1980, "Brother, 2 Sisters Reunited After 32-Year Separation."

119: "In at least one case . . . her actual expenses": *New York Post*, September 14, 1950.

120: "'Lose yourselves'": Letter from Nora Quain Deuel to Abe Waldauer, March 3, 1943.

120: "Adoptive parents also must . . . filed by birth parents": *Press-Scimitar*, November 20, 1937, "Dad Who Gave Away Children Wants Them Back—Court Says No"; *Press-Scimitar*, April 29, 1940, "Claims Society Misled Her and Took Child"; *Press-Scimitar*, 1947, "Unwed Mother Asks Return of Baby"; *The Commercial Appeal*, August 30, 1947, "Unwed Mother Plans New Fight for Child"; *Press-Scimitar*, March 24, 1951, "Child Placement Illegal, Welfare Chief Asserts"; *Press-Scimitar*, March 25, 1951, "Placing Children Described as Illegal"; *Press-Scimitar*, March 26, 1951, "Seeking Custody of Three Children"; *Nashville Tennessean*, April 3, 1951, "Couple Opens Fight to Regain Three Children"; *Nashville Tennessean*, April 4, 1951, "Court Delays Adoption Fight"; *Associated Press*, March 19, 1952 "Tann Victim Seeks Children's Return."

120: "The opportunity to . . . with Memphis couples": *Nashville Tennessean*, October 26, 1950, "Georgia Tann Campaigned Against Baby Rackets."

120: "By the late 1940s . . . out of state": *Nashville Tennessean*, September 22, 1950, "Sutton Asks Investigation of Baby Racketeering By House Committee."

121: "Pharmacist J. B. Martin . . . ejected from the ballpark": Allen, pp. 212-213.

121: "Attorney Ben W. Kohn . . . a Crump opponent": Oral History, interview with Mrs. Nell Aspero conducted by Charles W. Crawford, March 25, 1988, p. 24.

121: "Another attorney was . . . citizens: 'Boss'": Van Devander, p. 173.

122: "her staff of six women": January 20, 1937, letter from Georgia Tann to C. C. Carstens.

122–124: "One, an employee of . . . Saginaw, Michigan, couple'": Information regarding Grace Gribble was derived from Petition for Writ of Habeas Corpus, *State ex rel. Gribble v. Tennessee Children's Home Society et al.*, No. 41796—R45 (Prob. Ct., Shelby Co., TN, April 9, 1940). Also, Draft of brief in TN Sup. Ct., in *State ex rel. Gribble v. Tennessee Children's Home Society*, undated, c. 1941. Also, *Press-Scimitar*, April 29, 1940, "Claims Society Misled Her and Took Children"; interviews with three of Grace's children, Doris Ann Schaefer, David Gribble, and Charles Gribble.

124: "Regarding the children's . . . 'interests of her children'": Record, *State ex rel. Gribble v. Tennessee Children's Home Society*, p. 159 (No. 41796—Prob. Ct., Shelby Co., 1940).

125: "In a documentary . . . family to Arkansas": WSMV, Nashville, Tennessee, "Forgotten Families," Series, October 1990.

10. Georgia's Adults

127–128: "She must have . . . his little girl again": *Waggerman v. Tennessee Children's Home Society*, Bill, p. 1, No. 39939, Chancery Court, Shelby County, 1933; *Waggerman v. Tennessee Children's Home Society*, Bill of Exceptions, No. 39939, Chancery Court, Shelby County, 1933; *Waggerman v. Tennessee Children's Home Society*, Appeal To Petition to Re-Hear, No. 39939, Chancery Court, Shelby County.

128: "Eighteen-year-old Mary . . . 'this day,' Mary said": Memorandum, *State of Tennessee ex rel of Mary Aileen McIntosh, Petitioner, vs. Tennessee Children's Home Society and Miss Georgia Tann, Defendants*, No. 57412RD; *The Commercial Appeal*, "Hopes of Mother to Retain Child of 4 Rest With Judge," 1947; *The Commercial Appeal*, August 30, 1947, "Unwed Mother Plans New Fight for Child"; *The Commercial Appeal*, July 10, 1991, "Birth Mom, Son Unite Years After Custody Suit," interviews with Mary Reed, Sheila Brown, and Steve Popper, 1992.

129: "Irene Green was one . . . 'no one to love me now'": *St. Louis Post-Dispatch*, May 10, 1993, "Stolen Time"; interviews with Mary Margolis, Jim Lambert, Pat Spruill, and Betty Jo Mitchell, 1993-1994; interviews with Janice Lambert, 2006.

129: "When a twenty-seven-year-old . . . 'nervous breakdown'": Interview with Earline Phillips, 1992.

130–131: "She was a skillful . . . 'whole world to us'": *The Commercial Appeal*, September 18, 1950, "Hoodwinked Father Declares He'll Sue To Regain Children."

131: "But he'd lost . . . their adoptive parents": *Nashville Tennessean*, August 4, 1952, "Tennessee Mother Weeps As Court Takes 3 Children."

132: "The stock market . . . poor Memphians": Biles, p. 51.

132: "Employers cut workers' . . . jobs to men": Biles, p. 53.

132: "The city's financial . . . the Mississippi Delta": Biles, pp. 53-54.

132: "these institutions . . . Georgia's spotters": *The Commercial Appeal*, September 24, 1950, "Mothers Threatened, Taylor Says."

132: "'She knew how' . . . told me sadly": Interview with Alma Sipple, 1992.

133: "'excessively sexual equipment'": Schumacher, p. 780.

133: "'sexual deviants'": Duberman *et al.*, p. 291.

133: "'intermediate'": Smith-Rosenberg, p. 264.

133: "'third' sex": Duberman *et al.*, p. 289.

133–134: "He knocked on . . . and swiftly left": Interview with Vallie Miller, 1992.

134: "'Marriage Racket Laid' . . . to the unborn child": *Nashville Tennessean*, September 29, 1950, "Marriage Racket Laid to Miss Tann."

135: "'This child is 100 percent normal and healthy'": Georgia Tann said this to an adoptive mother, upon presentation of a child: Interview with Linda Myers, 1992.

135: "In the centuries . . . raise their children": Solinger, p. 285.

136: "Social workers more . . . children was adoption": Solinger, p. 173; Kunzel, p. 128.

136: "Enacted before adoption . . . to raise them": Solinger, p. 21.

136: "Some social workers . . . their baby's gender": Solinger, p. 161.

136: "By the time adoption . . . babies for adoption": Solinger, p. 149.

136: "endorsed by . . . Catholic Charities": Solinger, p. 26.

136–137: "Clark Vincent to predict . . . 'family and society'": Solinger, p. 186.

137: "in a 1955 article . . . babies for adoption": Buck, 1955.

137: "By the 1950s . . . children for adoption": Solinger, p. 164.

137: "Some suggested setting . . . they were joking": Perlman, 1964.

137: "Leontine Young . . . 'a means to an end'": Solinger, p. 28.

139: "'Two weeks went . . . and kill myself'": Solinger, p. 108.

139: "But she exploited . . . 'Miss Georgia Tann'": Interview with Barbara Sabin, 1992.

139: "She and her workers . . . of their pregnancies": Neill, October 1978, p. 51.

139: "She often told . . . keep their babies": *Daily News*, Los Angeles, April 2, 1951.

141–142: "'Giving up my baby . . . in thirty-seven years, we touched'": Livingston, 1977; interview with Gordon S. Livingston, 1993.

142–143: "Memphian Solon Freeman . . . 'a circle,' Ruby said": Interview with Solon Freeman, 1993; interview with Ruby Burdette, 1993.

11. Georgia's Children

147–151: Information about Mollie was gleaned from interviews with her son, Billy Hale; her brother, Harrison Moore; her sister, Frances Sylvie; and her sister-in-law, Stella Moore; as well as from Billy Hale's unpublished manuscript and unpublished journals, and from Mollie's scrapbook.

151: "She also denied . . . October of 1945": "Statement Answering Criticism Against Tennessee Children's Home Society," written by Georgia Tann, November 6, 1946, p. 4.

151: "A reporter for . . . the reporter believed": Letter from Mary E. Murray to author, May 18, 1993.

151: "'There were a lot' . . . said in 1950": *The Commercial Appeal*, September 18, 1950, "40 to 50 Babies Died at Children's Home, Medical Leader Says."

152: "The common practice . . . over five pounds": *The Commercial Appeal*, September 18, 1950, "40 to 50 Babies Died at Children's Home, Medical Leader Says."

152: "Georgia, however, sometimes . . . after birth": *Press-Scimitar*, October 19, 1950, "Tells of Keeping Unmarried Mothers for Miss Tann."

152: "Babies arrived at . . . and dehydrated": Interview with Lorene Cole, 1992.

152: "A hospital in . . . local adoptive parents": Interview with Lorene Cole, 1993.

152: "Physicians in these . . . of Public Welfare": *Nashville Tennessean*, September 22, 1950, "State Prober Charges Baby Records Moved"; interview with Edna Hughes, 1993.

152–153: "By 1932, only . . . soared even higher": Oppenheimer, p. 1.

153: "She found it . . . 'Mortality in Memphis'": Oppenheimer, p. 20.

153: "Dr. Oppenheimer also . . . Memphis General Hospital": Oppenheimer, p. 41.

153: "'On July 2' . . . Dr. Oppenheimer wrote": Oppenheimer, p. 67.

153: "In 'Infant Mortality' . . . unregulated boarding homes": Oppenheimer, pp. 66, 72, 76.

153: "She strongly urged . . . by the state": Oppenheimer, pp. 67, 68, 72, 74, 75.

154: "her attorney Abe . . . in Crump's Machine": Miller, W. 1964, pp. 142, 244, 247, 248, 254, 255.

154: "Some of the . . . collaborated with Georgia": Petition for Writ of Habeas Corpus, *State ex rel. Gribble v. Tennessee Children's Home Society et al.*, No. 41796-R45 (Prob. Ct., Shelby Co., TN, April 9, 1940); *Press-Scimitar*, April 29, 1940, "Claims Society Misled Her And Took Children"; interviews with Doris Ann Schaefer, David Gribble, Charles Gribble, and Cleveland Pannell.

154–155: "In preparation for . . . 'for babies and small children'": Wallis, pp. 17-18. See also Miller, R., pp. 7-8.

155: "Abe Waldauer wrote . . . Welfare William Shoaf": Letter from Abe Waldauer to William A. Shoaf, November 29, 1944.

155: "in 1945, the legislature . . . in Tennessee": Public Acts of Tennessee 1945, ch. 112; Wallis, p. 18.

155: "A subsection . . . agency from compliance": Public Acts of Tennessee, ch. 112, sec. 14a; Wallis, p. 18.

156: "A particularly severe . . . 'want to see it'": *The Commercial Appeal*, September 18, 1950, "40 to 50 Babies Died at Children's Home, Medical Leader Says"; *Nashville Tennessean*, September 18, 1950, "Doctor Charges Baby Deathtrap."

156–157: "Doctors Croswell and Carter . . . 'what it actually is'": Bates, pp. 1-6.

157: "Unless his charges": Bates did not mention some of Georgia's more serious crimes, such as her stealing and selling of children. He may have felt that, in Memphis' political climate, where many of the city's most prominent citizens had adopted through her, he had gone as far as he could. As it was, Bates paid for his criticism of Georgia by being forced to resign his long-held judgeship.

157: "Judge Bates's letter . . . approving her adoptions": Bates, p. 1.

158: "As the Commissioner . . . to do so": Public Acts of Tennessee 1937, ch. 48, subsection n., amended by Chapter 95, Public Acts of 1939; *Nashville Tennessean*, September 29, 1950, "Advisor Argues Charter Voided at Baby Home."

158: "Georgia's six-page rebuttal . . . 'an infamous attack'": "Statement Answering Criticisms

Against Tennessee Children's Home Society," written by Georgia Tann, undated, c. December 1946, p. 2.

158: "Abe Waldauer and other . . . 'beginning to end'": To the Board of Directors of Tennessee Children's Home Society, Supplemental Report, written by John Brown, December 28, 1946, pp. 1, 3; letter from John Brown to Board of Directors, December 10, 1946.

158: "The Public Welfare . . . Shoaf, did nothing": *Nashville Tennessean*, September 18, 1950.

158: "'Mr. Waldauer told'": *The Commercial Appeal*, September 18, 1950, "40 to 50 Babies Died at Children's Home, Medical Leader Says."

159: "the author of an . . . 'into garbage cans'": *Saturday Evening Post* 202, "The Baby Market," February 1, 1930, p. 25.

159: "The author contended . . . 'wants him at all'": *Saturday Evening Post* 202, "The Baby Market," February 1, 1930, p. 85.

160: "When the Christmas . . . League of America": Letter from Abe Waldauer to Dr. C. C. Carstens, December 28, 1937; Letter from Charles Cornelius to W. B. Herbert, February 9, 1938.

160: "which his successor . . . in their new homes": *The Commercial Appeal*, September 18, 1950, "40 to 50 Babies Died at Children's Home, Medical Leader Says."

160: "In typical fashion . . . 'not in agreement'": Letter from Abe Waldauer to William Shoaf, August 26, 1944.

160: "One of the more . . . reform adoptive legislation": Interview with Robert Taylor, 1992.

160: "Georgia sometimes sent . . . wanted to keep": Interview with Earline Phillips, 1992.

161: "'It is not' . . . clients in 1944": Letter from Abe Waldauer to Mrs. Leo Freeman, February 24, 1944.

161: "'This is one business' . . . that same year": Letter from Abe Waldauer to Horace L. Levy, May 26, 1944.

161: "In 1947 Abe . . . 'back, without question'": Letter from Abe Waldauer to Hyman L. Miller, October 8, 1947.

162: "In a letter . . . 'parents,' is destroyed'": *Press-Scimitar*, "Adoptions Are Final, and Finality Must Be Upheld, Miss Tann Says," December 30, 1938.

162: "misrepresenting her children in the first place": Interviews with Roy Dickinson, Barbara Davidson, Billy Hale, Linda Myers, Vallie Miller, Mary Margolis, Betty Jo Mitchell, Denny Glad, and Sen. John Hicks.

162: "considerably more than . . . clients were Jewish": E-mail from Denny Glad to member of the American Adoption Congress, February 23, 2004.

162: "so Georgia falsely . . . children as Jewish": *Press-Scimitar*, "Other Figure in Tann Case, Taylor Thinks: Report Suggests Confederates," June 27, 1951.

164: "Another child, adopted . . . happened to him": Letter from Rabbi Leo Stillpass to Abe Waldauer, September 26, 1947.

168: "Among the mail . . . in the 1940s": Letter to author, April 1, 1991.

168–169: "The twins had . . . with Georgia Tann": Interviews with twins, 1991, 1992; *The Pantagraph*, "Adoption Scandal Tangles Twins' Lives," June 23, 1991.

170: "Locking residents in . . . frequently used punishment": Interviews with Elizabeth Huber, Lynn Heinz, and Billy Hale.

171: "judging from his . . . 'orphanage got molested'": Interview with Roger Cleghorne, 1993.

171: "publication in 1961 . . . 'Battered Child Syndrome'": "The Battered Child Syndrome," C. Henry Kempe, Frederic N. Silverman, Brandt F. Steele, William Droegemueller, and Henry K. Silver, *Journal of the American Medical Association*, July 7, 1962, 181: 17-24.

176: "he was writing an article . . . *Missing Children's Bulletin*": *Missing Children's Bulletin*, Winter 1993, "Kidnapped, Abused and Molested, Then Sold to Adoptive Parents: A Portland, Oregon Man Tells His Shocking Story."

178: "*Good Housekeeping* published . . . been fatal abuse": "The Little Girl Who Refused To Die," *Good Housekeeping*, August 1991, pp. 90-91, 132-134.

178: "forty to fifty . . . of 1945": *The Commercial Appeal*, September 18, 1950, "40 to 50 Babies Died at Children's Home, Medical Leader Says."

178: "four more babies and . . . of Public Welfare": Bates, p. 4.

178: "the infant who . . . adoptive home": Bates, p. 4.

178: "premature twins, who . . . boarding home": , Deposition of May Hindman, taken in the Shelby County Courthouse, Memphis, Tennessee, October 23, 1950; accusation regarding the twins made by Robert Taylor, p. 7.

178: "and the babies . . . the broiling sun": Interview with Boo Cravens, 1992.

179: "'bad habit of . . . holding them down'": Besides Joe Pannell, three other people described this bathing technique—Lynn Heinz, Randall Gookin, and Barbara Davidson.

180: "or dangled down laundry chutes": Interview with Randall Gookin.

182: "'But the records . . . a brick wall'": *The Commercial Appeal*, January 1, 1980, "Brother, Two Sisters Reunited After 32 Years of Separation."

189: "homes in Memphis's best . . . in Biloxi, Mississippi": *Nashville Tennessean*, October 25, 1950, "Dead Past Rises Swiftly To Confront Georgia Tann."

190: "she and Ann . . . horses every morning": Interview with George Winfield, 1992.

190: "Instead of using . . . horses, and two dogs": *Press-Scimitar*, October 16, 1941, "Country Place That Pays, Run By a Lady."

190: "She even found . . . mother of quintuplets": *Press-Scimitar*, July 13, 1937, "Proxy Mother Proud of Quintuplets."

190: "'She became high' . . . taxi driver in 1950": *Nashville Tennessean*, October 24, 1950, "Adoption Home Head's Power Fostered Domineering Attitude."

190: "the reform-minded . . . 'that bunch'": Letter from Georgia Tann to Abe Waldauer, February 26, 1938.

191: "When another couple . . . back their adopted child": *Nashville Tennessean*, September 20, 1950, "Double-Cross Found in Baby Adoptions"; *Nashville Banner*, September 20, 1950, "Miss Martin Heads Home from Memphis"; interview with Nettie Creson, 1993.

191: "In 1949 a pediatrician . . . 'of the background'": *Press-Scimitar*, February 15, 1949, "Citizens Argue Merits of 2 Adoption Bills."

191–192: "In March of 1947 . . . 'symbol of sacrifice'": Letter from Mrs. W. A. Hachmeister to Senator Davis Wooten, March 19, 1949; letter from Randolph Johnson to Mrs. W. A. Hachmeister, March 16, 1949.

192: "whom she played off against each other": *Nashville Tennessean*, October 27, 1950, "Charity Forgotten in Miss Tann's Will."

192: "during June's honeymoon . . . she'd left at home": *Nashville Tennessean*, October 27, 1950, "Charity Forgotten in Miss Tann's Will"; interview with Robert Taylor, 1992.

192: "'almost to the breaking point'": Letter from Ann Atwood Hollinsworth to Abe Waldauer, August 3, 1934.

192: "Georgia herself told . . . by buying Tannwood": *Press-Scimitar*, October 16, 1941, "Country Place That Pays, Run By a Lady."

193: "heart attacks suffered in 1941": Letter from Abe Waldauer to Mrs. Maurice Emmich, April 15, 1941.

193: "and 1943": Letter from Abe Waldauer to Nathaniel Stewart, September 15, 1943.

193: "In 1945 doctors . . . with cancer": Interview with May Hindman, 1992; interview with Denny Glad, 1991.

193: "She refused surgery": Interview with May Hindman, 1992.

193: "relied upon narcotics for pain": *Nashville Tennessean*, October 27, 1950, "Charity Forgotten in Miss Tann's Will."

193: "Abe Waldauer dealt . . . cancellation of the proposed adoption": Letter from Abe Waldauer to Jerome M. Steiner, July 23, 1947.

193: "and a bill . . . reached the legislature": *The Commercial Appeal*, February 14, 1945, "Veteran Poll Tax Appeal, Children's Adoption Bill Feel Axe."

193: "Georgia worked furiously . . . opposing the bill": *Nashville Tennessean*, October 24, 1950, "Adoption Home Head's Power Fostered Domineering Attitude"; Kefauver Hearings, p. 193.

193–194: "and using her . . . the bill defeated": *The Commercial Appeal*, February 14, 1945, "Veteran's Poll Tax Appeal, Child Adoption Bill Feel Axe."

194: "In 1947 Tennessee . . . buried in committee": *The Commercial Appeal*, March 9, 1947, "Adoption Bill Tabled"; *The Commercial Appeal*, July 20, 1947, "Adoption Bill 'Lost.'"

194: "the Junior League": January 23, 1947, letter from Mrs. Eric Babenbeer to Harry Scruggs.

194: "Adoptive father Jesse . . . 'I did,' he said": *Nashville Tennessean*, October 25, 1950, "Dead Past Rises Swiftly To Confront Georgia Tann."

194–195: "During heated legislative fighting . . . burst into tears": Interview with the former Children's Bureau social worker whom Georgia threatened, 1992.

195: "The reform bill . . . it became law": *Nashville Tennessean*, September 28, 1950, "'Lost Paragraph' in 1949 State Adoption Act Could Have Blocked Alleged Racket—Inserted Words Pulled Teeth from Measure." In that politically charged period there was no mention of who had tampered with the Act; the perpetrator, the article read, remained "a mystery." Robert Taylor and Vallie Miller told me in 1992 that Abe Waldauer doctored the Act.

196: "she was confined . . . attended by a nurse": *Press-Scimitar*, September 15, 1950, "Miss Tann Dies During Inquiry."

196: "She sent her . . . most elegant hotels": Interview with Vicci Finn, 1993; *The Commercial Appeal*, October 7, 1979, "Estate Doesn't Hint Good Life for Georgia Tann."

196: "Her last purchases . . . a hospital bed": Kay Surgical, bill submitted September 30, 1950, Claim Against Estate of Georgia Tann, submitted in *Matter of Estate of Tann*, No. 62685, Prob. Ct., Shelby Co.

196: "including almost daily . . . to make the trip": Carney, Fred A., Affidavit to Claim Against Estate of Georgia Tann, sworn to September 26, 1950, submitted in *Matter of Estate of Tann*, No. 62685, Prob. Ct., Shelby Co.; C. F. Heackock (spelling of name may be wrong because the signature is difficult to decipher), Affidavit to Claim Against Georgia Tann, submitted in *Matter of Estate of Tann*, No. 62685, Prob. Ct., Shelby Co.

196: "She died at . . . four-poster bed": *St. Louis Post-Dispatch*, September 22, 1950, "Dealer of Babies in Black Market."

196: "at 4:20 A.M. . . . a few friends": *Press-Scimitar*, September 15, 1950, "Miss Tann Dies During Inquiry."

196: "'Sissy . . . didn't do that'": Interview with Mrs. William Tann Yates, 1993.

196: "Services were held . . . on September 17": *Press-Scimitar*, September 15, 1950, "Miss Tann Dies During Inquiry."

197: "And adoptive parents . . . were terrified": *Press-Scimitar*, September 1950, "New Angle Develops in Probe"; interview with Linda Myers, 1992.

197: "Actor Dick Powell . . . 'cannon,' he said": *Nashville Tennessean*, September 14,

1950, "State Launches Recovery Action for Baby Profits"; *Nashville Tennessean*, September 18, 1950, "Powell Says He'll Fight Return of Adopted Baby."

197: "only $80,000 worth . . . and property remained": *Press-Scimitar*, January 22, 1954, "Georgia Tann Estate To Be Settled Today."

197: "By the time . . . two-thirds of that": *State ex rel. Heisekll v. Tennessee Children's Home Society*, No. 53339 R.D. Cch. Ct. (Shelby Co., TN), Consent Decree (n.d.); *The Commercial Appeal*, October 7, 1979, "Estate Doesn't Hint Good Life for Georgia Tann."

197: "She left no . . . had consumed her": *Nashville Tennessean*, October 27, 1950, "Charity Forgotten in Miss Tann's Will."

12. Georgia's Lies

202: "A Georgia Tann adoptee living in . . . illegal transactions": Interview with Linda Myers, December 4, 1993.

203: "Few single mothers . . . access to their birth parents' names": Sachdev 1989, p. 56.

203: "But it wasn't until": Scotland, Finland, Israel, Wales: Sorosky *et al.*, p. 42. Holland, Germany, Belgium, the Scandinavian countries: Rene Hoksbergen, e-mail, November 7, 2006. New Zealand, Australia, Canadian provinces, China, Japan, Korea: "Statistics on U.S. Adoptions," L. Anne Babb, as published in "The Decree," the publication of the American Adoption Congress, 1996. Sweden: Brodzinsky, p. 89, fn. 2.

205: "a constant gnawing": Sorosky *et al.*, p. 131.

205: "No one has . . . my birthright": Sorosky *et al.*, p. 132.

205: "Typical was the reasoning of . . . 'a well established adoptive relationship'": Prentice, pp. 62-63.

205–206: "In a 1937 letter . . . 'very tempting morsel of gossip'": Letter from Georgia Tann to Abe Waldauer, December 16, 1937.

206: "Georgia's attorney was as . . . 'to accept children for adoption'": Letter from Abe Waldauer to Georgia Tann, April 25, 1940.

206–207: "On October 6, 1944, Abe . . . 'gossip for inquisitive women in a political set-up. . . .'": Letter from Abe Waldauer to E. W. McGovern, October 6, 1944.

207: "A desire to cater to adoptive parents . . . a large one": *The Commercial Appeal*, December 19, 1948, "Memphis Exports Twin Babies—And Awakens To A Controversy"; letter written by Georgia Tann to her Board of Directors, c. 1938.

208: "We never tell . . . interference and confusion": *The Commercial Appeal*, December 19, 1948, "Memphis 'Exports' Twin Babies—And Awakens a Controversy."

208: "Contemporary adoptive parents . . . of why it occurs": Interview with Pam Hasegawa, September, 2006.

208: "But over five decades later . . . 'or the threat of blackmail'": *Associated Press*, August 24, 1996, "Judge OK's Opening of Records."

209: "Another is that . . . was Alabama, not Tennessee": Colby, p. 73.

209: "'Secrecy in adoption does' . . . published in 1992": Aigner, p. 33.

209: "In 1928, three years . . . for her adoptees": *The Commercial Appeal*, September 29, 1939, "Finding Parents For Babies Is Task Of Children's Home"; *The Commercial Appeal*, January 28, 1948, "Adoption Law Defended By Miss Tann."

209: "Nine years later . . . the practice in Tennessee": Public Acts 1937, Ch. 310, Sec. 1; *The Commercial Appeal*, September 29, 1939, "Finding Parents For Babies Is Task Of Children's Home."

210: "But her purported . . . have sounded good": Letter from Georgia Tann to D. J. Gallert, April 23, 1935.

211: "By 1920, laws . . . Minnesota and New York": Carp 1998, p. 51.

211: "Ethical social workers . . . for historical purposes": Carp 1998, p. 52.

211: "She kept original birth certificates . . . her adoptees": Interview with Virginia Simmons, 1992.

211: "Ethical social workers . . . copies of their original birth certificates": Carp 1998, p. 55.

211: "Workers like Maud Morlock . . . 'who his parents were'": Morlock, p. 169.

211–212: "But by 1960 . . . find their families": Interview with Annette Baran, May 12, 1998; for discussion of growing reluctance of Children's Home Society of Washington social workers to give adoptees information about their identities, see Carp 1992, pp. 40-41.

212: "She couldn't threaten . . . to everyone in their home towns": Interview with Robert Taylor, 1993; *Nashville Tennessean*, October 26, 1950, "Georgia Tann Campaigned Against Baby Racket."

212–213: "In 1955 and 1956 . . . following her lead": Kefauver Hearings.

213: "A team very similar . . . had been stillborn": Solinger, p. 176.

213: "'Runners,' who scouted . . . 'a few bucks?'": Lake, p. 44.

213: "Operations of a . . . relinquishing their children": Solinger, pp. 169-170.

213: "If their babies had . . . require greater care": Solinger, p. 170.

213: "The committee also . . . for a poker debt": Mitler, p. 91.

213–214: "A Chicago woman. . . . as bonus": Mitler p. 91.

214: "A child was . . . to El Paso": *Ibid.*

214: "Less than one-third . . . accredited agencies": *New York Times Magazine*, April 2, 1950, p. 48, "Adoption Problems."

214: "Pregnant women who relinquished . . . and medical care": Solinger, p. 177.

214: "To Katherine B. Oettinger . . . wrote in 1958": Oettinger, pp. 123-128.

214–215: "Ten years earlier . . . 'vacuum we have left'": Solinger, p. 160.

215: "And the black market . . . in a new town": Lake, p. 44.

215: "Ethical professionals could . . . imitating them": Interview with Annette Baron, May 12, 1998.

215–216: "Ernest Mitler, special counsel . . . in Seattle had closed": Mitler, p. 94.

216: "But the Traveler's Aid . . . and other areas": Solinger, p. 159.

216: "Ethical social workers . . . information about their roots": Interview with Annette Baron, May 12, 1998.

217: "Composed of one thousand parents . . . California legislature herself": Interview with Lorene Cole, 1992.

217: "Passed in 1949 . . . none at all": Interview with Lorene Cole, 1992; *Nashville Tennessean*, September 22, 1950, "State Had No Right To Press Probe, Shoaf Says."

217–218: "'I bought into . . . request made sense,' she said": Interview with Annette Baron, October 16, 1998.

13. The Fallout

219: "'I remember looking . . . without knowing it'": Sorosky, p. 109.

220: "'I was forever . . . but who is it?'": Sorosky, p. 133.

220: "'I used to cry . . . to find her'": Sorosky, pp. 116-117.

220: "'I used to fantasize . . . from all angles'": Sorosky, p. 117.

221: "'. . . I worried about . . . my biological parents'": Sorosky, p. 132.

221: "'I have an . . . my biological relatives'": Sorosky, p. 127.

222: "'I am very . . . us have no lineage'": Sorosky, p. 134.

222: "'I have discovered . . . on to future generations'": Sorosky, p. 127.

222–223: "Testifying before a . . . 'well still be alive'": F. F. Greenman Jr., Testimony before Connecticut Select Committee on Children, February 16, 2006.

223: "'Some of the kids . . . their original parents are'": Krementz, p. 69.

224–225: "Years later, I . . . 'to be proud of'": CBS News, *60 Minutes*, originally aired January 12, 1992, "Black Market Babies," p. 7 transcript.

225: "As the twelve-year . . . are 'ridiculous'": Krementz, p. 69.

226: "Scores of Georgia Tann . . . identities and pasts": *The Commercial Appeal*, October 28, 1993, "Speakers Protest Secrecy in Tenn. Adoption Records"; *The Jackson Sun*, October 28, 1993, "For 60 Years, No Family, No Nothing."

14. The Beginning of the End

231: "Hundreds of adoptees . . . 'no parents, no nothing'": *The Commercial Appeal*, October 28, 1993, "Speakers Protest Secrecy in Tenn. Adoption Records"; *Jackson Sun*, October 28, 1993, "For 60 Years, No Family, No Nothing."

232: "On May 18 . . . a standing ovation": *Nashville Banner*, May 18, 1995, "House Unanimously Changes State Adoption Laws."

232: "Records would . . . indirect victims": Tennessee Public Laws 1995, ch. 532, sec. 1 (amending T.C.A. § 36-1-127) & sec. 20. The effective date for the pre-1951 adoptees was later delayed six months.

232–233: "Adoptee Carolyn Godeau . . . 'having a baby!'": *The Commercial Appeal*, July 24, 1996, "Most Wonderful Thing in the World: Mother and Daughter, Separated at Birth, Are Reunited."

233: "Pat Robertson, who . . . increase in abortions": PBS Online Newshour, January 15, 1997, "Opening Adoption Records," transcript.

233: "The adoptees consistently lost . . . sealing records": *Alma Society, Inc. v. Mellon*, 601 F.2d 1225 (2nd Cir. 1979), *cert. den.*, 444 U.S. 995 (1979); *In re Assalone*, 512 A.2d 1383 (R.I. 1986); *Bradey v. Children's Bureau*, 274 S.E.2d 418 (S.C. 1981); *Matter of Dixon*, 116 Mich. App. 763, 323 N.W.2d 549 (1982); *Kirsch v. Parker*, 383 So.2d 384 (La. 1980); *Massey v. Parker*, 369 So.2d 1310 (La. 1979); *Application of Maples*, 563 S.W.2d 760 (Mo. 1978); *Matter of Spinks*, 32 N.C. App. 422, 232 S.E.2d 479 (1977); *Mills v. Atlantic City Dept. of Vital Statistics*, 148 N.J. Super. 302, 372 A.2d 646 (1977).

234: "The veto had been invoked . . . would utilize the veto as well": New South Wales Law Reform Commission, Report 69, Review of the Adoption Information Act 1990, pp. 40, 44 (1992).

234–235: "Tennessee's contact veto . . . contact their parents": T.C.A. §§ 36-1-128, 36-1-132 (1999).

235: "In writing the new law . . . birth parents": T.C.A. § 36-127(e)(2) (1999).

235: "Unsealing birth records . . . Court of Appeals": American Center for Law and Justice, Plaintiffs' Memorandum in Support of Application for Preliminary Injunction, p. 24, *Doe v. Sundquist*, Case No. 3-96-0599 (U.S.D.C., M.D. Tenn.), quoting *Linda F. M. v. Dept. of Health of City of New York*, 418 N.E. 1302 (N.Y. 1981).

235: "Abe Waldauer's attorney's assertion . . . 'real [adoptive] parents'": Letter from Abe Waldauer to Georgia Tann, December 16, 1937.

236–237: "But 'very few . . . call home.'": F. F. Greenman Jr., Letter to the Editor, *New York Law Journal*, August 21, 2000.

237: "desired 'privacy'": F. F. Greenman Jr., *et al.*, Brief of Amici Curiæ Teresa Evetts Horton, pp. 30-32 (10/31/1996); *Doe v. Sundquist*, Case No. 96-6197 (U.S.C.A., 6th Cir.); Carp 1998, p. 104.

237–238: "The very opposite . . . that surrounded it": F. F. Greenman Jr., *et al.*, Brief of Amici Curiæ Teresa Evetts Horton, pp. 40-42 (10/31/1996); *Doe v. Sundquist*, Case No. 96-6197 (U.S.C.A., 6th Cir.); see also F. F. Greenman Jr., Affidavit sworn to July 17, 1996, *Doe v. Sundquist*, Case No. 3-96-0599 (U.S.D.C. M.D. Tenn.).

238: "On August 23, 1996 . . . accessing their records": *Doe v. Sundquist*, 943 F. Supp. 886 (M.D. Tenn., 1996).

238: "Then on February 11, 1997 . . . dissolving the stay": *Doe v. Sundquist*, 106 F.3d 702 (6th Cir., 1997).

238: "To adoptees' further joy . . . federal constitutional claims": *Id.*, 106 F.3d at 707-708.

238: "Writing for the court . . . 'babies are born'": *Id.* at 705.

238: "Judge Engel also praised . . . 'sound adoption system'": *Id.* at 707.

238: "ACLJ attorneys asked the U.S. . . . the court refused": *Doe v. Sundquist*, 522 U.S. 810 (1997).

239: "On March 26, 1997 . . . Davidson County, Tennessee": ACLJ, Motion for Temporary Restraining Order, *Doe v. Sundquist*, Case No. 97C-941 (Cir. Ct., Tenn., 3/26/97).

239: "The order was granted": Temporary Restraining Order, *Doe v. Sundquist*, Case No. 97C-941 (Cir. Ct., Tenn., 3/27/97).

239: "On May 2 . . . 'or her identity'": Memorandum and Order, *Doe v. Sundquist*, Case No. 97C-941 (Cir. Ct., Tenn., 5/2/97); 1997 WL 354786.

239: "ACLJ lawyers then appealed . . . (from their children.)": Opinion, p. 12, *Doe v. Sundquist*, Appeal No. 01-A-01-9705-CV-00209 (Court of Appeals, Tenn., 8/24/98).

240: "'This court battle' . . . had written in 1996": American Adoption Congress Newsletter, *The Decree*, July 1996, "Tennessee's Open Records Battle Heats Up."

240: "The courtroom was packed . . . the Coalition newsletter": Tennessee Coalition for Adoption Reform Newsletter, June 1999, "Supreme Court Weighs Constitutionality of New Adoption Law," p. 1.

240: "Issued on September 27 . . . open records": *Doe v. Sundquist*, 3 S.W.3d 919 (Tenn. 1999).

240: "No longer said, . . . 'cattle or property'": *Nashville Banner*, May 18, 1995, "House Unanimously Changes State Adoption Laws."

240: "'Victory in Tennessee!'": mood was euphoric: Pacer Newsletter, Fall 1999, "Victory in Tennessee!"

240: "In 1999 a group of . . . birth certificates": 71 Del. Laws, ch. 481, sec. 5 (1998); 72 Del. Laws, ch. 1, sec. 1 (1999).

240–241: "From 1998 to 2000 Helen Hill": Oregon Initiative Measure 58 (1998); *Does v. State of Oregon*, 164 Or. App. 543, 993 P.2d 822 (1999), *review den.*, 330 Or. 138, 6 P.3d 1098 (2000), *stay den.*, 530 U.S. 1228, 147 L. Ed. 2d 271 (2000).

241: "Bastard Nation caused . . . as well": Alabama Acts 2000, No. 00-794.

241: "In 2004, a successful campaign . . . New Hampshire": 2004 N. H., Ch. 99.

241: "Nine other states . . . their original birth certificates": CO sec. 19-5-305(2)(b)(I); HI sec. 578-15(3); IN secs. 31-19-25-1 to -3 and 31-19-25; MI sec. 710.68(7);

MT sec. 42-6-109(4); OH secs. 3107.39 and 3107.45-47; OK 10 Okl. St. 7505-1.1; VT 15A VSA sec. 6-105; WA sec. 26.33.345.

241: "As of January of 2007 . . . six more states": Maine, Minnesota, New Jersey, New York, and North Carolina.

Epilogue

244: "Despite the progress made since . . . in thirty-four states": Five states have recently granted adoptees access to their original birth certificates. Adoptees in nine other states who were born before or after certain dates have also recently won access to their original birth certificates. Two states—Alaska and Kansas—have always allowed adoptees access to their original birth certificates. This amounts to a total of sixteen states that grant full or limited access, leaving thirty-four states in which adoptees' original birth certificates remain sealed to all adoptees.

245: "Between 1997 and 2001 she . . . children by unwitting Americans": U.S. Immigration and Customs Enforcement, November 19, 2004, "Backgrounder: Operation Broken Hearts," pp. 1-2.

245: "including the actress Angelina Jolie . . . Galindo in 2003": ABC News, November 19, 2004, "Adoption Scanner Gets 18 Months in Jail"; *Seattle Post-Intelligencer*, December 17, 2003, "Feds Claim Adopted 'Orphans' Had Parents"; *Seattle Post-Examiner*, November 20, 2004, "Adoption Broker Gets 18 Months"; ABC Online, June 24, 2004, "Angelina Jolie's Adoption Agent Admits Fraud;" Reuters (Seattle), June 25, 2004, "Angelina Jolie's Adoption Agent Admits Fraud." There is no evidence that Jolie knew anything about Galindo's unethical or illegal practices. There is also no evidence that Maddox was obtained from his parents through any illegal means such as fraud or deceit.

246: "Like Georgia's birth mothers . . . giving them phony birth certificates": U.S. Immigration and Customs Enforcement, November 19, 2004, "Backgrounder: Operation Broken Hearts," pp. 1-2.

246: "sentenced by an American court . . . 'the highest integrity'": ABC News, November 19, 2004, "Adoption Scammer Gets 18 Months in Jail."

246–247: "'China has a' . . . *China Daily* wrote in 2006": *China Daily*, February 27, 2006, "Orphanage Director Jailed in Baby Selling Scam."

247: "But in 2004 over . . . 'or migrant workers'": BBC News, March 22, 2003, "Chinese Babies Found in Luggage."

247–248: "'China often balks at . . . taking care of her,' he said": *Los Angeles Times*, January 1, 2006, "Child-Theft Racket Growing in China."

248: "in countries where the average annual income is $1,800": $1,800 is the average income in Russia: *Way to Russia Travel and Business Guides*, "Russian Stereotypes," www.waytorussia.net, accessed December 6, 2006.

248–249: "'Last year, nearly 23,000 . . . eye to African countries'": *New York Sun*, November 2, 2006, "Madonna's Adoption in Malawi May Lead Others to Africa."

249: "There are often many . . . 'gangsters in a parking lot'": Reuters, November 12, 2001, "U. S. Hopes to Crack Down on Global Adoption Abuses."

249: "Such criminal operations also occur . . . 'then selling the babies'": ABC Radio Australia, September 27, 2005, "Malaysian Police Say Baby Selling Gangs Thriving."

249–250: "According to Interpol . . . even leave the hospital": *Belfast Telegraph*, July 18, 2006, "Bulgarian Mothers Tricked Into Selling Babies."

250: "'What you have is' . . . counsel to the American Adoption Congress": Reuters, December 12, 2001, "U. S. Hopes to Crack Down on Global Adoption Abuses."

250: "Even a perfunctory study of . . . testified against him at trial": Interview with Maureen Hogan, 2006.

250–251: "And on May 3, 2006 . . . 'no one seems to care about any of this'": Testimony Submitted by Masha Allen to the House Energy and Commerce Committee, Subcommittee on Oversight and Investigations, Oversight Hearing on Child Pornography on the Internet, May 3, 2006, Washington, D.C.

251: "The Hague Convention . . . and prohibition of child-buying": Interview with F. F. Greenman Jr., 2006.

252: "But, according to Trish Maskew . . . the State Department estimated in 2003": Ethica Website, "20/20 FAQs," Report interview given by Trish Maskew, president of Ethica, for ABC 20/20 segment about baby trafficking in Cambodia, www.ethicanet.org/item.php?recordid=20/20FAQs&pagestyle=default.

Sources

Much of my information was derived from interviews with people directly affected by Georgia Tann—adoptees, birth parents, and adoptive parents. I also spoke with dozens of pediatricians and social workers who were contemporaries of Georgia, and with twenty-four of her former neighbors. During the course of my research, I conducted over one thousand interviews.

I also drew upon newspaper and magazine articles, court records, correspondence, books, journals, and records of Senate Subcommittee Hearings. Following are the principal sources:

Aigner, Hal. *Adoption in America Coming of Age*. Paradigm Press, 1992.

Alabama. Alabama Acts 2000, No. 00-794.

Allen, Col. Robert S., ed. *Our Fair City*. New York: The Vanguard Press, 1947.

Aspero, Nell. Interviewed by S. Glenda Maness, Oral History: "Memphis Politics During the Crump Era." Oral History Research Office, Memphis State University, interviewed on March 25, 1988.

Bates, Memphis Probate Court Judge Samuel O. Letter to William A. Shoaf, May 28, 1946.

Berebitsky, Julie. *Like Our Very Own*. Lawrence: University Press of Kansas, 2000.

Biles, Roger. *Memphis in the Great Depression*. Knoxville: University of Tennessee Press, 1986.

Brace, Charles Loring. *The Dangerous Classes of New York and Twenty Years' Work Among Them*. New York: Wynkoop & Hallenback, Publishers, 1872.

Brodzinsky, David M. and Marshall D. Schechter, eds. *The Psychology of Adoption*. New York and Oxford: Oxford University Press, 1990.

Browning, Gordon. Papers of Governor Gordon Browning, Tennessee State Library and Archives.

Buck, Pearl S. "The Child Waiting," *Woman's Home Companion*, Vol. 28, September 1955.

Capers, Gerald M. Jr. *The Biography of a River Town*. Chapel Hill: University of North Carolina Press, 1939.

Capers, Gerald M. Jr. "Memphis—Satrapy of a Benevolent Despot," *Our Fair City*, edited by Col. Robert S. Allen. New York: The Vanguard Press, 1947, pp. 211-234.

Caplan, Lincoln, *An Open Adoption*. New York: Farrar, Strauss and Giroux, 1990.

Carp, E. Wayne. *Family Matters*. Cambridge: Harvard University Press, 1998.

Carp, E. Wayne. "The Sealed Records Controversy in Historical Perspective: The Case of the Children's Home Society of Washington, 1895-1988," *Journal of Sociology and Social Welfare*, Vol. 19, June 1992.

CBS News, *60 Minutes*. "Black Market Babies," originally aired January 12, 1992.

Colby, Ruth. "Progress in Adoption Legislation," *Social Services Review*, March 16, 1942.

Collins, S. H. (Dr.). "Original Communications," *The Cincinnati Lancet and Clinic, A Weekly Journal of Medicine and Surgery*, New Series, Vol. 1, Whole Vol. XL, 1878, pp. 265–268.

Colorado, CO sec. 19-5-305(2)(b)(I).

Commercial Appeal, The: 1878 to 2006.

Coppock, Paul R. Interviewed by Charles W. Crawford, "An Oral History of the Crump Era and TVA," Oral History Research Office, Memphis State University, interviewed on June 29, 1967.

Coppock, Paul R. *Memphis Memoirs*. Memphis: Memphis State University Press, 1980.

Coulter, Col. Ernest K. "The Baby Farm and Its Victims," *The National Humane Review*, January 1926.

Crosby, Molly Caldwell. *The American Plague*. New York: Berkley Books, 2006.

Daniels, Jonathan. "He Suits Memphis," *Saturday Evening Post*, June 10, 1939.

Delaware, 71 Del. Laws, ch 481, sec. 5 (1998); 72 Del. Laws, ch. 1, sec. 1 (1999).

Doe v. Sundquist, 943 F. Supp. 886 (M.D. Tenn., 1996), *affd.* 106 F.3rd 702 (6th Cir., 1997), *cert. den.* 522 U.S. 810 (1997).

Doe v. Sundquist, 1997 WL 354786 (Cir. Ct., Tenn.), *revd.* 1998 WL 1988596 (Ct. Of App., Tenn), *revd.* 3 S.W.3rd 919 (Tenn., 1999).

Does v. State of Oregon, 164 Or. App. 543, 993 P.2d 822 (1999), *review den.*, 330 Or. 138, 6 P.3rd 1098 (2000), *stay den.*, 530 U.S. 1228 (2000).

Dorr, Louise. "A Study of Private Institutions for Dependent Children in Tennessee," a Thesis Submitted to the Department of Sociology of Vanderbilt University in Partial Fulfullment for the Degree of Master of Arts, May 1930.

Dowdy, G. Wayne. *Mayor Crump Don't Like It*. Memphis: University of Memphis Press, 2006.

Duberman, Martin; Vicinius, Martha; Chauncey, George Jr., eds. *Hidden from History: Reclaiming the Gay and Lesbian Past*. New York: NAL Books, 1989.

The Economist (a correspondent in Tennessee). "Manipulation in Memphis," August 21, 1943, pp. 235-236.

Evans, Mary. *Feminism: Critical Concepts of Literary and Cultural Studies*. London: Routledge, 2001.

Faderman, Lillian. *Odd Girls and Twilight Lovers*. New York: Columbia University Press, 1992.

Federal Bureau of Investigation (FBI). File on E.H. Crump, 9-14073.

Federal Bureau of Investigation (FBI). File on Juvenile Court Judge Camille Kelley, 94-4, sub 2569.

Finger, Michael. "The Martyrs of Memphis," *Memphis Magazine*, Vol. XVIII, No. 3, June/July 1993.

Fisher, Charles G. Papers of Charles G. Fisher, University of Memphis.

Foreman-Peck, James. *New Perspectives on the Late Victorian Economy*. Cambridge and New York: Cambridge University Press, 1991.

Forman, Rachel Zinober. *Let Us Now Praise Obscure Women: A Comparative Study of Publicly Supported Unmarried Mothers in Government Housing in the United States and Britain*. Washington, D.C.: University Press of America, 1982.

Frazer, Elizabeth. "The Baby Market." *The Saturday Evening Post*, 202, February 1, 1930.

Glad, Denny. "The Tennessee Children's Home Society Scandal." Paper presented at the American Adoption Congress Conference, April 11, 1991.

Gunther, John. "Last of the Big-Time Bosses." *Reader's Digest*, May 1947.

Hale, Billy. *Lost Love*, manuscript.

Hale, Billy. Journal, unpublished.

Hale, Mollie. Scrapbook.

Harkins, John E. *Metropolis of the American Nile*. Woodland Hills, CA: Windsor Publications, 1982.

Hawaii, HI sec. 578-15(3).

Hinton, Harold B. "Crump of Memphis: Portrait of a Boss." *New York Times Magazine*, September 29, 1946.

Holloran, Peter C. *Boston's Wayward Children: Social Services for Homeless Children, 1830–1930*. Rutherford, NJ: Fairleigh Dickinson University Press, 1989.

Holt, Marilyn Irvin. *The Orphan Trains: Placing Out in America*. Lincoln: University of Nebraska Press, 1994.

Indiana, IN secs. 31-19-25-1 to -3 and 31-19-25.

Kammerer, Percy Gamble. *The Unmarried Mother: A Study of 500 Cases*. Boston: Little, Brown & Co., 1918.

Keating, J. M. *A History of the Yellow Fever Epidemic of 1878 in Memphis, Tennessee*. Printed for the Howard Association, 1879.

Kefauver Hearing. U.S. Senate, 84th Congress, Jud. Comm., Subcommittee to Investigate Juvenile Delinquency. Hearings, July 15 and 16, 1955.

Krementz, Jill. *How It Feels to Be Adopted*. New York: Alfred A. Knopf, Inc., 1982.

Kunzel, Regina G. *Fallen Women, Problem Girls: Unmarried Mothers and the Professionalization of Social Work*. New Haven, CT: Yale University Press, 1993.

La Pointe, Patricia. *From Saddlebags to Science: A Century of Health Care in Memphis, 1830-1930*. Memphis: Health Sciences Museum Foundation, 1984.

Lake, Alice. "Why Young Girls Sell Their Babies." *Cosmopolitan*, December 1956.

Leake, George Craig. Presentation of the Script and Production Background for the Television Documentary, "The Once and Always Mr. Crump," A Supplement to the Production Thesis, presented to the Department of Speech and Drama, Memphis State University, August 1968.

Livingston, Gordon S. "Search for a Stranger," *Reader's Digest*, 110, June 1977.

Maine Department of Human Resources, Task Force on Adoption. *Adoption, A Life Long Process*. Portland: Maine, 1989.

McIlwaine, Shields. *Memphis Down in Dixie*. New York: E. P. Dutton & Co., Inc., 1948.

Michigan, MI sec. 710.68(7).

Miller, Roberta. "Boarding Homes for Children." *Tennessee Public Welfare Record*, Vol. 7, Issue 10, October 1944.

Miller, Vallie. Report to J. O. McMahon, Commissioner, Department of Public Welfare, State of Tennessee by Vallie S. Miller, Supervisor of Adoptions, on the Tennessee Children's Home Society Shelby County Branch, Administration and Placement Practices and Services to Children under Care, June 12, 1951.

Miller, William D. *Memphis During the Progressive Era*. Memphis: Memphis State University Press, 1957.

Miller, William D. *Mr. Crump of Memphis*. Memphis: Louisiana State Press, 1964.

Mitler, Ernest A. "Babies: Our One Remaining Black Market." *Look Magazine*, December 28, 1954.

Montana, MT sec. 42-6-109(4).

Morlock, Maud. "Wanted: A Square Deal for the Baby Born Out of Wedlock." *The Child*, 10, May 1946, pp. 167-168.

Neill, Kenneth. "Adoption for Profit: Conspiracy and Cover-Up." Part I, *Memphis Magazine*, Vol. III, No. 7, October 1978.

Neill, Kenneth. "Adoption for Profit: Conspiracy and Cover-Up." Part II, *Memphis Magazine*, Vol. III, No. 8, November 1978.

Neill, Kenneth. "Mr. Crump: The Making of a Boss," *Memphis Magazine*, October 1979.

Nelson, Claudia. *Little Strangers: Portrayal of Adoption and Foster Care in America, 1850-1929*. Bloomington: Indiana University Press, 2003.

New Hampshire, 2004 N.H., Ch. 99.

North Carolina, Acts of North Carolina, 1741, Ch. 14, Sec. 10, as quoted in Scott Edward, Laws of the State of Tennessee Including Those of North Carolina Now in Force in This State from the Year 1715 to the Year 1820 Inclusive. Knoxville: Heiskell and Brown, 1921, Vol. I, 55-57.

O'Conner, Stephen. *Orphan Trains: The Story of Charles Loring Brace and the Children He Saved and Failed*. University of Chicago Press, 2004.

Oettinger, Katherine B. "Current Concerns of the Children's Bureau." *Children*, 5, May-June 1958, pp. 123-128.

O'Hagan, Anne. "The Biography of a Foundling." *Munsey's Magazine*, 25, June 1901.

Ohio, OH secs. 3107.39 and 3107.45-47.

Oklahoma, OK 10 Okl. St. 7505-1.1.

Olson, Kristin. *Chronology of Women's History*. Westport, CT: Greenwood Press, 1994.

Oppenheimer, Ella, M.D. *Infant Mortality in Memphis*. Washington: United States Children's Bureau Publication No. 233, 1937.

Oregon, Oregon Initiative Measure 58 (1998); *Does v. State of Oregon*, 164 Or. App. 543, 993 P.2d 822 (1999), *review den.*, 330 Or. 138, 6P.3d 1098 (2000), *stay den.*, 530 U.S. 1228, 147 L. Ed. 2d 271 (2000).

Patrick, Michael; Sheets, Evelyn; and Trickel, Evelyn. *We Are a Part of History: The Story of the Orphan Trains*. Santa Fe: The Lightning Tree, 1990.

Perlman, Helen H. "Unmarried Mothers," *Social Work and Social Problems*. Nathan E. Cohen, ed. New York: National Association of Social Work, 1964.

Perry, Jennings. *Democracy Begins at Home*. Nashville, TN: Williams Publishing Company, 1947.

Prentice, Carol S. *An Adopted Child Looks at Adoption*. New York: Appleton-Century, 1940.

Press-Scimitar, Memphis, 1878 to 1983.

Robbins, Peggy. "Alas, Memphis!" *American History Illustrated*, January 1982.

Rowland, Dunbar. *The Official and Statistical Register of the State of Mississippi* (Centennial Edition, Jackson, 1917). p. 545. Biographical Sketch by George C. Tann, undated, Mississippi State Archives, Jackson, Mississippi.

Sachdev, Paul. "Achieving Openness in Adoption: Some Critical Issues in Policy Formulation." *American Journal of Orthopsychiatry*, 61(2), 1991, pp. 241-249.

Sachdev, Paul. *Unlocking the Adoption Files*. Lexington Books, 1989.

Schumacher, Henry C., M.D. "The Unmarried Mother: A Socio-Psychiatric Viewpoint," *Mental Hygiene*, 4, October 1927, pp. 775-782.

Shannon, B. Clay. *Still Casting Shadows: A Shared Mosaic of U.S. History*. iUniverse, Inc. 2006.

Smith-Rosenberg, Carroll. "Discourses of Sexuality and Subjectivity: The New Woman 1870-1936," in *Hidden From History: Reclaiming the Gay and Lesbian Past* (pp. 264-280). Duberman *et al.*, eds. New York: NAL Books, 1989.

Solinger, Rickie. *Wake Up Little Susie: Single Pregnancy and Race Before* Roe v. Wade. New York and London: Routledge, 1992.

Sorosky, Arthur D.; Baron, Annette; and Pannor, Reuben. *The Adoption Triangle*. New York: Doubleday, 1978.

Sory, Anne. The Development of Public Child Welfare Services in Tennessee, 1937-1942, A Field Study Submitted to the Faculty of the School of Social Service Administration in Candidacy for the Degree of Master of Arts, unpublished, Chicago, Illinois, 1944.

Street, James. "Mista Crump Keeps Rollin' Along." *Colliers Magazine*, April 9, 1938.

Taylor, Robert. Report to J.O. McMahan, Commissioner of Public Welfare of the State of Tennessee by Robert L. Taylor, Special Counsel on the Investigation of Tennessee Children's Home Society, May 21, 1951.

Tennessee, Public Acts of Tennessee 1851-1852, ch. 338, sec.2

Tennessee, Public Acts of Tennessee 1917, ch. 120, House Bill 1276.

Tennessee, Public Acts of Tennessee 1937, ch. 310, House Bill No. 1712.

Tennessee, Public Acts of Tennessee 1937, ch. 310, sec. N.

Tennessee, Public Acts of Tennessee 1937, ch. 310, sec. 1.

Tennessee, Public Acts of Tennessee 1941, ch. 151, House Bill 964.

Tennessee, Public Acts of Tennessee 1945, ch. 112.

Tennessee, Public Acts of Tennessee 1945, ch. 112, sec. 14 a.

Tennessee, Public Acts of Tennessee 1951, ch. 202, 36-1-136.

Tennessee, *Doe v. Sundquist*, 943 F. Supp. 886 (M.D. Tenn., 1996), *affd.* 106 F.3rd 702 (6th Cir., 1997), *cert. den.* 522 U.S. 810 (1997).

Tennessee, *Doe v. Sundquist*, 1997 WL 354786 (Cir. Ct., Tenn.), *revd.* 1998 WL 1988596 (Ct. Of App., Tenn), revd. 3 S.W.3rd 919 (Tenn., 1999).

Van Devander, Charles. "The Big Bosses." New York: Howell, Saskin Publishers, 1944.

Van Devander, Charles. "Mailed Fist in Tennessee." *American Mercury*, 1944, pp. 539-546.

Vansant, Martha. "The Life of An Adopted Child," *American Mercury*, 28, February 1933.

Vermont, VT 15A VSA sec. 6-105.

Vincent, Clark. "Unwed Mothers and the Adoption Market: Psychological and Familial Factors." *Journal of Marriage and Family Living*, 22, May 1960.

Wallis, Faye. "Children's Boarding Homes in Shelby Co." *Tennessee Public Welfare Record*, Vol. 8, Issue 12, December 1945.

Washington, WA sec. 26.33.345.

Weisberger, Bernard A. "Epidemic," *American Heritage: A Medical Picture of the United States*. October/November 1984.

Sources

White, Mimi. "Memphis Ignored Repeated Warnings of Peril." *The Commercial Appeal*, October 31, 1978, pp. 2A-8A.

Williams, Thomas E. The Dependent Child in Mississippi 1900-1972, Dissertation Presented in Partial Fulfillment of the Requirements for the Degree Doctor of Philosophy in the Graduate School of The Ohio State University, 1972.

WSMV, Nashville, TN. "Forgotten Families," series aired in October 1990.

Yellow Fever Collection. Memphis, Tennessee Library and Information Center.

Zelizer, Viviana A. *Pricing the Priceless Child*. New York: Basic Books, 1985.

Zimmerman, Waldo. "Mr. Crump's Legacy," *Memphis Magazine*, October 1984.

Acknowledgments

Hundreds of people helped me write this book. I am more grateful to them than I can express.

There are two people I spoke with most frequently. One was the late Billy Hale, who generously shared with me his story, as well as his journals, poems, and his mother Mollie's scrapbook. Billy helped several other Georgia Tann adoptees, and, toward the end of his life, searched for children who'd been abducted, as he'd been. He read the book in manuscript form. I am very sorry he cannot see it in print.

The other person I talked to most often was Barbara Davidson. Revisiting the past was not easy for Barbara, or for most others I spoke with. She hoped that telling her story would help prevent other children from being harmed by child traffickers today. Regarding the book's publication, she said, "Now the story will be out there. People will no longer be able to pretend it didn't happen." Her strength, and that of the other Georgia Tann victims I spoke with, will always astound me.

I am particularly thankful also for the help of Cleveland Panell, who searched for his missing sister for more than thirty-seven years; and Joy

Barner and Grady Earrey, who also found each other after decades of searching. I deeply appreciated being able to interview people like Randall Gookin and Eugene Calhoun, who survived so much, and came out not only whole but strong. Thanks also to reunited sibling groups such as Mary Margolis, Betty Jo Mitchell, Jim Lambert, and Pat Spruill; Heidi Naylor, Judy Young, and Arthur East; David Gribble, Doris Ann Shaefer, Charles Gribble, and Roland Gribble.

And I am grateful to so many other people who told me about their experiences with Georgia Tann. In no particular order, they are: Alma Sipple, Lynn Heinz, Christine Nilan, Virginia Simmons, Wilhemina Newsome, Steve Popper, Mary Reed, Solon Freeman, Ruby Burdette, Gordon Livingston, Mrs. Leon Sims, Elizabeth Huber, Marie Long, Joe Pannell, Bill Layton, Hilda Martin, Helen Greer, Andre Bond, Barbara Savin, Harrison Moore, Stella Moore, Frances Sylvie, Ruby Burdette, Solon Freeman, Roy Dickinson, June Jardin, Roger Cleghorne, Josephine Statler, Jean Stewart, Linda Myers, Lorene Cole, Candy Debs, Joy West, Marie Long, Nell Aspero, Cynthia Lupresto, Evelyn Quillen, George Winfield, Larry Nelson, Sam Rutherford, Nettie Creson, Jim Creson, Lyle Dorsett, Louise Davis, Barbara June Boros, Lou Bates, B.B. Bagett, Lane Driscoll, Roy Dickson, Hilda Deane, Wyeth Chandler, Ruth Cook, Ruth Crawford, Mary Crenshaw, Charles Crump, Mrs. C.P. Davis, W.B. Fowler, John Easley, Debbie Easley, Mrs. Haguewood, Jim Henry, Jenny Gardner, Butch Hobbs, David Hill, Jan Green, Maxine Hansberger, Pam Gorham, Jim Gallaspy, Robin Hooper, Alena Hutchinson, William Moxley, Jean Norris, Lucille Madden, Sandra Kimbrell, Harry Laughlin, J. Richard Matthews, Leon Levy, Vivian Lutrell, Walter Armstrong, Clyde Porteous, Karen Wickham, Barbara Nikulski, Lowell Schultz, Walter Armstrong, Frank Alghren, Jean Stewart, Van Stewart, Norma Stiles, Cathy Vaughn, Janey Vick, and Joe Wilkerson.

Acknowledgments

I am deeply indebted to many other interviewees: Robert Taylor, who tried in vain to conduct a thorough investigation of Georgia Tann; and Vallie Miller, who helped Georgia's last remaining wards. And to the physicians who tried to save children who were dying of neglect: Charles Carter, Ben Goodman, B.C. Collins, Jimmy Hughes, George Lovejoy, and Clifton Wooley.

Thank you also to the social workers who were contemporaries of Georgia Tann, and who described their attempts to stop her: besides Vallie Miller, these include Boo Cravens, Mary E. Murray, Fay Wallis, Edna Hughes, Miriam Kelly, and Mildred Stoves.

My deepest thanks also to Steve McFarland of Memphis, who saved many important papers from ruin, and helped me in so many ways. He and his wife were also wonderful, considerate hosts.

I am very grateful for the help of Vicci Finn, and of Jack Tann Watson.

Thank you, also, to Rosetta Hale and to Janeice Lambert. And to Eva Callahan, Norma Tillman, Hazel Fath, Regina Hines, Roswell Stratton, Lucius Burch, Lewis Donelson, and Jimmye Pidgeon.

I want to thank the twenty-three residents of Hickory, Mississippi who spoke with me, particularly several of the women, who were extremely kind.

Richard Panell is truly his father Cleveland's son—thoughtful, generous of his time, and very helpful. Thank you also to his wife, Janet, and to his mother, Gloria.

I greatly appreciate also the help of Maureen Wood and Mike Landwehr.

I am indebted to Denny Glad, Caprice East, and Bob Tuke. They have done much to help adoptees reunite with their families of birth.

I want to thank everyone affiliated with Adoption Network Cleveland, especially executive director Betsie Norris, for helping my daughter find her family. Betsie's organization is the best adoption-related search, support, and advocacy group in the United States.

Thank you also, to two great photographers, Pam Hasegawa and Carol Schaefer, and to others in the adoption community: Adam Pertman, Pat Lubarsky, Amy Winn, Janine Baer, Marley Greiner, and Maureen Flatley.

Ed Frank and Chris Ratliff of the Mississippi Valley Collection at the University of Memphis were always helpful. So too was Jim Johnson of the Memphis Room at the Memphis/Shelby County Library and Information Center.

Thank you also to those who read my manuscript. My best and oldest friend, Kappy Peters, read several versions, always enthusiastically and with great insight. Bob Raymond also read many versions, and gave thoughtful, sound advice. Thank you also to Don McKinney, my former magazine editor, who read an early draft, and to Joan Thursh, my former editor at *Good Housekeeping*. I am also very grateful to Alan Sachs, and to Tim Raymond, Beth Raymond Good, and Fred Greenman.

Lynn Franklin is a wonderful agent, and a friend who has always believed in this book.

I am very grateful to Philip Turner for his enthusiastic acquisition of the book, his editing, and his support. He's an editor in the old-fashioned sense.

Thank you also to everyone at Carroll & Graf, particularly my editor, Bill Strachan, and Adelaide Docx and Keith Wallman.

Gail and Salvatore Amato are warm, funny, wonderful people. I am very lucky to know them.

Thank you, Tim Good.

And finally, I want to thank the most important people in my life: Beth Raymond Good, Tim Raymond, Bob Raymond, and Fred Greenman. I could not have completed this project without their support and love.

To all of these, and those I do not have the space to name, the most heartfelt thanks.

Index